마이갓 5 Step 모의고사 공부

● **Vocabulary** 필수 단어 암기 & Test
① 단원별 필수 단어 암기 ② 영어 → 한글 Test ③ 한글 → 영어 Test

2 ● **Text** 지문과 해설
① 전체 지문 해석 ② 페이지별 필기 공간 확보 ③ N회독을 통한 지문 습득

3 ● **Practice 1** 빈칸 시험 (w/ 문법 힌트)
① 해석 없는 반복 빈칸 시험 ② 문법 힌트를 통한 어법 숙지
③ 주요 문법과 암기 내용 최종 확인

4 ● **Practice 2** 빈칸 시험 (w/ 해석)
① 주요 내용/어법/어휘 빈칸 ② 한글을 통한 내용 숙지
③ 반복 시험을 통한 빈칸 암기

5 ● **Quiz** 객관식 예상문제를 콕콕!
① 수능형 객관식 변형문제 ② 100% 자체 제작 변형문제 ③ 빈출 내신 문제 유형 연습

영어 내신의 끝
마이갓 모의고사 고1,2

1 등급을 위한 5단계 노하우
2 모의고사 연도 및 시행월 별 완전정복
3 내신변형 완전정복

영어 내신의 끝
마이갓 교과서 고1,2

1 등급을 위한 10단계 노하우
2 교과서 레슨별 완전정복
3 영어 영역 마스터를 위한 지름길

마이갓 교재
보듬책방 온라인 스토어 (https://smartstore.naver.com/bdbooks)

🌱 마이갓 10 Step 영어 내신 공부법

ⓞ Vocabulary ⓞ Grammar ⓞ Text

필수 단어 암기 & Test
① 단원별 필수 단어 암기
② 영어 → 한글 Test
③ 한글 → 영어 Test

단원별 중요 문법과 연습 문제
① 기초 문법 설명
② 교과서 적용 예시 소개
③ 기초/ Advanced Test

지문과 해설
① 전체 지문 해석
② 페이지별 필기 공간 확보
③ N회독을 통한 지문 습득

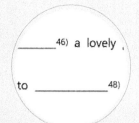

ⓞ Practice 3 ⓞ Practice 2 ⓞ Practice 1

빈칸 시험 (w/ 해석)
① 주요 내용/어법/어휘 빈칸
② 한글을 통한 내용 숙지
③ 반복 시험을 통한 빈칸 암기

빈칸 시험 (w/ 해석)
① 주요 내용/어법/어휘 빈칸
② 한글을 통한 내용 숙지
③ 반복 시험을 통한 빈칸 암기

어휘 & 어법 선택 시험
① 시험에 나오는 어법 어휘 공략
② 중요 어법/어휘 선택형 시험
③ 반복 시험을 통한 포인트 숙지

ⓞ Quiz ⓞ Final Test ⓞ 전체 영작 연습 ⓞ 학교 기출 문제

객관식 예상문제를 콕콕!
① 수능형 객관식 변형문제
② 100% 자체 제작 변형문제
③ 빈출 내신 문제 유형 연습

주관식 서술형 예상문제
① 어순/영작/어법 등
   주관식 서술형 문제 대비!
② 100% 자체 제작 변형문제

직접 영작 해보기
① 주어진 단어를 활용한
   전체 서술형 영작 훈련
② 쓰기를 통한 내용 암기

지문과 해설
① 단원별 실제 학교 기출
   문제 모음
② 객관식부터 서술형까지
   완벽 커버!

24년 고1
6월 모의고사

마
이
갓

연습과 실전 모두 잡는 내신대비 완벽
| workbook |

보듬영어

2024 고1

6월

WORK BOOK

―――――

2024년 고1 6월 모의고사 내신대비용 WorkBook & 변형문제

CONTENTS

2024 고1 6월 WORK BOOK

Voca

18	appreciate	진가를 알아보다, 이해하다, 감사하다		state	상태, 국가, 주; 진술하다
	support	지지[부양]하다; 지지, 후원, 도움		professional	프로, 전문가; 전문적인, 직업의
	switch	바꾸다, 전환하다; 스위치, 개폐기		tidy	말쑥한, 단정한, 상당한; 정돈하다
	current	현재의; 흐름, 해류, 기류, 경향		expert	전문가, 숙련가, 권위자
	access	접근, 이용; 접근하다, 이용하다		perspective	관점, 시각, 전망, 경치, 원근법
	via	경유하여, ~을 거쳐, ~에 의해		surroundings	환경, 주위의 상황, 처지
	editor	편집자, 교정자		atmosphere	대기, 분위기
	selection	선택, 선별, 선발		efficiently	능률[효율]적으로
	article	(신문 등의) 기사, 글, 조항, 물품		organize	정리하다, 체계화[구조화]하다
19	beat	치다, 때리다, 패배시키다; 고동, 맥박, 박자		arrange	정리[준비]하다, 배열[배치]하다, 각색하다
	rapidly	빨리, 급속히	21	force	강요하다; 힘, 세력
	apply to	~에 적용되다		environment	환경, 주위(의 상황)
	application	신청(서), 지원(서), 적용, 응용 프로그램		monoculture	단일 작물 재배
	carefully	주의 깊게, 신중히		growth	성장, 발육, 발전
	envelope	봉투		achieve	달성하다, 이루다, 성취하다
	emerge	나오다, 나타나다, 드러나다		nutrient	영양소, 영양분
	phrase	구(문장 구성 단위), 어구, 문구, 말		form	형태, 모양, 양식; 형성하다, 만들다
	pleasure	즐거움		by way of	~로, ~을 통해, ~을 거쳐[경유하여]
	faraway	먼, 멀리서		irrigation	(논, 밭에) 물을 댐; 관개
20	add up to	(합계, 결과 등이) ~가 되다		crop	(농)작물, 수확(량)
	destructive	파괴적인		efficient	유능한, 능률적인, 효율적인
	psychologist	심리학자		supply	공급하다, 주다; 공급
	disorderly	무질서한		usage	사용, 활용, 관습, 취급, 용법
	indicate	말하다, 나타내다, 표시하다		global	세계적인, 전 세계의, 전체적인
	mental	마음의, 정신의		capacity	용량, 수용력, 능력

Voca

❶ voca	❷ text	❸ [/]	❹ _____	❺ quiz 1	❻ quiz 2	❼ quiz 3	❽ quiz 4	❾ quiz 5

	feed	먹이를 주다, 먹이다; 먹이		path	(작은) 길, 진로, 보도, 경로
	unfortunately	불행하게도, 안타깝게도		resistance	저항(력), 반항, 반대
	luxurious	호화로운, 사치스러운	24	reflection	반영, 반사, 숙고, 반성
	attention	주의(력), 집중(력), 관심		identity	정체(성), 신원, 고유성, 독자성
	agricultural	농경의, 농업의		consciously	의식적으로
	be loaded with	~로 가득 차 있다, ~을 가득 싣고 있다		believe in	~을 믿다, 신뢰하다
	relative	상대적[비교적]인, 관련된; 친척, 동족		particular	특정한, 개개의; 사항, 상세
	surround	둘러싸다, 에워싸다; 주위, 분위기		aspect	측면, 면, 양상, 관점
	luxury	호화, 사치(品); 사치(品)의		according to	~에 의하면, ~에 따라
	random	무작위의, 임의의		identify	알아보다, 확인하다, 동일시하다
22	when it comes to -ing	~에 관해서 이야기하면		vote	투표하다, 제안하다; 투표, 표결, 선거권
	notice	알아채다, 주목하다; 공지, 안내문, 주목		claim	주장[요구]하다, 차지하다; 요구, 주장
	by oneself	홀로, 저절로		perform	수행하다, 행동하다, 공연[연주]하다
	owe	(~에게) 빚지고 있다; (~의) 덕분이다		similarly	유사하게, 마찬가지로
	pass by	옆을 지나다, 스쳐 지나가다		accept	받아들이다, 인정하다
23	take ~ to ...	~을 ...에 데려다주다		convince	납득시키다, 설득하다
	strength	장점, 강점, 힘, 강도, 내구력		after all	(예상과 달리) 마침내, 결국, 어쨌든
	compete	다투다, 겨루다, 경쟁하다		match	경기, 시합, 호적수; 경쟁시키다, 어울리다
	mastery	숙달, 통달, 지배		no longer	더 이상 ~아닌[하지 않는]
	tool	도구, 연장		pursue	추구하다, 쫓다
	prosperity	번영	25	collection	수집, 소장품, 수금, 징수
	equipment	장비, 장치, 기구		recycling	재활용
	hardship	고난, 역경		region	지역, 지방
	strategy	전략, 전술, 계획, 방법		lower	낮은, 하부의; 낮추다, 내리다, 떨어뜨리다
	struggle	싸우다, 분투하다; 투쟁, 노력, 고투		respectively	각각, 각기, 저마다

Voca

	gap	격차		souvenir	기념품
26	memorable	기억할 만한, 인상적인		participant	참여자, 참가자
	coin	(새로운 낱말.어구를) 만들다	28	detail	세부 (항목); 자세히 말하다, 열거하다
	term	기간, 용어, (-s) 조건, 관점; 말하다		figure	생각[계산]하다; 수치, 숫자, 인물, 모양
	Czech	체코인; 체코(사람)의	29	describe	묘사하다, 기술하다, 설명하다
	look after	돌보다		recommend	추천하다; 권고하다
	receive	받다, 받아들이다		remains	유적, 유해
	advanced	발달한, 진보된, 고급의		suggest	제안하다, 암시하다, 시사하다
	physics	물리(학)		ancestor	조상, 선조
	emigrate	(타국으로) 이주하다		excessive	과도한, 지나친, 터무니없는
	develop	발달[개발]하다, (병에) 걸리다		suffer	시달리다, 고통 받다
	numerous	수많은, 다수의		disease	질병, 질환
	theory	이론, 학설, 견해		settle in	적응하다, 자리 잡다
	influence	영향을 미치다; 영향(력)		permanent	영구적인, 영속적인
	universe	우주, 은하계, 세계		agriculture	농업, 농경, 농사
	appoint	임명[지명]하다, 정하다, 약속하다		domesticate	길들이다
	astronomy	천문학		cultivate	경작[재배]하다, 함양[양성]하다, 구축하다
	patent	특허(권)		epidemic	전염병, 유행(병); 유행성의
	propulsion	추진(력)		root	뿌리, 근원; 뿌리를 내리다
27	competition	경쟁, 시합		immediate	즉각적인, 직접의, 인접한
	dust off	(다시 쓰기 위해) 방치했던 것을 오랜 만에 꺼내다		effect	결과, 영향, 효과; 초래하다, 이루다
	recipe	조리법, 요리법		development	발달, 발전, 성장
	registration	등록 (서류), 기재		settlement	정착지, 합의, 해결
	register	등록하다, 기재하다; 등록부, 명부		lead to	~을 낳다, ~으로 이어지다
	participate in	~에 참여[참가]하다		increase	(수량이) 늘다, 증가하다; 증가

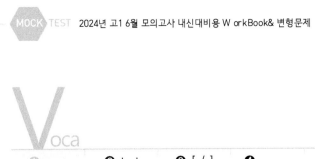

❶ voca		❷ text	❸ [/]	❹ _____	❺ quiz 1	❻ quiz 2	❼ quiz 3	❽ quiz 4	❾ quiz 5

	population	인구, 개체 수	
	density	밀도	
	major	주요한, 대다수의; 전공; 전공하다	
	eventually	결국, 마침내	
	settle	해결[결정]하다, 정착하다, 진정시키다	
30	commodity	물건	
	consumption	소비, 소모	
	reveal	드러내다, 폭로하다	
	preference	선호, 애호	
	delay	연기하다, 미루다; 지연, 지체	
	reward	보상, 보답; 보상[보답]하다	
	give up	포기하다, 그만두다	
	in exchange for	~ 대신에, ~와 교환하여	
	present	제공하다, 주다; 현재의, 출석한; 현재, 선물	
	envision	계획하다	
	occasion	행사, 경우, 중요한 때	
	weakness	약점, 결점	
	judge	판단하다, 심사하다; 판사, 심판	
	resolve	결심[결정]하다, 해결하다, 용해하다	
	benefit	이익, 이득; 이익이 되다	
31	lament	슬퍼하다	
	poem	시(詩)	
	literary	문학의, 문학적인	
	unexpected	예기치 않은, 뜻밖의	
	coincidence	우연의 일치, 동시에 일어남, 공존함	

	particularly	특히, 상세히	
	inspiration	영감, 고무, 감화	
	document	기록하다	
	significant	상당한, 중요한, 의미심장한	
	consequence	결과, 영향(력), 중요성	
	critical	중요한, 비판적인	
	impact	영향, 효과, 충격; 영향[충격]을 주다	
	slow down	느리게 하다, 늦추다	
	productivity	생산성	
	generally	일반적으로, 대개, 보통	
32	evidence	증거, 징후	
	demonstrate	입증[설명]하다, 보여 주다, 시위하다	
	focus	집중하다, 초점을 맞추다; 중심, 초점	
	avoid	피하다, 막다	
	auditory	청각의	
	eyesight	시력, 시야, 시각	
	dramatic	급격한, 극적인, 연극의	
	expansion	확대, 확장, 팽창	
	cortex	(대뇌) 피질	
	represent	표현하다, 나타내다	
	string	끈, 줄; 묶다, 꿰다, 연결하다	
	hippocampus	(대뇌 측두엽의) 해마	
	vital	중대한, 생명의, 활기 있는	
	spatial	공간의, 공간적인	
	physical	물리적인, 육체의	

Voca

| ❶ voca | ❷ text | ❸ [/] | ❹ _____ | ❺ quiz 1 | ❻ quiz 2 | ❼ quiz 3 | ❽ quiz 4 | ❾ quiz 5 |

	architecture	건축, 건축물	shift	(근무) 교대
	direct	직접의, 솔직한; 지시[감독]하다, 향하다	process	과정, 절차; 처리하다, 가공하다
	practice	습관, 관례, 실행[실천], 연습	initial	최초의, 초기의; 머리글자(의)
33	evolve	진화하다, (서서히) 발전하다	generate	발생시키다, 만들어내다, (감정을) 일으키다
	conflict	분쟁, 충돌, 갈등; 충돌하다, 다투다	separately	제각각, 각자, 따로따로
	tribe	부족, 종족	share	지분, 몫, 주식; 공유하다, 나누다
	outthink	~보다 우수한 생각을 하다	anonymously	익명으로
	enemy	적, 원수	preserve	보존[보호]하다, 저장하다; 금렵 지구
	slightly	약간, 조금	independent	독립적인
	possess	소유하다, ~의 마음을 사로잡다	judgment	판단, 판결, 견해
	advantage	이익, 이점; 이롭게 하다	evaluate	평가하다, 감정하다
	strike	치다, 떠오르다, 노력하다; 타격, 공격, 파업	on one's own	혼자, 혼자 힘으로
	accordingly	그에 따라, 그래서	promising	유망한
	military	군(대)의, 군사(상)의; 군대	assess	(자질 등을) 재다, 평가[가늠]하다
	weapon	무기, 병기, 공격 수단; 무장하다	individually	개별적으로, 개인적으로
	survival	생존, 생존자; 생존을 위한	elaborate	정교한, 공들인; 정교하게 만들다[말하다]
	decisive	결단력 있는, 단호한, 결정적인	surface	드러내다
	apply	지원[신청]하다, 적용하다, 바르다	advance	사전의; 진보, 전진; 진보하다, 제기하다
	succeeding	다음의	otherwise	그렇지 않으면, ~와 다르게
	generation	세대, 대, 발생	make sure	반드시 (~하도록) 하다, 확인하다, 확신하다
	opponent	상대, 반대자; 반대하는	effective	효과적인, 유효한, 시행되는
	pass on	속이다, 이용하다, 물려주다	in groups	떼를 지어, 삼삼오오
	responsible	책임있는	struggle to V	~하려고 몸부림치다[투쟁하다]
34	hide	숨기다, 감추다	intelligence	지성, 지능, 정보
	potential	가능성이 있는, 잠재적인; 가능성, 잠재력		

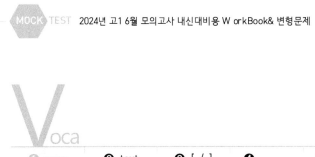

❶ voca	❷ text	❸ [/]	❹ _____	❺ quiz 1	❻ quiz 2	❼ quiz 3	❽ quiz 4	❾ quiz 5
35	sense	느끼다, 감지하다; 감각, 느낌, 분별		emission	배출(물), 배출량, 발산			
	agency	대리점, 대행사, 기관	37	exotic	이국적인, 진기한, 외래의, 이국의			
	genuine	진실한, 진정한, 진짜의		species	종, 종류			
	decision-making	의사 결정		suddenly	갑자기, 불시에			
	authority	권위, 권한, 당국, 기관		ecosystem	생태계			
	radically	급격하게		habitat	서식지, 거주지			
	manufacture	제조하다, 생산하다; 제조, 제품		pressure	압력, 압박, 스트레스; 압력을 가하다			
	plant	식물, 공장; 심다, 이식하다, 설치하다		edge	이점, 우위, 모서리, 끝, 가장자리, 날			
	for instance	예를 들면		adapt	조정하다, 적응시키다, 개작하다			
	examine	검사[조사]하다, 진찰하다		acorn	도토리			
	empower	(권한을) 부여하다		mature	성숙한, 원숙한; 성숙해지다			
	decision	결정, 결심, 판결		destroy	파괴하다, 논파하다, 죽이다			
	improve	향상[개선]시키다, 향상하다		varied	다양한, 다채로운			
36	archive	기록 (보관소), 아카이브; 보관하다		survive	살아남다, 생존하다			
	assume	추정하다, (태도 등을) 취하다, 맡다		as a result	그 결과			
	threaten	협박[위협]하다, 위태롭게 하다	38	force A to V	A가 ~하도록 강요하다			
	hazardous	위험한		typically	전형적으로, 대표적으로, 대체로, 보통			
	used to V	~하곤 했다		frequently	자주, 흔히, 빈번히			
	shift from A to B	A에서 B로 옮겨가다		possession	소유(권), (-s) 소지품, 재산			
	electricity	전기, 전류		in particular	특히, 특별히			
	neglect	무시[방치]하다; 소홀, 무시		so ~ that ...	아주 ~해서 ...하다			
	declare	선언하다, 신고하다, 분명하게 말하다		at a time	한 번에, 한꺼번에			
	source	원천, 근원, (-s) 출처, 정보원		on the other hand	한편, 반면에			
	fossil fuel	화석 연료		transport	운송, 수송; 운반[수송]하다			
	carbon	탄소		distance	거리, 간격, 차이			

Voca

❶ voca　　❷ text　　❸ [/]　　❹ _____　　❺ quiz 1　　❻ quiz 2　　❼ quiz 3　　❽ quiz 4　　❾ quiz 5

	counterpart	(대응 관계에 있는) 상대		progress	진보[발전]하다, 전진하다; 진보, 발전
	in turn	결과적으로, 차례차례		fail to V	~하지 못하다
	result in	(결과적으로) ~을 낳다[야기하다]		account	기술, 설명, 계좌; 설명[생각]하다, 차지하다
	rapid	빠른, 신속한, 급한		embrace	포옹하다, 수용하다; 포옹, 수용
	require	필요로 하다, 요구하다		ensure	확실하게 하다, 보장하다
	labor	노동, 산고; 노동하다		product	생산물, 상품, 산물
39	flexible	융통성이 있는, 유연한, 탄력적인		serve	제공[기여]하다, 복무하다, 적합하다
	migrate	이동하다, 이주하다		overlook	간과하다, 눈감아 주다, 내려다보다
	instruction	수업, 교육, 지시, 설명		adopt	(채)택하다, 선정하다, 취하다
	inefficient	비효율적인	41-42	seek	추구하다, 찾다, 노력하다
	migration	이주, 이동		degree	정도, 도, 학위
	keep -ing	계속 ~하다		in order to V	~하기 위해, ~하려고
	comparison	비교, 비유		spicy	매운, 향신료를 넣은
	tend to V	~하는 경향이 있다		threat	위협, 협박
	facilitate	촉진[조장]하다, 용이하게 하다		perceive	인지하다, 감지하다
	flexibility	유연성		stimulus	자극, 격려, 고무 ((복수형 stimuli))
40	standard	표준, 기준; 표준의, 보통의		painful	아픈, 괴로운
	for the most part	대부분은, 대개는, 주로		ultimately	최후로, 마침내, 궁극적으로
	resource	수단, 기지 (-s) 자원, 소질; 자원을 제공하다		similar to	~와 비슷한
	useless	쓸모없는, 소용없는, 헛된		violate	어기다, 위반하다, 침해하다
	A as well as B	B뿐만 아니라 A도		uncomfortable	불편한
	vision	미래상, 비전, 시야, 시력; 상상하다		context	상황, 배경, 맥락, 문맥
	have difficulty -ing	~하는 것에 어려움을 겪다		suffering	고통, 괴로움, 고난; 괴로워하는, 고통을 겪는
	educational	교육(상)의, 교육적인		punishment	처벌, 형벌
	commercial	광고(방송); 상업적인		remarkable	놀랄 만한, 주목할 만한, 훌륭한

❶ voca	❷ text	❸ [/]	❹ _____	❺ quiz 1	❻ quiz 2	❼ quiz 3	❽ quiz 4	❾ quiz 5

	ingredient	재료, 성분, 구성 요소	instrument	악기, 기구, 도구
	chilly	냉담한, 쌀쌀한	at a loss	당황하여, 어찌할 바를 몰라, 밑지고
	tongue	혀, 언어	steady	한결같은, 확고한, 안정된, 착실한
	stimulate	자극하다, 활성화시키다, 흥분시키다	focus on	~에 집중하다, 초점을 맞추다
	receptor	수용체	encourage	장려[격려]하다, 촉구하다
	activate	작동시키다, 활성화시키다	search for	~을 찾다
	tissue	(세포)조직	safety	안전
	completely	완전히, 충분히	relief	안도(감), 경감, 완화, 구호, 구제
	produce	생산[제조]하다, 초래하다; 농산물	proudly	자랑스럽게, 위풍당당하게
	start off	움직이기 시작하다		
	derive	비롯되다, 유래하다, 끌어내다		
	repeat	되풀이하다, 반복하다; 반복		
	exposure	노출, 폭로, 직접적인 체험		
	directly	곧장, 똑바로, 직접(적)으로, 즉시		
	associate	연관[제휴]시키다, 교제하다; 동료		
43-45	far from	전혀[결코] ~이 아닌		
	flight	비행, 항공편		
	instructor	강사, 교사		
	be filled with	~로 가득차다		
	wonder	궁금해하다, 경탄하다; 경이		
	appreciation	평가, 인정, 이해, 감탄, 감사		
	emergency	긴급, 긴급 상황, 응급		
	a bit of	한 조각의, 소량의		
	turbulence	난(亂)기류		
	flash	번쩍임, 섬광; 갑자기 비추다		

Voca Test

영 〉 한

❶ voca	❷ text	❸ [/]	❹ ____	❺ quiz 1	❻ quiz 2	❼ quiz 3	❽ quiz 4	❾ quiz 5
18 appreciate				state				
support				professional				
switch				tidy				
current				expert				
access				perspective				
via				surroundings				
editor				atmosphere				
selection				efficiently				
article				organize				
19 beat				arrange				
rapidly		**21**		force				
apply to				environment				
application				monoculture				
carefully				growth				
envelope				achieve				
emerge				nutrient				
phrase				form				
pleasure				by way of				
faraway				irrigation				
20 add up to				crop				
destructive				efficient				
psychologist				supply				
disorderly				usage				
indicate				global				
mental				capacity				

Voca Test

❶ voca	❷ text	❸ [/]	❹ _____	❺ quiz 1	❻ quiz 2	❼ quiz 3	❽ quiz 4	❾ quiz 5
	feed				path			
	unfortunately				resistance			
	luxurious			24	reflection			
	attention				identity			
	agricultural				consciously			
	be loaded with				believe in			
	relative				particular			
	surround				aspect			
	luxury				according to			
	random				identify			
22	when it comes to -ing				vote			
	notice				claim			
	by oneself				perform			
	owe				similarly			
	pass by				accept			
23	take ~ to ...				convince			
	strength				after all			
	compete				match			
	mastery				no longer			
	tool				pursue			
	prosperity			25	collection			
	equipment				recycling			
	hardship				region			
	strategy				lower			
	struggle				respectively			

Voca Test

	voca	❷ text	❸ [/]	❹ ____	❺ quiz 1	❻ quiz 2	❼ quiz 3	❽ quiz 4	❾ quiz 5

	❶ voca					❶ voca				
	gap					souvenir				
26	memorable					participant				
	coin			28		detail				
	term					figure				
	Czech			29		describe				
	look after					recommend				
	receive					remains				
	advanced					suggest				
	physics					ancestor				
	emigrate					excessive				
	develop					suffer				
	numerous					disease				
	theory					settle in				
	influence					permanent				
	universe					agriculture				
	appoint					domesticate				
	astronomy					cultivate				
	patent					epidemic				
	propulsion					root				
27	competition					immediate				
	dust off					effect				
	recipe					development				
	registration					settlement				
	register					lead to				
	participate in					increase				

Voca Test

	❶ voca	❷ text	❸ [/]	❹ _____	❺ quiz 1	❻ quiz 2	❼ quiz 3	❽ quiz 4	❾ quiz 5
	population					particularly			
	density					inspiration			
	major					document			
	eventually					significant			
	settle					consequence			
30	commodity					critical			
	consumption					impact			
	reveal					slow down			
	preference					productivity			
	delay					generally			
	reward				32	evidence			
	give up					demonstrate			
	in exchange for					focus			
	present					avoid			
	envision					auditory			
	occasion					eyesight			
	weakness					dramatic			
	judge					expansion			
	resolve					cortex			
	benefit					represent			
31	lament					string			
	poem					hippocampus			
	literary					vital			
	unexpected					spatial			
	coincidence					physical			

Voca Tes

영 한

❶ voca	❷ text	❸ [/]	❹ _____	❺ quiz 1	❻ quiz 2	❼ quiz 3	❽ quiz 4	❾ quiz 5

	architecture		shift			
	direct		process			
	practice		initial			
33	evolve		generate			
	conflict		separately			
	tribe		share			
	outthink		anonymously			
	enemy		preserve			
	slightly		independent			
	possess		judgment			
	advantage		evaluate			
	strike		on one's own			
	accordingly		promising			
	military		assess			
	weapon		individually			
	survival		elaborate			
	decisive		surface			
	apply		advance			
	succeeding		otherwise			
	generation		make sure			
	opponent		effective			
	pass on		in groups			
	responsible		struggle to V			
34	hide		intelligence			
	potential					

Voca Test

 영 한

❶ voca	❷ text	❸ [/]	❹ _____	❺ quiz 1	❻ quiz 2	❼ quiz 3	❽ quiz 4	❾ quiz 5
35 sense								
agency								
genuine								
decision-making								
authority								
radically								
manufacture								
plant								
for instance								
examine								
empower								
decision								
improve								
36 archive								
assume								
threaten								
hazardous								
used to V								
shift from A to B								
electricity								
neglect								
declare								
source								
fossil fuel								
carbon								
emission								
37 exotic								
species								
suddenly								
ecosystem								
habitat								
pressure								
edge								
adapt								
acorn								
mature								
destroy								
varied								
survive								
as a result								
38 force A to V								
typically								
frequently								
possession								
in particular								
so ~ that ...								
at a time								
on the other hand								
transport								
distance								

Voca Test

영 한

	① voca	② text	③ [/]	④ ____	⑤ quiz 1	⑥ quiz 2	⑦ quiz 3	⑧ quiz 4	⑨ quiz 5
	counterpart				progress				
	in turn				fail to V				
	result in				account				
	rapid				embrace				
	require				ensure				
	labor				product				
39	flexible				serve				
	migrate				overlook				
	instruction				adopt				
	inefficient			41-42	seek				
	migration				degree				
	keep -ing				in order to V				
	comparison				spicy				
	tend to V				threat				
	facilitate				perceive				
	flexibility				stimulus				
40	standard				painful				
	for the most part				ultimately				
	resource				similar to				
	useless				violate				
	A as well as B				uncomfortable				
	vision				context				
	have difficulty -ing				suffering				
	educational				punishment				
	commercial				remarkable				

Voca Test

영 한

❶ voca	❷ text	❸ [/]	❹ _____	❺ quiz 1	❻ quiz 2	❼ quiz 3	❽ quiz 4	❾ quiz 5

	ingredient		instrument	
	chilly		at a loss	
	tongue		steady	
	stimulate		focus on	
	receptor		encourage	
	activate		search for	
	tissue		safety	
	completely		relief	
	produce		proudly	
	start off			
	derive			
	repeat			
	exposure			
	directly			
	associate			
43-45	far from			
	flight			
	instructor			
	be filled with			
	wonder			
	appreciation			
	emergency			
	a bit of			
	turbulence			
	flash			

oca Test

영 〉 한

❶ voca	❷ text	❸ [/]	❹ ____	❺ quiz 1	❻ quiz 2	❼ quiz 3	❽ quiz 4	❾ quiz 5
18		진가를 알아보다, 이해하다, 감사하다				상태, 국가, 주; 진술하다		
		지지[부양]하다; 지지, 후원, 도움				프로, 전문가; 전문적인, 직업의		
		바꾸다, 전환하다; 스위치, 개폐기				말쑥한, 단정한, 상당한; 정돈하다		
		현재의; 흐름, 해류, 기류, 경향				전문가, 숙련가, 권위자		
		접근, 이용; 접근하다, 이용하다				관점, 시각, 전망, 경치, 원근법		
		경유하여, ~을 거쳐, ~에 의해				환경, 주위의 상황, 처지		
		편집자, 교정자				대기, 분위기		
		선택, 선별, 선발				능률[효율]적으로		
		(신문 등의) 기사, 글, 조항, 물품				정리하다, 체계화[구조화]하다		
19		치다, 때리다, 패배시키다; 고동, 맥박, 박자				정리[준비]하다, 배열[배치]하다, 각색하다		
		빨리, 급속히	21			강요하다; 힘, 세력		
		~에 적용되다				환경, 주위(의 상황)		
		신청(서), 지원(서), 적용, 응용 프로그램				단일 작물 재배		
		주의 깊게, 신중히				성장, 발육, 발전		
		봉투				달성하다, 이루다, 성취하다		
		나오다, 나타나다, 드러나다				영양소, 영양분		
		구(문장 구성 단위), 어구, 문구, 말				형태, 모양, 양식; 형성하다, 만들다		
		즐거움				~로, ~을 통해, ~을 거쳐[경유하여]		
		먼, 멀리서				(논, 밭에) 물을 댐; 관개		
20		(합계, 결과 등이) ~가 되다				(농)작물, 수확(량)		
		파괴적인				유능한, 능률적인, 효율적인		
		심리학자				공급하다, 주다; 공급		
		무질서한				사용, 활용, 관습, 취급, 용법		
		말하다, 나타내다, 표시하다				세계적인, 전 세계의, 전체적인		
		마음의, 정신의				용량, 수용력, 능력		

Voca Test

❶ voca	❷ text	❸ [/]	❹ _____	❺ quiz 1	❻ quiz 2	❼ quiz 3	❽ quiz 4	❾ quiz 5
		먹이를 주다, 먹이다; 먹이				(작은) 길, 진로, 보도, 경로		
		불행하게도, 안타깝게도				저항(력), 반항, 반대		
		호화로운, 사치스러운	24			반영, 반사, 숙고, 반성		
		주의(력), 집중(력), 관심				정체(성), 신원, 고유성, 독자성		
		농경의, 농업의				의식적으로		
		~로 가득 차 있다, ~을 가득 싣고 있다				~을 믿다, 신뢰하다		
		상대적[비교적]인, 관련된; 친척, 동족				특정한, 개개의; 사항, 상세		
		둘러싸다, 에워싸다; 주위, 분위기				측면, 면, 양상, 관점		
		호화, 사치(품); 사치(품)의				~에 의하면, ~에 따라		
		무작위의, 임의의				알아보다, 확인하다, 동일시하다		
22		~에 관해서 이야기하면				투표하다, 제안하다, 투표, 표결, 선거권		
		알아채다, 주목하다; 공지, 안내문, 주목				주장[요구]하다, 차지하다; 요구, 주장		
		홀로, 저절로				수행하다, 행동하다, 공연[연주]하다		
		(~에게) 빚지고 있다; (~의) 덕분이다				유사하게, 마찬가지로		
		옆을 지나다, 스쳐 지나가다				받아들이다, 인정하다		
23		~을 ...에 데려다주다				납득시키다, 설득하다		
		장점, 강점, 힘, 강도, 내구력				(예상과 달리) 마침내, 결국, 어쨌든		
		다투다, 겨루다, 경쟁하다				경기, 시합, 호적수; 경쟁시키다, 어울리다		
		숙달, 통달, 지배				더 이상 ~아닌[하지 않는]		
		도구, 연장				추구하다, 쫓다		
		번영	25			수집, 소장품, 수금, 징수		
		장비, 장치, 기구				재활용		
		고난, 역경				지역, 지방		
		전략, 전술, 계획, 방법				낮은, 하부의; 낮추다, 내리다, 떨어뜨리다		
		싸우다, 분투하다; 투쟁, 노력, 고투				각각, 각기, 저마다		

Voca Test

❶ voca	❷ text	❸ [/]	❹ _____	❺ quiz 1	❻ quiz 2	❼ quiz 3	❽ quiz 4	❾ quiz 5
		격차				기념품		
26		기억할 만한, 인상적인				참여자, 참가자		
		(새로운 낱말.어구를) 만들다	28			세부 (항목); 자세히 말하다, 열거하다		
		기간, 용어, (-s) 조건, 관점; 말하다				생각[계산]하다; 수치, 숫자, 인물, 보양		
		체코인; 체코(사람)의	29			묘사하다, 기술하다, 설명하다		
		돌보다				추천하다; 권고하다		
		받다, 받아들이다				유적, 유해		
		발달한, 진보된, 고급의				제안하다, 암시하다, 시사하다		
		물리(학)				조상, 선조		
		(타국으로) 이주하다				과도한, 지나친, 터무니없는		
		발달[개발]하다, (병에) 걸리다				시달리다, 고통 받다		
		수많은, 다수의				질병, 질환		
		이론, 학설, 견해				적응하다, 자리 잡다		
		영향을 미치다; 영향(력)				영구적인, 영속적인		
		우주, 은하계, 세계				농업, 농경, 농사		
		임명[지명]하다, 정하다, 약속하다				길들이다		
		천문학				경작[재배]하다, 함양[양성]하다, 구축하다		
		특허(권)				전염병, 유행(병); 유행성의		
		추진(력)				뿌리, 근원; 뿌리를 내리다		
27		경쟁, 시합				즉각적인, 직접의, 인접한		
		(다시 쓰기 위해) 방치했던 것을 오랜 만에 꺼내다				결과, 영향, 효과; 초래하다, 이루다		
		조리법, 요리법				발달, 발전, 성장		
		등록 (서류), 기재				정착지, 합의, 해결		
		등록하다, 기재하다; 등록부, 명부				~을 낳다, ~으로 이어지다		
		~에 참여[참가]하다				(수량이) 늘다, 증가하다; 증가		

Voca Test

❶ voca	❷ text	❸ [/]	❹ _____	❺ quiz 1	❻ quiz 2	❼ quiz 3	❽ quiz 4	❾ quiz 5
		인구, 개체 수				특히, 상세히		
		밀도				영감, 고무, 감화		
		주요한, 대다수의; 전공; 전공하다				기록하다		
		결국, 마침내				상당한, 중요한, 의미심장한		
		해결[결정]하다, 정착하다, 진정시키다				결과, 영향(력), 중요성		
30		물건				중요한, 비판적인		
		소비, 소모				영향, 효과, 충격; 영향[충격]을 주다		
		드러내다, 폭로하다				느리게 하다, 늦추다		
		선호, 애호				생산성		
		연기하다, 미루다; 지연, 지체				일반적으로, 대개, 보통		
		보상, 보답; 보상[보답]하다	32			증거, 징후		
		포기하다, 그만두다				입증[설명]하다, 보여 주다, 시위하다		
		~ 대신에, ~와 교환하여				집중하다, 초점을 맞추다; 중심, 초점		
		제공하다, 주다; 현재의, 출석한; 현재, 선물				피하다, 막다		
		계획하다				청각의		
		행사, 경우, 중요한 때				시력, 시야, 시각		
		약점, 결점				급격한, 극적인, 연극의		
		판단하다, 심사하다; 판사, 심판				확대, 확장, 팽창		
		결심[결정]하다, 해결하다, 용해하다				(대뇌) 피질		
		이익, 이득; 이익이 되다				표현하다, 나타내다		
31		슬퍼하다				끈, 줄; 묶다, 꿰다, 연결하다		
		시(詩)				(대뇌 측두엽의) 해마		
		문학의, 문학적인				중대한, 생명의, 활기 있는		
		예기치 않은, 뜻밖의				공간의, 공간적인		
		우연의 일치, 동시에 일어남, 공존함				물리적인, 육체의		

Voca Test

❶ voca	❷ text	❸ [/]	❹ ____	❺ quiz 1	❻ quiz 2	❼ quiz 3	❽ quiz 4	❾ quiz 5
		건축, 건축물				(근무) 교대		
		직접의, 솔직한; 지시[감독]하다, 향하다				과정, 절차; 처리하다, 가공하다		
		습관, 관례, 실행[실천] ,연습				최초의, 초기의; 머리글자(의)		
33		진화하다, (서서히) 발전하다				발생시키다, 만들어내다, (감정을) 일으키다		
		분쟁, 충돌, 갈등; 충돌하다, 다투다				제각각, 각자, 따로따로		
		부족, 종족				지분, 몫, 주식; 공유하다, 나누다		
		~보다 우수한 생각을 하다				익명으로		
		적, 원수				보존[보호]하다, 저장하다; 금렵 지구		
		약간, 조금				독립적인		
		소유하다, ~의 마음을 사로잡다				판단, 판결, 견해		
		이익, 이점; 이롭게 하다				평가하다, 감정하다		
		치다, 떠오르다, 노력하다; 타격, 공격, 파업				혼자, 혼자 힘으로		
		그에 따라, 그래서				유망한		
		군(대)의, 군사(상)의; 군대				(자질 등을) 재다, 평가[가늠]하다		
		무기, 병기, 공격 수단; 무장하다				개별적으로, 개인적으로		
		생존, 생존자; 생존을 위한				정교한, 공들인; 정교하게 만들다[말하다]		
		결단력 있는, 단호한, 결정적인				드러내다		
		지원[신청]하다, 적용하다, 바르다				사전의; 진보, 전진; 진보하다, 제기하다		
		다음의				그렇지 않으면, ~와 다르게		
		세대, 대, 발생				반드시 (~하도록) 하다, 확인하다, 확신하다		
		상대, 반대자; 반대하는				효과적인, 유효한, 시행되는		
		속이다, 이용하다, 물려주다				떼를 지어, 삼삼오오		
		책임있는				~하려고 몸부림치다[투쟁하다]		
34		숨기다, 감추다				지성, 지능, 정보		
		가능성이 있는, 잠재적인; 가능성, 잠재력						

Voca Test

❶ voca	❷ text	❸ [/]	❹ _____	❺ quiz 1	❻ quiz 2	❼ quiz 3	❽ quiz 4	❾ quiz 5
35			느끼다, 감지하다; 감각, 느낌, 분별				배출(물) ,배출량, 발산	
			대리점, 대행사, 기관	37			이국적인, 진기한, 외래의, 이국의	
			진실한, 진정한, 진짜의				종, 종류	
			의사 결정				갑자기, 불시에	
			권위, 권한, 당국, 기관				생태계	
			급격하게				서식지, 거주지	
			제조하다, 생산하다; 제조, 제품				압력, 압박, 스트레스; 압력을 가하다	
			식물, 공장; 심다, 이식하다, 설치하다				이점, 우위, 모서리, 끝, 가장자리, 날	
			예를 들면				조정하다, 적응시키다, 개작하다	
			검사[조사]하다, 진찰하다				도토리	
			(권한을) 부여하다				성숙한, 원숙한; 성숙해지다	
			결정, 결심, 판결				파괴하다, 논파하다, 죽이다	
			향상[개선]시키다, 향상하다				다양한, 다채로운	
36			기록 (보관소) ,아카이브; 보관하다				살아남다, 생존하다	
			추정하다, (태도 등을) 취하다, 맡다				그 결과	
			협박[위협]하다, 위태롭게 하다	38			A가 ~하도록 강요하다	
			위험한				전형적으로, 대표적으로, 대체로, 보통	
			~하곤 했다				자주, 흔히, 빈번히	
			A에서 B로 옮겨가다				소유(권) ,(-s) 소지품, 재산	
			전기, 전류				특히, 특별히	
			무시[방치]하다; 소홀, 무시				아주 ~해서 ...하다	
			선언하다, 신고하다, 분명하게 말하다				한 번에, 한꺼번에	
			원천, 근원, (-s) 출처, 정보원				한편, 반면에	
			화석 연료				운송, 수송; 운반[수송]하다	
			탄소				거리, 간격, 차이	

Voca Test

❶ voca	❷ text	❸ [/]	❹ _____	❺ quiz 1	❻ quiz 2	❼ quiz 3	❽ quiz 4	❾ quiz 5
		(대응 관계에 있는) 상대				진보[발전]하다, 전진하다; 진보, 발전		
		결과적으로, 차례차례				~하지 못하다		
		(결과적으로) ~을 낳다[야기하다]				기술, 설명, 계좌; 설명[생각]하다, 차지하다		
		빠른, 신속한, 급한				포옹하다, 수용하다; 포옹, 수용		
		필요로 하다, 요구하다				확실하게 하다, 보장하다		
39		노동, 산고; 노동하다				생산물, 상품, 산물		
		융통성이 있는, 유연한, 탄력적인				제공[기여]하다, 복무하다, 적합하다		
		이동하다, 이주하다				간과하다, 눈감아 주다, 내려다보다		
		수업, 교육, 지시, 설명				(채)택하다, 선정하다, 취하다		
		비효율적인	41-42			추구하다, 찾다, 노력하다		
		이주, 이동				정도, 도, 학위		
		계속 ~하다				~하기 위해, ~하려고		
		비교, 비유				매운, 향신료를 넣은		
		~하는 경향이 있다				위협, 협박		
		촉진[조장]하다, 용이하게 하다				인지하다, 감지하다		
		유연성				자극, 격려, 고무 ((복수형 stimuli))		
40		표준, 기준; 표준의, 보통의				아픈, 괴로운		
		대부분은, 대개는, 주로				최후로, 마침내, 궁극적으로		
		수단, 기지 (-s) 자원, 소질; 자원을 제공하다				~와 비슷한		
		쓸모없는, 소용없는, 헛된				어기다, 위반하다, 침해하다		
		B뿐만 아니라 A도				불편한		
		미래상, 비전, 시야, 시력; 상상하다				상황, 배경, 맥락, 문맥		
		~하는 것에 어려움을 겪다				고통, 괴로움, 고난; 괴로워하는, 고통을 겪는		
		교육(상)의, 교육적인				처벌, 형벌		
		광고(방송) ;상업적인				놀랄 만한, 주목할 만한, 훌륭한		

Voca Test

❶ voca	❷ text	❸ [/]	❹ _____	❺ quiz 1	❻ quiz 2	❼ quiz 3	❽ quiz 4	❾ quiz 5
		재료, 성분, 구성 요소			악기, 기구, 도구			
		냉담한, 쌀쌀한			당황하여, 어찌할 바를 몰라, 밑지고			
		혀, 언어			한결같은, 확고한, 안정된, 착실한			
		자극하다, 활성화시키다, 흥분시키다			~에 집중하다, 초점을 맞추다			
		수용체			장려[격려]하다, 촉구하다			
		작동시키다, 활성화시키다			~을 찾다			
		(세포)조직			안전			
		완전히, 충분히			안도(감), 경감, 완화, 구호, 구제			
		생산[제조]하다, 초래하다; 농산물			자랑스럽게, 위풍당당하게			
		움직이기 시작하다						
		비롯되다, 유래하다, 끌어내다						
		되풀이하다, 반복하다; 반복						
		노출, 폭로, 직접적인 체험						
		곧장, 똑바로, 직접(적)으로, 즉시						
		연관[제휴]시키다, 교제하다; 동료						
43-45		전혀[결코] ~이 아닌						
		비행, 항공편						
		강사, 교사						
		~로 가득차다						
		궁금해하다, 경탄하다; 경이						
		평가, 인정, 이해, 감탄, 감사						
		긴급, 긴급 상황, 응급						
		한 조각의, 소량의						
		난(亂)기류						
		번쩍임, 섬광; 갑자기 비추다						

2024 고1 6월 모의고사

① voca ② text ❸ [/] ❹ ＿＿＿ ❺ quiz 1 ❻ quiz 2 ❼ quiz 3 ❽ quiz 4 ❾ quiz 5

18 목적

❶ Dear Reader,

독자분께,

❷ We always appreciate your support.

보내주신 성원에 항상 감사드립니다.

❸ As you know, our service is now available through an app.

아시다시피, 이제 앱을 통해서도 저희 서비스를 이용하실 수 있습니다.

❹ There has never been a better time to switch to an online membership of TourTide Magazine.

TourTide Magazine의 온라인 회원으로 전환하기에 이보다 더 좋은 시기는 없습니다.

❺ At a 50% discount off your current print subscription, you can access a full year of online reading.

신의 현재 인쇄본 구독료에서 50% 할인된 가격으로 1년 치를 온라인으로 구독할 수 있습니다.

❻ Get new issues and daily web pieces at TourTide.com, read or listen to TourTide Magazine via the app, and get our members only newsletter.

TourTide.com에서 신간호와 일일 웹 기사를 받아보고, 앱을 통해 TourTide Magazine을 읽거나 청취해 보고, 회원 전용 뉴스레터도 받아보세요.

❼ You'll also gain access to our editors' selections of the best articles. Join today!

편집자들이 선정한 최고의 기사도 받아볼 수 있습니다. 오늘 가입하세요!

❽ Yours, TourTide Team

TourTide 팀 드림

19 심경

❶ As I walked from the mailbox, my heart was beating rapidly.
우체통에서 걸어올 때 내 심장은 빠르게 뛰고 있었다.

❷ In my hands, I held the letter from the university I had applied to.
내 손에는 지원했던 대학에서 보낸 편지가 들려있었다.

❸ I thought my grades were good enough to cross the line and my application letter was well-written, but was it enough?
내 생각에는 합격할 만큼 성적이 좋았고 지원서도 잘 썼지만, 그것으로 충분했을까?

❹ I hadn't slept a wink for days.
며칠 동안 한숨도 잘 수 없었다.

❺ As I carefully tore into the paper of the envelope, the letter slowly emerged with the opening phrase, "It is our great pleasure.."
봉투의 종이를 조심스럽게 찢자 "매우 기쁘게도..."라는 첫 문구와 함께 편지가 천천히 모습을 드러냈다.

❻ I shouted with joy, "I am in!" As I held the letter, I began to make a fantasy about my college life in a faraway city.
나는 기뻐서 소리질렀다. "합격이야!" 나는 편지를 손에 쥐고 집에서 멀리 떨어진 도시에서의 대학 생활에 대해 상상하기 시작했다.

20 요지

❶ Having a messy room can add up to negative feelings and destructive thinking.
방이 지저분한 것은 결국 부정적인 감정과 파괴적인 사고로 이어질 수 있다.

❷ Psychologists say that having a disorderly room can indicate a disorganized mental state.
심리학자들은 방이 무질서하다는 것은 정신 상태가 혼란스럽다는 것을 나타낼 수 있다고 말한다.

❸ One of the professional tidying experts says that the moment you start cleaning your room, you also start changing your life and gaining new perspective.
정리 전문가 중 한 명은 방 청소를 시작하는 순간 당신은 인생을 변화시키고 새로운 관점을 얻기 시작한다고 말한다.

❹ When you clean your surroundings, positive and good atmosphere follows.
주변을 청소하면 긍정적이고 좋은 분위기가 따라온다.

❺ You can do more things efficiently and neatly.
당신은 더 많은 일을 효율적이고 깔끔하게 할 수 있다.

❻ So, clean up your closets, organize your drawers, and arrange your things first, then peace of mind will follow.
그러니 먼저 옷장을 청소하고, 서랍을 정리하고, 물건을 정돈한다면 마음의 평화가 따라올 것이다.

21 주장

❶ The soil of a farm field is forced to be the perfect environment for monoculture growth.
농지의 토양은 단일 작물 재배를 위한 완벽한 환경이어야 한다.

❷ This is achieved by adding nutrients in the form of fertilizer and water by way of irrigation.
이것은 비료 형태로 양분을 더하고 관개로 물을 댐으로써 이루어진다.

❸ During the last fifty years, engineers and crop scientists have helped farmers become much more efficient at supplying exactly the right amount of both.
지난 50년 동안 기술자와 농작물 연구자들은 농부들이 양쪽 모두의 정확한 적정량을 공급하는 데 훨씬 더 효율적일 수 있도록 도움을 주었다.

❹ World usage of fertilizer has tripled since 1969, and the global capacity for irrigation has almost doubled; we are feeding and watering our fields more than ever, and our crops are loving it.
전 세계 비료 사용량은 1969년 이래로 세 배가 되었고, 전체 관개 능력은 거의 두 배가 되었다. 우리는 그 어느 때보다도 들판을 기름지게 하고 물을 대고 있으며, 우리의 농작물은 이를 좋아한다.

❺ Unfortunately, these luxurious conditions have also excited the attention of certain agricultural undesirables.
불행히도, 이러한 호사스러운 상황은 농업에서는 달갑지 않은 것들의 관심도 끌어들였다.

❻ Because farm fields are loaded with nutrients and water relative to the natural land that surrounds them, they are desired as luxury real estate by every random weed in the area.
농지는 주위를 둘러싼 자연 지대에 비해 영양분과 물이 풍족히 채워져 있기 때문에 그 지역의 어떤 잡초라도 원하는 고급 부동산이 된다.

22 의미

❶ When it comes to helping out, you don't have to do much.
도움을 주는 것에 관해서 당신은 많은 것을 할 필요는 없다.

❷ All you have to do is come around and show that you care.
그저 다가가서 관심을 갖고 있다는 것을 보여주기만 하면 된다.

❸ If you notice someone who is lonely, you could go and sit with them.
외로운 사람을 발견하면 가서 함께 앉아 있으면 된다.

❹ If you work with someone who eats lunch all by themselves, and you go and sit down with them, they will begin to be more social after a while, and they will owe it all to you.
혼자서 점심을 먹는 사람과 함께 일한다면, 그리고 그 사람에게 다가가서 함께 앉는다면 얼마 지나지 않아 그 사람은 더 사교적으로 변하기 시작할 것이고, 이 모든 것을 당신 덕분이라고 할 것이다.

❺ A person's happiness comes from attention.
한 사람의 행복은 관심에서 비롯된다.

❻ There are too many people out in the world who feel like everyone has forgotten them or ignored them.
세상에는 모든 이가 자신을 잊었거나 무시한다고 느끼는 사람들이 너무 많다.

❼ Even if you say hi to someone passing by, they will begin to feel better about themselves, like someone cares.
지나가는 사람들에게 인사만 건네도, 누군가 (그들에게) 관심을 가져주는 것처럼, 그들은 자기 자신에 대해 기분이 좋아지기 시작할 것이다.

23 주제

❶ We often try to make cuts in our challenges and take the easy route.
우리는 종종 우리의 도전을 멈추고, 쉬운 길을 택하려고 한다.

❷ When taking the quick exit, we fail to acquire the strength to compete.
쉬운 길을 택하면 경쟁할 수 있는 힘을 얻지 못한다.

❸ We often take the easy route to improve our skills.
우리는 종종 실력을 향상하기 위해 쉬운 길을 택한다.

❹ Many of us never really work to achieve mastery in the key areas of life.
우리 중 다수가 인생의 핵심이 되는 영역에서 숙달을 위한 노력을 하지 않는다.

❺ These skills are key tools that can be useful to our career, health, and prosperity.
이러한 기술은 경력, 건강, 번영에 도움이 될 수 있는 핵심 도구이다. 성공한 운동선수들은 더 좋은 장비 때문에 승리하는 것이 아니다.

❻ Highly successful athletes don't win because of better equipment; they win by facing hardship to gain strength and skill.
그들은 힘과 실력을 얻기 위해 고난에 맞섬으로써 승리한다. 그들은 힘과 실력을 얻기 위해 고난에 맞섬으로써 승리한다.

❼ They win through preparation.
그들은 준비를 통해 승리한다.

❽ It's the mental preparation, winning mindset, strategy, and skill that set them apart.
그들을 돋보이게 하는 것은 바로 정신적 준비, 승리하는 마음가짐, 전략, 그리고 기술이다.

❾ Strength comes from struggle, not from taking the path of least resistance.
힘은 저항이 가장 적은 길을 택하는 것이 아니라 맞서 싸우는 데서 나온다.

❿ Hardship is not just a lesson for the next time in front of us.
고난은 단지 우리 앞에 놓인 다음을 위한 교훈만은 아니다.

⓫ Hardship will be the greatest teacher we will ever have in life.

고난은 우리 인생에서 가장 위대한 스승이 될 것이다.

24 제목

❶ Your behaviors are usually a reflection of your identity.
당신의 행동은 대개 당신의 정체성을 반영한다.

❷ What you do is an indication of the type of person you believe that you are — either consciously or nonconsciously.
당신이 하는 행동은 의식적으로든 무의식적으로든 당신이 스스로를 어떤 사람이라고 믿고 있는지를 나타낸다.

❸ Research has shown that once a person believes in a particular aspect of their identity, they are more likely to act according to that belief.
연구에 따르면 자신의 정체성의 특정 측면을 믿는 사람은 그 믿음에 따라 행동할 가능성이 더 높다.

❹ For example, people who identified as "being a voter" were more likely to vote than those who simply claimed "voting" was an action they wanted to perform.
예를 들어, 자신을 "유권자"라고 느끼는 사람은 단순히 "투표"가 자신이 하고 싶은 행동이라고 주장하는 사람보다 투표할 가능성이 더 높았다.

❺ Similarly, the person who accepts exercise as the part of their identity doesn't have to convince themselves to train.
마찬가지로, 운동을 자신의 정체성의 일부로 받아들이는 사람은 훈련하라고 스스로를 설득할 필요가 없다.

❻ Doing the right thing is easy.
옳은 일을 하는 것은 쉽다.

❼ After all, when your behavior and your identity perfectly match, you are no longer pursuing behavior change.
결국, 자신의 행동과 정체성이 완벽하게 일치하면 더이상 행동 변화를 추구하지 않아도 된다.

❽ You are simply acting like the type of person you already believe yourself to be.
당신은 그저 당신 스스로가 그렇다고 이미 믿고 있는 유형의 사람처럼 행동하고 있을 뿐이다.

25 도표

❶ The above graph shows the electronic waste collection and recycling rate by region in 2016 and 2019.
위 도표는 2016년과 2019년의 지역별 전자 폐기물 수거율 및 재활용률을 보여준다.

❷ In both years, Europe showed the highest electronic waste collection and recycling rates.
두 해 모두 유럽이 가장 높은 전자 폐기물 수거율 및 재활용률을 보였다.

❸ The electronic waste collection and recycling rate of Asia in 2019 was lower than in 2016.
2019년 아시아의 전자 폐기물 수거율 및 재활용률은 2016년보다 낮았다.

❹ The Americas ranked second in 2016 and third in 2019, with 17 percent and 9 percent respectively.
(남·북·중앙)아메리카는 2016년에 2위, 2019년은 3위를 기록했으며, 그 비율은 각각 17퍼센트와 9퍼센트였다.

❺ In both years, the electronic waste collection and recycling rates in Oceania remained under 10 percent.
오세아니아의 전자 폐기물 수거율 및 재활용률은 두 해 모두 10퍼센트 아래에 머물렀다.

❻ Africa had the lowest electronic waste collection and recycling rates in both 2016 and 2019, showing the smallest gap between 2016 and 2019.
아프리카는 2016년과 2019년 모두 가장 낮은 전자 폐기물 수거율 및 재활용률을 기록했으며, 두 해 사이의 비율 격차가 가장 적었다.

26 일치

❶ Fritz Zwicky, a memorable astrophysicist who coined the term 'supernova', was born in Varna, Bulgaria to a Swiss father and a Czech mother.

'초신성'이라는 용어를 만든 유명한 천체 물리학자 Fritz Zwicky는 불가리아의 Varna에서 스위스인 아버지와 체코인 어머니 사이에서 태어났다.

❷ At the age of six, he was sent to his grandparents who looked after him for most of his childhood in Switzerland.

여섯 살이 되던 해, 그는 스위스에서 보낸 어린 시절의 대부분 동안 그를 돌봐준 조부모에게 보내졌다.

❸ There, he received an advanced education in mathematics and physics.

그곳에서, 그는 수학과 물리학에 대한 고급 교육을 받았다.

❹ In 1925, he emigrated to the United States and continued his physics research at California Institute of Technology (Caltech).

1925년 미국으로 이주하여 California Institute of Technology(Caltech)에서 물리학 연구를 이어갔다.

❺ He developed numerous theories that have had a profound influence on the understanding of our universe in the early 21st century.

그는 21세기 초 우주에 대한 이해에 지대한 영향을 미친 수많은 이론을 발전시켰다.

❻ After being appointed as a professor of astronomy at Caltech in 1942, he developed some of the earliest jet engines and holds more than 50 patents, many in jet propulsion.

1942년 Caltech의 천문학 교수로 임용된 후 그는 초창기 제트 엔진을 개발했고, 50개 이상의 특허를 보유하고 있으며, 이 중 많은 부분이 제트 추진 분야의 특허이다.

29 어법

❶ The hunter-gatherer lifestyle, which can be described as "natural" to human beings, appears to have had much to recommend it.

수렵 채집 생활 방식은 인류에게 "자연스러운" 것으로 묘사될 수 있으며, 그것을 추천할 만한 많은 것(장점)이 있는 것으로 보인다.

❷ Examination of human remains from early hunter-gatherer societies has suggested that our ancestors enjoyed abundant food, obtainable without excessive effort, and suffered very few diseases.

초기 수렵 채집 사회의 유적 조사는 인류의 조상들이 과도한 노력 없이도 구할 수 있는 풍족한 식량을 누릴 수 있었고 질병에 걸리는 일도 거의 없었다는 것을 알려준다.

❸ If this is true, it is not clear why so many humans settled in permanent villages and developed agriculture, growing crops and domesticating animals: cultivating fields was hard work, and it was infarming villages that epidemic diseases first took root.

이것이 사실이라면, 왜 그렇게 많은 인류가 영구적으로 마을에 정착하여 농작물을 재배하고 동물을 기르면서 농업을 발달시켰는지는 분명하지 않다. 밭을 경작하는 것은 힘든 일이었고, 전염병이 처음 뿌리를 내린 곳은 농경 마을이었다.

❹ Whatever its immediate effect on the lives of humans, the development of settlements and agriculture undoubtedly led to a high increase in population density.

인간의 삶에 미치는 즉각적인 영향이 무엇이든, 정착지와 농업의 발전은 의심의 여지 없이 인구 밀도의 높은 증가로 이어졌다.

❺ This period, known as the New Stone Age, was a major turning point in human development, opening the way to the growth of the first towns and cities, and eventually leading to settled "civilizations."

신석기 시대로 알려진 이 시기는 인류 발전의 중요한 전환점으로, 최초의 마을과 도시가 성장하는 길을 열었고, 결국 정착된 "문명"으로 이어졌다.

30 어휘

❶ Many human and nonhuman animals save commodities or money for future consumption.
많은 인간과 인간이 아닌 동물은 물건이나 돈을 미래의 소비를 위해 저축한다.

❷ This behavior seems to reveal a preference of a delayed reward over an immediate one: the agent gives up some immediate pleasure in exchange for a future one.
이러한 행동은 즉각적인 보상보다 지연된 보상을 선호하는 것을 드러내는 듯하다. 즉, 행위자는 미래의 보상을 위해 당장의 쾌락을 포기하는 것이다.

❸ Thus the discounted value of the future reward should be greater than the undiscounted value of the present one.
그러므로 미래 보상의 하락된 가치는 하락되지 않은 현재의 가치보다 더 커야만 한다.

❹ However, in some cases the agent does not wait for the envisioned occasion but uses their savings prematurely.
그러나, 어떤 경우 행위자가 계획한 일을 기다리지 않고 그들의 저축을 조기에 사용하는 경우도 있다.

❺ For example, early in the year an employee might set aside money to buy Christmas presents but then spend it on a summer vacation instead.
예를 들어, 연초에 한 직원이 자기 돈을 크리스마스 선물을 사기 위해 모아두었지만 대신 여름 휴가에 사용할 수 있다.

❻ Such cases could be examples of weakness of will.
이러한 사례는 의지의 약함의 예시가 될 수 있다.

❼ That is, the agents may judge or resolve to spend their savings in a certain way for the greatest benefit but then act differently when temptation for immediate pleasure appears.
즉, 행위자는 그들의 저축을 가장 큰 이익을 위해 특정 방식으로 사용하기로 판단하거나 결심했으나 즉각적인 즐거움에 대한 유혹이 생기면 다르게 행동할 수도 있다.

31 빈칸

❶ The costs of interruptions are well-documented.
방해로 인한 대가는 잘 기록되어 있다.

❷ Martin Luther King Jr. lamented them when he described "that lovely poem that didn't get written because someone knocked on the door."
Martin Luther King Jr.는 "누군가 문을 두드리는 바람에 쓰여지지 못한 사랑스러운 시"를 묘사하며 이를 슬퍼했다.

❸ Perhaps the most famous literary example happened in 1797 when Samuel Taylor Coleridge started writing his poem Kubla Khan from a dream he had but then was visited by an unexpected guest.
아마도 가장 유명한 문학적 사례는 1797년 Samuel Taylor Coleridge가 꿈을 꾸고 Kubla Khan이 라는 시를 쓰기 시작했는데 뜻밖의 손님이 찾아왔을 때 일어났던 일일 것이다.

❹ For Coleridge, by coincidence, the untimely visitor came at a particularly bad time.
공교롭게도 Coleridge에게 이 불청객은 특히 좋지 않은 시기에 찾아왔다.

❺ He forgot his inspiration and left the work unfinished.
그는 영감을 잊고 작품을 미완성으로 남겼다.

❻ While there are many documented cases of sudden disruptions that have had significant consequences for professionals in critical roles such as doctors, nurses, control room operators, stock traders, and pilots, they also impact most of us in our everyday lives, slowing down work productivity and generally increasing stress levels.
의사, 간호사, 관제실 운영자, 주식 거래자, 조종사와 같은 중요한 역할을 담당하는 전문가들에게 심각한 결과를 초래한 갑작스러운 방해의 사례가 많이 기록되어 있지만, 갑작스러운 방해는 일상 생활에서 대부분의 사람들에게도 영향을 미쳐 업무 생산성을 떨어뜨리며 일반적으로 스트레스 수준을 높인다.

32 빈칸

❶ There's a lot of scientific evidence demonstrating that focused attention leads to the reshaping of the brain.

주의 집중이 뇌의 재구조화로 이어진다는 과학적 증거는 많이 있다.

❷ In animals rewarded for noticing sound (to hunt or to avoid being hunted for example), we find much larger auditory centers in the brain.

(예를 들어 사냥하거나 사냥감이 되는 것을 피하기 위해) 소리를 알아채는 것에 대한 보상을 받은 동물에서 우리는 뇌의 청각 중추가 훨씬 더 큰 것을 발견한다.

❸ In animals rewarded for sharp eyesight, the visual areas are larger.

예리한 시력에 대한 보상을 받은 동물은 시각 영역이 더 크다.

❹ Brain scans of violinists provide more evidence, showing dramatic growth and expansion in regions of the cortex that represent the left hand, which has to finger the strings precisely, often at very high speed.

바이올린 연주자의 뇌 스캔 결과는 더 많은 증거를 제공해서 종종 매우 빠른 속도로 현을 정확하게 켜야 하는 왼손을 나타내는 피질 영역의 극적인 성장과 확장을 보여준다.

❺ Other studies have shown that the hippocampus, which is vital for spatial memory, is enlarged in taxi drivers. The point is that the physical architecture of the brain changes according to where we direct our attention and what we practice doing.

다른 연구는 공간 기억에 필수적인 해마가 택시 운전사에게서 확대되는 것을 보여준다. 요점은 우리가 어디에 주의를 기울이고 무엇을 연습하느냐에 따라 뇌의 물리적 구조가 달라진다는 것이다.

33 빈칸

❶ How did the human mind evolve? One possibility is that competition and conflicts with other human tribes caused our brains to evolve the way they did.
인간의 생각은 어떻게 진화했을까? 한 가지 가능성은 다른 인간 부족과의 경쟁과 갈등이 우리 두뇌가 그렇게 진화하도록 했다는 것이다.

❷ A human tribe that could out-think its enemies, even slightly, possessed a vital advantage.
적보다 조금이라도 더 우수한 생각을 할 수 있는 인간 부족은 중요한 우위를 점했다.

❸ The ability of your tribe to imagine and predict where and when a hostile enemy tribe might strike, and plan accordingly, gives your tribe a significant military advantage.
적대적인 적 부족이 언제 어디서 공격할지 상상하고 예측하며 그에 따라 계획을 세울 수 있는 능력은 부족에게 상당한 군사적 우위를 가져다준다.

❹ The human mind became a weapon in the struggle for survival, a weapon far more decisive than any before it.
인간의 생각은 생존을 위한 투쟁에서 그 이전의 어떤 무기보다 훨씬 더 결정적인 무기가 되었다.

❺ And this mental advantage was applied, over and over, within each succeeding generation.
그리고 이러한 정신적 우위는 다음 세대에 걸쳐 계속해서 적용되었다.

❻ The tribe that could out-think its opponents was more likely to succeed in battle and would then pass on the genes responsible for this mental advantage to its offspring. You and I are the descendants of the winners.
상대보다 더 우수한 생각을 할 수 있는 부족은 전투에서 승리할 확률이 높았고, 이러한 정신적 우위를 담당하는 유전자를 자손에게 물려주었다. 당신과 나는 승자의 후손이다.

34 빈칸

❶ To find the hidden potential in teams, instead of brainstorming, we're better off shifting to a process called brainwriting.
팀의 숨겨진 잠재력을 찾으려면 브레인스토밍 대신 브레인라이팅이라는 과정으로 전환하는 것이 좋다.

❷ The initial steps are solo.
초기 단계는 혼자서 진행한다.

❸ You start by asking everyone to generate ideas separately.
먼저 모든 사람에게 개별적으로 아이디어를 내도록 요청한다.

❹ Next, you pool them and share them anonymously among the group.
그런 다음, 아이디어를 모아 익명으로 그룹에 공유한다.

❺ To preserve independent judgment, each member evaluates them on their own.
독립적인 판단을 유지하기 위해 각 구성원이 스스로 그 아이디어를 평가한다.

❻ Only then does the team come together to select and refine the most promising options.
그리고 나서야 팀이 함께 모여 가장 유망한 옵션을 선택하고 다듬는다.

❼ By developing and assessing ideas individually before choosing and elaborating them, teams can surface and advance possibilities that might not get attention otherwise.
아이디어를 선택하고 구체화하기 전에 개별적으로 아이디어를 전개하고 평가함으로써 팀은 다른 방법으로는 주목받지 못했을 가능성을 드러내고 발전시킬 수 있다.

❽ This brainwriting process makes sure that all ideas are brought to the table and all voices are brought into the conversation. It is especially effective in groups that struggle to achieve collective intelligence.
이 브레인라이팅 과정은 모든 아이디어를 테이블에 올려놓고 모든 의견을 대화에 반영할 수 있도록 한다. 특히 집단 지성을 달성하는 데 어려움을 겪는 그룹에서 효과적이다.

35 무관

❶ Simply giving employees a sense of agency — a feeling that they are in control, that they have genuine decision-making authority — can radically increase how much energy and focus they bring to their jobs.

단순히 직원들에게 주인의식(그들이 통제하고 있는 느낌, 진정한 의사 결정 권한이 있다는 느낌)을 주는 것만으로도 그들이 자신의 업무에 쏟는 에너지와 집중력을 급격하게 높일 수 있다.

❷ One 2010 study at a manufacturing plant in Ohio, for instance, carefully examined assembly-line workers who were empowered to make small decisions about their schedules and work environment.

예를 들어, 오하이오주의 한 제조 공장에서 진행된 2010년의 한 연구는 그들의 일정과 작업 환경에 대한 작은 결정 권한을 부여받은 조립 라인 근로자를 주의 깊게 살펴보았다.

❸ They designed their own uniforms and had authority over shifts while all the manufacturing processes and pay scales stayed the same.

그들은 그들 자신의 유니폼을 디자인했고, 근무 교대에 대한 권한을 가진 반면에, 모든 생산 과정과 임금규모는 동일하게 유지되었다.

❹ Within two months, productivity at the plant increased by 20 percent, with workers taking shorter breaks and making fewer mistakes. Giving employees a sense of control improved how much self-discipline they brought to their jobs.

두 달 만에 직원들은 휴식 시간을 더 짧게 가졌고, 실수를 더 적게 하였으며, 그 공장의 생산성은 20퍼센트 증가했다. 자신들이 통제권을 쥐고 있다는 느낌을 직원들에게 부여한 것이 그들이 업무에 끌어들이는 자기 통제력을 향상시켰다.

36 순서

❶ As businesses shift some core business activities to digital, such as sales, marketing, or archiving, it is assumed that the impact on the environment will be less negative.
기업이 영업, 마케팅, 파일 보관 등 일부 핵심 비즈니스 활동을 디지털로 전환함에 따라 환경에 미치는 영향이 덜 부정적일 것으로 예상된다.

❷ However, digital business activities can still threaten the environment.
그러나 디지털 비즈니스 활동은 여전히 환경을 위협할 수 있다.

❸ In some cases, the harm of digital businesses can be even more hazardous.
경우에 따라서는 디지털 비즈니스가 끼치는 해악이 훨씬 더 위험할 수 있다.

❹ A few decades ago, offices used to have much more paper waste since all documents were paper based.
수십 년 전만 해도 사무실에서는 모든 문서가 종이로 작성되었기 때문에 종이 폐기물이 훨씬 더 많았다.

❺ When workplaces shifted from paper to digital documents, invoices, and emails, it was a promising step to save trees.
직장에서 종이를 디지털 문서, (디지털) 송장, 이메일로 전환한 것은 나무를 보호할 수 있는 유망한 조치였다.

❻ However, the cost of the Internet and electricity for the environment is neglected. A recent Wired report declared that most data centers' energy source is fossil fuels.
하지만 인터넷과 전기가 환경에 입히는 손실은 간과되고 있다. 최근 Wired의 보고서에 따르면 대부분의 데이터 센터의 에너지원은 화석 연료이다.

❼ When we store bigger data on clouds, increased carbon emissions make our green clouds gray.
클라우드에 더 많은 데이터를 저장할수록 탄소 배출량이 증가하여 녹색 구름을 회색으로 변하게 만든다.

❽ The carbon footprint of an email is smaller than mail sent via a post office, but still, it causes four grams of CO_2, and it can be as much as 50 grams if the attachment is big.
이메일의 탄소 발자국은 우체국을 통해 보내는 우편물보다 적지만 여전히 4g의 이산화탄소를 유발하며 첨부 파일이 크면 50g에 달할 수 있다.

37 순서

❶ Problems often arise if an exotic species is suddenly introduced to an ecosystem.
외래종이 갑자기 생태계에 유입되면 문제가 종종 발생한다.

❷ Britain's red and grey squirrels provide a clear example.
영국의 붉은색 다람쥐와 회색 다람쥐가 명확한 예를 제공한다.

❸ When the grey arrived from America in the 1870s, both squirrel species competed for the same food and habitat, which put the native red squirrel populations under pressure.
1870년대 미국에서 회색 다람쥐가 왔을 때, 두 다람쥐 종은 동일한 먹이와 서식지를 놓고 경쟁했고, 이것이 토종의 붉은 다람쥐 개체군을 압박했다.

❹ The grey had the edge because it can adapt its diet; it is able, for instance, to eat green acorns, while the redcan only digest mature acorns.
회색 다람쥐는 먹이를 조절할 수 있기 때문에 우위를 점했다. 예를 들어 회색 다람쥐는 설익은 도토리를 먹을 수 있는 반면, 붉은 다람쥐는 다 익은 도토리만 소화할 수 있다.

❺ Within the same area of forest, grey squirrels can destroy the food supply before red squirrels even have a bite.
숲의 같은 지역 내에서 회색 다람쥐는 붉은 다람쥐가 한 입 먹기도 전에 식량 공급을 파괴할 수 있다.

❻ Greys can also live more densely and in varied habitats, so have survived more easily when woodland has been destroyed. As a result, the red squirrel has come close to extinction in England.
회색 다람쥐는 또한 더 밀집하며 다양한 서식지에서 살 수 있어서 삼림이 파괴되었을 때 더 쉽게 살아남았다. 그 결과, 붉은 다람쥐는 영국에서 거의 멸종 위기에 이르렀다.

38 삽입

❶ Growing crops forced people to stay in one place.
농작물 재배는 사람들이 한곳에 머무르게 했다.

❷ Hunter-gatherers typically moved around frequently, and they had to be able to carry all their possessions with them every time they moved.
수렵 채집인들은 일반적으로 자주 이동해야 했고, 이동할 때마다 모든 소유물을 가지고 다닐 수 있어야 했다.

❸ In particular, mothers had to carry their young children.
특히, 어머니들은 어린아이를 업고 이동해야 했다.

❹ As a result, hunter-gatherer mothers could have only one baby every four years or so, spacing their births so that they never had to carry more than one child at a time.
그 결과, 수렵 채집인 어머니들은 대략 4년마다 한 명의 아이만 낳을 수 있었고, 한 번에 한 명 이상의 아이를 업고 다닐 필요가 없도록 출산 간격을 두었다.

❺ Farmers, on the other hand, could live in the same place year after year and did not have to worry about transporting young children long distances.
반면, 농부들은 매년 같은 장소에서 살 수 있었고 어린아이를 장거리 이동시켜야 하는 걱정을 하지 않아도 되었다.

❻ Societies that settled down in one place were able to shorten their birth intervals from four years to about two.
한곳에 정착하게 된 사회는 출산 간격을 4년에서 약 2년으로 단축할 수 있었다.

❼ This meant that each woman could have more children than her hunter-gatherer counterpart, which in turn resulted in rapid population growth among farming communities.
이는 여성 한 명이 수렵 채집인인 상대보다 더 많은 아이를 낳을 수 있다는 것을 의미했고, 그 결과 그것은 농경 사회에서 급격한 인구 증가를 야기했다.

❽ An increased population was actually an advantage to agricultural societies, because farming required large amounts of human labor.
인구 증가는 실제로 농경 사회에 유리했는데, 왜냐하면 농사는 많은 인간의 노동력을 필요로 했기 때문이다.

39 삽입

❶ Spending time as children allows animals to learn about their environment.
동물은 유년기를 보내면서 환경에 대해 배울 수 있다.

❷ Without childhood, animals must rely more fully on hardware, and therefore be less flexible.
유년기가 없으면, 동물은 하드웨어에 더 많이 의존해야 하므로 유연성이 떨어질 수밖에 없다.

❸ Among migratory bird species, those that are born knowing how, when, and where to migrate — those that are migrating entirely with instructions they were born with — sometimes have very inefficient migration routes.
철새 중에서도 언제, 어디로, 어떻게 이동해야 하는지를 알고 태어나는 새들, 즉 전적으로 태어날 때부터 주어진 지침에 따라 이동하는 새들은 때때로 매우 비효율적인 이동 경로를 가지고 있다.

❹ These birds, born knowing how to migrate, don't adapt easily.
이동 방법을 알고 태어난 새들은 쉽게 적응하지 못한다.

❺ So when lakes dry up, forest becomes farmland, or climate change pushes breeding grounds farther north, those birds that are born knowing how to migrate keep flying by the old rules and maps.
따라서 호수가 마르거나 숲이 농지로 바뀌거나 기후 변화로 번식지가 더 북쪽으로 밀려났을 때, 이동하는 방법을 알고 태어난 새들은 기존의 규칙과 지도를 따라 계속 날아간다.

❻ By comparison, birds with the longest childhoods, and those that migrate with their parents, tend to have the most efficient migration routes.
이에 비해 유년기가 가장 길고 부모와 함께 이동하는 새는 가장 효율적인 이동 경로를 가지고 있는 경향이 있다.

❼ Childhood facilitates the passing on of cultural information, and culture can evolve faster than genes.
유년기는 문화적 정보의 전달을 촉진하며, 문화는 유전자보다 더 빠르게 진화할 수 있다.

❽ Childhood gives flexibility in a changing world.
유년기는 변화하는 세상에서 유연성을 제공한다.

40 요약

❶ Over the last several decades, scholars have developed standards for how best to create, organize, present, and preserve digital information for future generations.

지난 수십 년 동안 학자들은 미래 세대를 위해 디지털 정보를 가장 잘 만들고, 정리하고, 제시하고, 보존하는 방법에 대한 표준을 개발해 왔다.

❷ What has remained neglected for the most part, however, are the needs of people with disabilities.

그러나 대부분의 경우 장애가 있는 사람들의 요구는 여전히 무시되어 왔다.

❸ As a result, many of the otherwise most valuable digital resources are useless for people who are deaf or hard of hearing, as well as for people who are blind, have low vision, or have difficulty distinguishing particular colors.

그 결과, 청각 장애가 있거나 듣는 것이 힘든 사람, 시각 장애가 있거나 시력이 낮거나 특정 색상을 구분하기 어려운 사람에게는 그렇지 않은 경우라면 가장 가치 있었을 디지털 자원 중 상당수가 무용지물이 되고 있다.

❹ While professionals working in educational technology and commercial web design have made significant progress in meeting the needs of such users, some scholars creating digital projects all too often fail to take these needs into account.

교육 기술 및 상업용 웹디자인에 종사하는 전문가들은 이러한 사용자의 요구를 충족시키는 데 상당한 진전을 이루었지만, 디지털 프로젝트를 만드는 일부 학자들은 이러한 요구를 고려하지 못하는 경우가 너무 많다.

❺ This situation would be much improved if more projects embraced the idea that we should always keep the largest possible audience in mind as we make design decisions, ensuring that our final product serves the needs of those with disabilities as well as those without.

더 많은 프로젝트에서 디자인을 결정할 때 최대한 많은 사용자를 항상 염두에 두고 최종 제품이 장애가 있는 사람들과 그렇지 않은 사람들 모두의 요구를 충족시킬 수 있도록 해야 한다는 생각을 받아들인다면 이러한 상황은 훨씬 개선될 것이다.

41~42 제목, 어휘

❶ All humans, to an extent, seek activities that cause a degree of pain in order to experience pleasure, whether this is found in spicy food, strong massages, or stepping into a too-cold or too-hot bath.
모든 인간은 어느 정도는 쾌락을 경험하기 위해 약간의 고통을 유발하는 활동을 추구한다. 이것이 매운 음식 또는 강한 마사지, 너무 차갑거나 뜨거운 욕조에 들어가기 중 어디에서 발견되든지 간에 말이다.

❷ The key is that it is a 'safe threat'.
핵심은 그것이 '안전한 위협'이라는 점이다.

❸ The brain perceives the stimulus to be painful but ultimately nonthreatening.
뇌는 자극이 고통스럽지만 궁극적으로 위협적이지 않은 것으로 인식한다.

❹ Interestingly, this could be similar to the way humor works: a 'safe threat' that causes pleasure by playfully violating norms.
흥미롭게도 이것은 유머가 작동하는 방식, 즉 규범을 장난스럽게 위반함으로써 쾌락을 유발하는 '안전한 위협'과 유사할 수 있다.

❺ We feel uncomfortable, but safe. In this context, where survival is clearly not in danger, the desire for pain is actually the desire for a reward, not suffering or punishment.
우리는 불편하지만 안전하다고 느낀다. 생존이 위험하지 않은 이런 상황에서 고통에 대한 욕구는 실제로는 고통이나 처벌이 아닌 보상에 대한 욕구이다.

❻ This reward-like effect comes from the feeling of mastery over the pain.
이러한 보상과 같은 효과는 고통에 대한 숙달된 느낌에서 비롯된다.

The closer you look at your chilli-eating habit, the more remarkable it seems.
칠리를 먹는 습관을 자세히 들여다볼수록 이는 더욱 분명하게 드러난다.

❼ When the active ingredient of chillies — capsaicin — touches the tongue, it stimulates exactly the same receptor that is activated when any of these tissues are burned.
칠리의 활성 성분인 캡사이신이 혀에 닿으면 피부 조직이 화상을 입었을 때 활성화되는 것과 똑같은 수용체를 자극한다.

❽ Knowing that our body is firing off danger signals, but that we are actually completely safe, produces pleasure.
우리 몸이 위험 신호를 보내고 있지만 실제로는 완전히 안전하다는 것을 알면 쾌감이 생긴다.

❾ All children start off hating chilli, but many learn to derive pleasure from it through repeated exposure and knowing that they will never experience any real harm.

모든 아이들은 처음에는 칠리를 싫어하지만, 반복적인 노출과 실질적인 해를 경험하지 않는다는 것을 알게 됨을 통해 그것에서 쾌락을 얻는 방법을 배우게 된다.

❿ Interestingly, seeking pain for the pain itself appears to be uniquely human. The only way scientists have trained animals to have a preference for chilli or to self-harm is to have the pain always directly associated with a pleasurable reward.

흥미롭게도 고통 그 자체를 위해 고통을 추구하는 것은 인간만이 할 수 있는 행동으로 보인다. 동물이 칠리를 선호하게 하거나 스스로에게 해를 가하도록 과학자들이 훈련시키는 유일한 방법은 고통을 항상 즐거운 보상과 직접적으로 연관시키는 것이다.

43~45 순서, 지칭, 세부 내용

❶An airplane flew high above the deep blue seas far from any land.
비행기가 육지에서 멀리 떨어진 깊고 푸른 바다 위를 높이 날고 있었다.

❷ Flying the small plane was a student pilot who was sitting alongside an experienced flight instructor.
소형 비행기를 조종하고 있는 것은 노련한 비행 교관과 나란히 앉아 있는 한 파일럿 교육생이었다.

❸ As the student looked out the window, she was filled with wonder and appreciation for the beauty of the world.
교육생이 창문 밖을 바라볼 때, 그녀는 세상의 아름다움에 대한 경이로움과 감탄으로 가득 찼다.

❹ Her instructor, meanwhile, waited patiently for the right time to start a surprise flight emergency training exercise.
한편, 비행 교관은 비행 중 돌발 비상 상황 대처 훈련을 시작할 적절한 때를 인내심을 가지고 기다리고 있었다.

❺ When the plane hit a bit of turbulence, the instructor pushed a hidden button.
비행기가 약간의 난기류를 만났을 때, 교관은 숨겨진 버튼을 눌렀다.

❻ Suddenly, all the monitors inside the plane flashed several times then went out completely!
갑자기, 비행기 안의 모든 모니터가 여러 번 깜박이다가 완전히 꺼졌다!

❼ Now the student was in control of an airplane that was flying well, but she had no indication of where she was or where she should go.
이제 교육생은 잘 날고 있는 비행기를 조종하고 있었지만, 그녀는 자신이 어디에 있는지, 어디로 가야 하는지 알 방도가 없었다.

❽ She did have a map, but no other instruments.
교육생은 지도는 가지고 있었지만, 다른 도구는 가지고 있지 않았다.

❾ She was at a loss and then the plane shook again.
그녀는 어쩔 줄 몰라 했고 그때 비행기가 다시 흔들렸다.

❿ When the student began to panic, the instructor said, "Stay calm and steady. You can do it." Calm as ever, the instructor told her student, "Difficult times always happen during flight. The most important thing is to focus on your flight in those situations."
교육생이 당황하기 시작하자 교관은 "침착하세요. 당신은 할 수 있습니다." 여느 때처럼 침착한 교관은 교육생에게 "비행 중에는 항상 어려운 상황이 발생합니다. 그러한 상황에서는 비행에 집중하는 것이 가장 중요합니다."라고 말했다.

⓫ Those words encouraged the student to focus on flying the aircraft first. "Thank you, I think I can make it," she said, "As I've been trained, I should search for visual markers."
그 말이 교육생이 먼저 비행에 집중할 수 있게끔 용기를 주었다. "감사합니다. 제가 해낼 수 있을 것 같아요."라고 그녀는 말했다. "훈련받은 대로, 저는 시각 표식을 찾아야겠어요."

⓬ Then, the student carefully flew low enough to see if she could find any ships making their way across the surface of the ocean.
그런 다음 교육생은 바다 표면을 가로지르는 배가 보이는지 확인할 수 있을 정도로 충분히 낮게 조심히 비행하였다.

⓭ Now the instructor and the student could see some ships.
이제 교관과 교육생은 배 몇 척을 볼 수 있었다.

⓮ Although the ships were far apart, they were all sailing in a line.
배들은 멀리 떨어져 있었지만 모두 한 줄을 이루고 항해하고 있었다.

⓯ With the line of ships in view, the student could see the way to home and safety.
배들이 줄을 지어있는 것이 보이자, 교육생은 안전하게 복귀하는 길을 알 수 있었다.

⓰ The student looked at her in relief, who smiled proudly back at her student.
교육생은 안도하며 그녀를 바라봤고, 그녀도 교육생을 향해 자랑스럽게 웃어보였다.

2024 고1 6월 모의고사　❶ 회차 :　점 / 200점

18.

Dear Reader,

We always appreciate your support. As you know, our service is now available through an app. There [**have / has**]¹⁾ never been a better time to switch to an online membership of TourTide Magazine. At a 50% discount off your current print [**description / subscription**]²⁾, you can [**access / assess**]³⁾ a full year of online reading. Get new issues and daily web pieces at TourTide.com, read or listen to TourTide Magazine via the app, and [**get / to get**]⁴⁾ our membersonly newsletter. You'll also gain access to our editors' selections of the best articles. Join today!

Yours, TourTide Team

독자분께, 보내주신 성원에 항상 감사드립니다. 아시다시피, 이제 앱을 통해서도 저희 서비스를 이용하실 수 있습니다. TourTide Magazine의 온라인 회원으로 전환하기에 이보다 더 좋은 시기는 없습니다. 신의 현재 인쇄본 구독료에서 50% 할인된 가격으로 1년 치를 온라인으로 구독할 수 있습니다. TourTide.com에서 신간호와 일일 웹 기사를 받아보고, 앱을 통해 TourTide Magazine을 읽거나 청취해 보고, 회원 전용 뉴스레터 도 받아보세요. 편집자들이 선정한 최고의 기사도 받아볼 수 있습니다. 오늘 가입하세요! / TourTide 팀 드림

19.

As I walked from the mailbox, my heart was beating [**rapid / rapidly**]⁵⁾. In my hands, I held the letter from the university I had applied to. I thought my grades were good enough to [**cross / crossing**]⁶⁾ the line and my application letter was well-written, but was it enough? I hadn't slept a wink for days. As I carefully tore into the paper of the envelope, the letter slowly emerged [**from / with**]⁷⁾ the opening phrase, "It is our great pleasure..." I shouted with joy, "I am in!" As I held the letter, I began [**x / to**]⁸⁾ make a fantasy about my college life in a faraway city.

우체통에서 걸어올 때 내 심장은 빠르게 뛰고 있었다. 내 손에는 지원했던 대학에서 보낸 편지가 들려있었다. 내 생각에는 합격할 만큼 성적이 좋았고 지원서도 잘 썼지만, 그것으로 충분했을까? 며칠 동안 한 숨도 잘 수 없었다. 봉투의 종이를 조심스럽게 찢자 "매우 기쁘게도..."라는 첫 문구와 함께 편지가 천천히 모습을 드러냈다. 나는 기뻐서 소리질렀다. "합격이야!" 나는 편지를 손에 쥐고 집에서 멀리 떨어진 도시에서의 대학 생활에 대해 상상하기 시작했다.

20.

Having a [**mess / messy**]⁹⁾ room can add up to [**negative / positive**]¹⁰⁾ feelings and [**constructive / destructive**]¹¹⁾ thinking. Psychologists say that having a disorderly room can indicate a [**disorganized / disorganizing**]¹²⁾ mental state. One of the professional tidying experts [**say / says**]¹³⁾ that the moment you start cleaning your room, you also start changing your life and [**gain / gaining**]¹⁴⁾ new perspective. When you clean your surroundings, positive and good atmosphere follows. You can do more things [**effective / efficiently**]¹⁵⁾ and [**neat / neatly**]¹⁶⁾. So, clean up your closets, organize your drawers, and [**arrange / arranging**]¹⁷⁾ your things first, then peace of mind will follow.

방이 지저분한 것은 결국 부정적인 감정과 파괴적 인 사고로 이어질 수 있다. 심리학자들은 방이 무질서하다는 것은 정신 상태가 혼란스럽다는 것을 나타낼 수 있다고 말한다. 정리 전문가 중 한 명은 방청소를 시작하는 순간 당신은 인생을 변화시키고 새로운 관점을 얻기 시작한다고 말한다. 주변을 청소하면 긍정적이고 좋은 분위기가 따라온다. 당신은 더 많은 일을 효율적이고 깔끔하게 할 수 있다. 그러니 먼저 옷장을 청소하고, 서랍을 정리하고, 물건을 정돈한다면 마음의 평화가 따라올 것이다.

21.

The soil of a farm field is forced to be the perfect environment for monoculture growth. This [**achieved / is achieved**]18) by adding nutrients in the form of fertilizer and water by way of irrigation. [**During / While**]19) the last fifty years, engineers and crop scientists have helped farmers [**become / becoming**]20) much more efficient at supplying [**exact / exactly**]21) the right amount of both. World usage of fertilizer has tripled since 1969, and the global capacity for irrigation has almost doubled; we are feeding and [**water / watering**]22) our fields more than ever, and our crops are loving it. [**Fortunately / Unfortunately**]23), these luxurious conditions have also excited the attention of certain agricultural undesirables. [**Because / Because of**]24) farm fields are loaded with nutrients and water [**relative / relatively**]25) to the natural land that surrounds them, they [**are desired / desired**]26) as luxury real estate by every random weed in the area.

농지의 토양은 단일 작물 재배를 위한 완벽한 환경이어야 한다. 이것은 비료 형태로 양분을 더하고 관개로 물을 댐으로써 이루어진다. 지난 50년 동안 기술자와 농작물 연구자들은 농부들이 양쪽 모두의 정확한 적정량을 공급하는 데 훨씬 더 효율적일 수 있도록 도움을 주었다. 전 세계 비료 사용량은 1969년 이래로 세 배가 되었고, 전체 관개 능력은 거의 두 배가 되었다. 우리는 그 어느 때보다도 들판을 기름지게 하고 물을 대고 있으며, 우리의 농작물은 이를 좋아한다. 불행히도, 이러한 호사스러운 상황은 농업에서는 달갑지 않은 것들의 관심도 끌어들였다. 농지는 주위를 둘러싼 자연 지대에 비해 영양분과 물이 풍족히 채워져 있기 때문에 그 지역의 어떤 잡초라도 원하는 고급 부동산이 된다.

22.

When it comes to [**help / helping**]27) out, you don't have to do much. All you have to do is come around and [**show / to show**]28) that you care. If you notice someone who is lonely, you could go and sit with [**them / themselves**]29). If you work with someone who eats lunch all by themselves, and you go and sit down with them, they will begin to be more [**social / sociable**]30) after a while, and they will owe [**it / them**]31) all to you. A person's happiness comes from attention. There are too many people out in the world [**who / whom**]32) feel like everyone [**has / have**]33) forgotten them or ignored them. Even if you say hi to someone passing by, they will begin to feel better about [**them / themselves**]34), like someone cares.

도움을 주는 것에 관해서 당신은 많은 것을 할 필요는 없다. 그저 다가가서 관심을 갖고 있다는 것을 보여주기만 하면 된다. 외로운 사람을 발견하면 가서 함께 앉아 있으면 된다. 혼자서 점심을 먹는 사람과 함께 일한다면, 그리고 그 사람에게 다가가서 함께 앉는다면 얼마 지나지 않아 그 사람은 더 사교적으로 변하기 시작할 것이고, 이 모든 것을 당신 덕분이라고 할 것이다. 한 사람의 행복은 관심에서 비롯된다. 세상에는 모든 이가 자신을 잊었거나 무시한다고 느끼는 사람들이 너무 많다. 지나가는 사람들에게 인사만 건네도, 누군가 (그들에게) 관심을 가져주는 것처럼, 그들은 자기 자신에 대해 기분이 좋아지기 시작할 것이다.

23.

We often try [**making / to make**]35) cuts in our challenges and take the easy route. When [**taking / took**]36) the quick exit, we fail to acquire the strength to compete. We often take the easy route to [**improve / involve**]37) our skills. Many of us never really work to achieve mastery in the key areas of life. These skills are key tools that can be useful to our career, health, and [**property / prosperity**]38). Highly successful athletes don't win [**because / because of**]39) better equipment; they win by facing hardship to gain strength and skill. They win through preparation. It's the [**mental / physical**]40) preparation, winning mindset, strategy, and skill that [**set / sets**]41) them apart. Strength comes from struggle, not from [**take / taking**]42) the path of least resistance. Hardship is not just a lesson for the next time in front of us. Hardship will be the greatest teacher we will ever [**had / have**]43) in life.

우리는 종종 우리의 도전을 멈추고, 쉬운 길을 택하려고 한다. 쉬운 길을 택하면 경쟁할 수 있는 힘을 얻지 못한다. 우리는 종종 실력을 향상하기 위해 쉬운 길을 택한다. 우리 중 다수가 인생의 핵심이 되는 영역에서 숙달을 위한 노력을 하지 않는다. 이러한 기술은 경력, 건강, 번영에 도움이 될 수 있는 핵심 도구이다. 성공한 운동선수들은 더 좋은 장비 때문에 승리하는 것이 아니다. 그들은 힘과 실력을 얻기 위해 고난에 맞섬으로써 승리한다. 그들은 준비를 통해 승리한다. 그들을 돋보이게 하는 것은 바로 정신적 준비, 승리하는 마음가짐, 전략, 그리고 기술이다. 힘은 저항이 가장 적은 길을 택하는 것이 아니라 맞서 싸우는 데서 나온다. 고난은 단지 우리 앞에 놓인 다음을 위한 교훈만은 아니다. 고난은 우리 인생에서 가장 위대한 스승이 될 것이다.

24.

Your behaviors are usually a reflection of your [**identify / identity**]44). What you do is an indication of the type of person you believe [**that / what**]45) you are — [**neither / either**]46) consciously [**nor / or**]47) nonconsciously. Research has shown that once a person believes in a particular aspect of their identity, they are [**less / more**]48) likely to act according to that belief. For example, people who [**identified / identify**]49) as "being a voter" were more likely to vote than those who simply claimed "voting" was an action they wanted [**performing / to perform**]50). Similarly, the person who accepts exercise as the part of their identity doesn't have to convince [**them / themselves**]51) to train. [**Do / Doing**]52) the right thing is easy. After all, when your behavior and your identity perfectly [**match / matches**]53), you are no longer pursuing behavior change. You are simply acting like the type of person you already believe [**you / yourself**]54) to be.

당신의 행동은 대개 당신의 정체성을 반영한다. 당신이 하는 행동은 의식적으로든 무의식적으로든 당신이 스스로를 어떤 사람이라고 믿고 있는지를 나타낸다. 연구에 따르면 자신의 정체성의 특정 측면을 믿는 사람은 그 믿음에 따라 행동할 가능성이 더 높다. 예를 들어, 자신을 "유권자"라고 느끼는 사람은 단순히 "투표"가 자신이 하고 싶은 행동이라고 주장하는 사람보다 투표할 가능성이 더 높았다. 마찬가지로, 운동을 자신의 정체성의 일부로 받아들이는 사람은 훈련하라고 스스로를 설득할 필요가 없다. 옳은 일을 하는 것은 쉽다. 결국, 자신의 행동과 정체성이 완벽하게 일치하면 더 이상 행동 변화를 추구하지 않아도 된다. 당신은 그저 당신 스스로가 그렇다고 이미 믿고 있는 유형의 사람처럼 행동하고 있을 뿐이다.

25.

The above graph shows the electronic waste collection and recycling rate by region in 2016 and 2019. In [**both / either**]55) years, Europe showed the highest electronic waste collection and recycling rates. The electronic waste collection and recycling [**rate / rates**]56) of Asia in 2019 was lower than in 2016. The Americas ranked second in 2016 and third in 2019, with 17 percent and 9 percent [**respectable / respectively**]57). In both years, the electronic waste collection and recycling rates in Oceania [**remained / remaining**]58) under 10 percent. Africa had the lowest electronic waste collection and recycling rates in both 2016 and 2019, [**showing / shown**]59) the smallest gap between 2016 and 2019.

위 도표는 2016년과 2019년의 지역별 전자 폐기물 수거율 및 재활용률을 보여준다. 두 해 모두 유럽이 가장 높은 전자 폐기물 수거율 및 재활용률을 보였다. 2019년 아시아의 전자 폐기물 수거율 및 재활용률은 2016년보다 낮았다. (남·북·중앙)아메리카는 2016년에 2위, 2019년은 3위를 기록했으며, 그 비율은 각각 17퍼센트와 9퍼센트였다. 오세아니아의 전자 폐기물 수거율 및 재활용률은 두 해 모두 10퍼센트 아래에 머물렀다. 아프리카는 2016년과 2019년 모두 가장 낮은 전자 폐기물 수거율 및 재활용률을 기록했으며, 두 해 사이의 비율 격차가 가장 적었다.

26.

Fritz Zwicky, a memorable astrophysicist who coined the term 'supernova', [**born / was born**]60) in Varna, Bulgaria to a Swiss father and a Czech mother. At the age of six, he was sent to his grandparents who looked after him for [**almost / most**]61) of his childhood in Switzerland. There, he received an [**advanced / advancing**]62) education in mathematics and physics. In 1925, he emigrated to the United States and [**continued / continuing**]63) his physics research at California Institute of Technology (Caltech). He developed numerous theories that have had a profound influence on the understanding of our universe in the early 21st century. After [**be / being**]64) appointed as a professor of [**astrology / astronomy**]65) at Caltech in 1942, he developed some of the earliest jet engines and [**hold / holds**]66) more than 50 patents, many in jet propulsion.

'초신성'이라는 용어를 만든 유명한 천체 물리학자 Fritz Zwicky는 불가리아의 Varna에서 스위스인 아버지와 체코인 어머니 사이에서 태어났다. 여섯 살이 되던 해, 그는 스위스에서 보낸 어린 시절의 대부분 동안 그를 돌봐준 조부모에게 보내졌다. 그곳에서, 그는 수학과 물리학에 대한 고급 교육을 받았다. 1925년 미국으로 이주하여 California Institute of Technology(Caltech)에서 물리학 연구를 이어갔다. 그는 21세기 초 우주에 대한 이해에 지대한 영향을 미친 수많은 이론을 발전시켰다. 1942년 Caltech의 천문학 교수로 임용된 후 그는 초창기 제트 엔진을 개발했고, 50개 이상의 특허를 보유하고 있으며, 이 중 많은 부분이 제트 추진 분야의 특허이다.

29.

The hunter-gatherer lifestyle, which can [**be described / describe**]67) as "natural" to human beings, appears to have had much to recommend it. Examination of human remains from early hunter-gatherer societies [**has / have**]68) suggested that our ancestors enjoyed abundant food, obtainable without excessive effort, and [**suffer / suffered**]69) very few diseases. If this is true, it is not clear why so many humans settled in [**permanent / permanently**]70) villages and developed agriculture, growing crops and [**domesticated / domesticating**]71) animals: cultivating fields was hard work, and it was in farming villages that epidemic diseases first took root. [**However / Whatever**]72) its immediate effect on the lives of humans, the development of settlements and agriculture undoubtedly led to a high increase in population density. This period, known as the New Stone Age, was a major turning point in human development, opening the way to the growth of the first towns and cities, and eventually [**leading / led**]73) to settled "civilizations."

수렵 채집 생활 방식은 인류에게 "자연스러운" 것으로 묘사될 수 있으며, 그것을 추천할 만한 많은 것(장점)이 있는 것으로 보인다. 초기 수렵 채집 사회의 유적 조사는 인류의 조상들이 과도한 노력 없이도 구할 수 있는 풍족한 식량을 누릴 수 있었고 질병에 걸리는 일도 거의 없었다는 것을 알려준다. 이것이 사실이라면, 왜 그렇게 많은 인류가 영구적으로 마을에 정착하여 농작물을 재배하고 동물을 기르면서 농업을 발달시켰는지는 분명하지 않다. 밭을 경작하는 것은 힘든 일이었고, 전염병이 처음 뿌리를 내린 곳은 농경 마을이었다. 인간의 삶에 미치는 즉각적인 영향이 무엇이든, 정착지와 농업의 발전은 의심의 여지 없이 인구 밀도의 높은 증가로 이어졌다. 신석기 시대로 알려진 이 시기는 인류 발전의 중요한 전환점으로, 최초의 마을과 도시가 성장하는 길을 열었고, 결국 정착된 "문명"으로 이어졌다.

30.

[**Many / Much**]74) human and nonhuman animals save commodities or money for future consumption. This behavior seems to reveal a preference of a delayed reward over an immediate one: the agent gives up some immediate pleasure in exchange for a future [**one / ones**]75). Thus the discounted value of the future reward should be greater than the undiscounted value of the present one. However, in some cases the agent does not wait for the envisioned occasion but [**used / uses**]76) their savings [**premature / prematurely**]77). For example, early in the year an employee might set aside money to buy Christmas presents but then spend [**it / them**]78) on a summer vacation instead. Such cases could be examples of weakness of will. That is, the agents may judge or resolve to spend their savings in a certain way for the greatest benefit but then act [**different / differently**]⁷⁹⁾ when temptation for immediate pleasure [**appear / appears**]⁸⁰⁾.

많은 인간과 인간이 아닌 동물은 물건이나 돈을 미래의 소비를 위해 저축한다. 이러한 행동은 즉각적인 보상보다 지연된 보상을 선호하는 것을 드러내는 듯하다. 즉, 행위자는 미래의 보상을 위해 당장의 쾌락을 포기하는 것이다. 그러므로 미래 보상의 하락된 가치는 하락되지 않은 현재의 가치보다 더 커야만 한다. 그러나, 어떤 경우 행위자가 계획한 일을 기다리지 않고 그들의 저축을 조기에 사용하는 경우도 있다. 예를 들어, 연초에 한 직원이 자기 돈을 크리스마스 선물을 사기 위해 모아두었지만 대신 여름 휴가에 사용할 수 있다. 이러한 사례는 의지의 약함의 예시가 될 수 있다. 즉, 행위자는 그들의 저축을 가장 큰 이익을 위해 특정 방식으로 사용하기로 판단하거나 결심했으나 즉각적인 즐거움에 대한 유혹이 생기면 다르게 행동할 수도 있다.

31.

The costs of interruptions are well-documented. Martin Luther King Jr. lamented [**it / them**]⁸¹⁾ when he described "that lovely poem that didn't get written because someone knocked on the door." Perhaps the most famous [**literary / literate**]⁸²⁾ example happened in 1797 when Samuel Taylor Coleridge started writing his poem Kubla Khan from a dream he had but then [**was visited / visited**]⁸³⁾ by an unexpected guest. For Coleridge, by [**coincidence / coincident**]⁸⁴⁾, the untimely visitor came at a particularly bad time. He forgot his inspiration and [**leave / left**]⁸⁵⁾ the work unfinished. While there are [**many / much**]⁸⁶⁾ documented cases of sudden disruptions that have had significant consequences for professionals in critical roles such as doctors, nurses, control room operators, stock traders, and pilots, they also impact most of us in our everyday lives, [**slowing / slows**]⁸⁷⁾ down work productivity and generally [**increases / increasing**]⁸⁸⁾ stress levels.

방해로 인한 대가는 잘 기록되어 있다. Martin Luther King Jr.는 "누군가 문을 두드리는 바람에 쓰여지지 못한 사랑스러운 시"를 묘사하며 이를 슬퍼했다. 아마도 가장 유명한 문학적 사례는 1797년 Samuel Taylor Coleridge가 꿈을 꾸고 Kubla Khan이 라는 시를 쓰기 시작했는데 뜻밖의 손님이 찾아왔을 때 일어났던 일일 것이다. 공교롭게도 Coleridge에게 이 불청객은 특히 좋지 않은 시기에 찾아왔다. 그는 영감을 잊고 작품을 미완성으로 남겼다. 의사, 간호사, 관제실 운영자, 주식 거래자, 조종사와 같은 중요한 역할을 담당하는 전문가들에게 심각한 결과를 초래한 갑작스러운 방해의 사례가 많이 기록되어 있지만, 갑작스러운 방해는 일상 생활에서 대부분의 사람들에게도 영향을 미쳐 업무 생산성을 떨어뜨리며 일반적으로 스트레스 수준을 높인다.

32.

There's a lot of scientific evidence demonstrating [**that / what**]⁸⁹⁾ focused attention leads to the reshaping of the brain. In animals [**rewarded / rewarding**]⁹⁰⁾ for noticing sound (to hunt or to avoid being hunted for example), we find much larger auditory centers in the brain. In animals [**rewarded / rewarding**]⁹¹⁾ for sharp eyesight, the visual areas are larger. Brain scans of violinists [**provide / providing**]⁹²⁾ more evidence, showing dramatic growth and expansion in regions of the cortex that [**represent / represents**]⁹³⁾ the left hand, [**that / which**]⁹⁴⁾ has to finger the strings precisely, often at very high speed. [**Other / The other**]⁹⁵⁾ studies have shown that the hippocampus, which is vital for [**spacious / spatial**]⁹⁶⁾ memory, is enlarged in taxi drivers. The point is [**that / what**]⁹⁷⁾ the physical architecture of the brain changes according to [**where / which**]⁹⁸⁾ we direct our attention and [**that / what**]⁹⁹⁾ we practice doing.

주의 집중이 뇌의 재구조화로 이어진다는 과학적 증거는 많이 있다. (예를 들어 사냥하거나 사냥감이 되는 것을 피하기 위해) 소리를 알아채는 것에 대한 보상을 받은 동물에서 우리는 뇌의 청각 중추가 훨씬 더 큰 것을 발견한다. 예리한 시력에 대한 보상을 받은 동물은 시각 영역이 더 크다. 바이올린 연주자의 뇌 스캔 결과는 더 많은 증거를 제공해서 종종 매우 빠른 속도로 현을 정확하게 켜야 하는 왼손을 나타내는 피질 영역의 극적인 성장과 확장을 보여준다. 다른 연구는 공간 기억에 필수적인 해마가 택시 운전사에게서 확대되는 것을 보여준다. 요점은 우리가 어디에 주의를 기울이고 무엇을 연습하느냐에 따라 뇌의 물리적 구조가 달라진다는 것이다.

33.

How did the human mind [**evolve** / **revolve**]^100)? One possibility is that competition and conflicts with other human tribes caused our brains to evolve the way they [**did** / **had**]^101). A human tribe that could out-think its enemies, even slightly, [**possess** / **possessed**]^102) a vital advantage. The ability of your tribe to imagine and [**predict** / **predicting**]^103) where and when a hostile enemy tribe might strike, and [**plan** / **planning**]^104) accordingly, [**give** / **gives**]^105) your tribe a significant military advantage. The human mind became a weapon in the struggle for survival, a weapon far more decisive than any before [**it** / **them**]^106). And this mental advantage [**applied** / **was applied**]^107), over and over, within each [**succeeding** / **successful**]^108) generation. The tribe that could out-think [**its** / **their**]^109) opponents [**was** / **were**]^110) more likely to succeed in battle and would then pass on the genes responsible for this mental advantage to [**its** / **their**]^111) offspring. You and I are the [**descendants** / **predecessors**]^112) of the winners.

인간의 생각은 어떻게 진화했을까? 한 가지 가능성은 다른 인간 부족과의 경쟁과 갈등이 우리 두뇌가 그렇게 진화하도록 했다는 것이다. 적보다 조금이라도 더 우수한 생각을 할 수 있는 인간 부족은 중요한 우위를 점했다. 적대적인 적 부족이 언제 어디서 공격할지 상상하고 예측하며 그에 따라 계획을 세울 수 있는 능력은 부족에게 상당한 군사적 우위를 가져다준다. 인간의 생각은 생존을 위한 투쟁에서 그 이전의 어떤 무기보다 훨씬 더 결정적인 무기가 되었다. 그리고 이러한 정신적 우위는 다음 세대에 걸쳐 계속해서 적용되었다. 상대보다 더 우수한 생각을 할 수 있는 부족은 전투에서 승리할 확률이 높았고, 이러한 정신적 우위를 담당하는 유전자를 자손에게 물려주었다. 당신과 나는 승자의 후손이다.

34.

To find the hidden potential in teams, instead of brainstorming, we're better off shifting to a [**process** / **progress**]^113) called brainwriting. The [**initial** / **initiative**]^114) steps are solo. You start by asking everyone to generate ideas [**separate** / **separately**]^115). Next, you pool them and share them [**anonymously** / **unanimously**]^116) among the group. To preserve [**dependent** / **independent**]^117) judgment, each member evaluates them on their own. Only then does the team come together to select and [**define** / **refine**]^118) the most promising options. By developing and assessing ideas individually before choosing and elaborating [**them** / **themselves**]^119), teams can surface and advance possibilities that might not get attention otherwise. This brainwriting process makes sure [**that** / **what**]^120) all ideas are brought to the table and all voices [**are brought** / **brought**]^121) into the conversation. It is especially effective in groups that [**struggle** / **struggles**]^122) to achieve collective intelligence.

팀의 숨겨진 잠재력을 찾으려면 브레인스토밍 대신 브레인라이팅이라는 과정으로 전환하는 것이 좋다. 초기 단계는 혼자서 진행한다. 먼저 모든 사람에게 개별적으로 아이디어를 내도록 요청한다. 그런 다음, 아이디어를 모아 익명으로 그룹에 공유한다. 독립적인 판단을 유지하기 위해 각 구성원이 스스로 그 아이디어를 평가한다. 그러고 나서야 팀이 함께 모여 가장 유망한 옵션을 선택하고 다듬는다. 아이디어를 선택하고 구체화하기 전에 개별적으로 아이디어를 전개하고 평가함으로써 팀은 다른 방법으로는 주목받지 못했을 가능성을 드러내고 발전시킬 수 있다. 이 브레인라이팅 과정은 모든 아이디어를 테이블에 올려놓고 모든 의견을 대화에 반영할 수 있도록 한다. 특히 집단 지성을 달성하는 데 어려움을 겪는 그룹에서 효과적이다.

35.

Simply [**give** / **giving**]^123) employees a sense of agency — a feeling that they are in control, [**that** / **what**]^124) they have genuine decision-making authority — can radically [**decrease** / **increase**]^125) how much energy and focus they bring to their jobs. One 2010 study at a manufacturing plant in Ohio, for instance, carefully examined assembly-line workers who [**empowered** / **were empowered**]^126) to make small decisions about their schedules and work environment. They designed their own uniforms and [**had** / **have**]^127) authority over shifts while all the manufacturing processes and pay scales stayed the same. Within two months, productivity at the plant [**increasing** / **increased**]^128) by 20 percent, with workers [**taken** / **taking**]^129) shorter breaks and making fewer mistakes. Giving [**employees** / **employers**]^130) a sense of control improved how much self-discipline they brought to their jobs.

단순히 직원들에게 주인의식(그들이 통제하고 있는 느낌, 진정한 의사 결정 권한이 있다는 느낌)을 주는 것만으로도 그들이 자신의 업무에 쏟는 에너지와 집중력을 급격하게 높일 수 있다. 예를 들어, 오하이오주의 한 제조 공장에서 진행된 2010년의 한 연구는 그들의 일정과 작업 환경에 대한 작은 결정 권한을 부여받은 조립 라인 근로자를 주의 깊게 살펴보았다. 그들은 그들 자신의 유니폼을 디자인했고, 근무 교대에 대한 권한을 가진 반면에, 모든 생산 과정과 임금규모는 동일하게 유지되었다. 두 달 만에 직원들은 휴식 시간을 더 짧게 가졌고, 실수를 더 적게 하였으며, 그 공장의 생산성은 20퍼센트 증가했다. 자신들이 통제권을 쥐고 있다는 느낌을 직원들에게 부여한 것이 그들이 업무에 끌어들이는 자기 통제력을 향상시켰다.

36.

As businesses shift some core business activities to digital, such as sales, marketing, or archiving, it is assumed [**that / what**]131) the impact on the environment will be [**less / more**]132) negative. However, digital business activities can still [**threaten / threatens**]133) the environment. In some cases, the harm of digital businesses can be even [**less / more**]134) hazardous. A few decades ago, offices used to [**have / having**]135) much more paper waste since all documents were paper based. [**When / While**]136) workplaces shifted from paper to digital documents, invoices, and emails, it was a promising step to save trees. However, the cost of the Internet and electricity for the environment [**neglected / is neglected**]137). A recent Wired report declared [**that / what**]138) most data centers' energy source is fossil fuels. When we store bigger data on clouds, [**increased / increasing**]139) carbon emissions make our green clouds gray. The carbon footprint of an email is smaller than mail sent via a post office, but still, it causes four grams of CO_2, and it can be as much as 50 grams if the attachment [**is / was**]140) big.

기업이 영업, 마케팅, 파일 보관 등 일부 핵심 비즈니스 활동을 디지털로 전환함에 따라 환경에 미치는 영향이 덜 부정적일 것으로 예상된다. 그러나 디지털 비즈니스 활동은 여전히 환경을 위협할 수 있다. 경우에 따라서는 디지털 비즈니스가 끼치는 해악이 훨씬 더 위험할 수 있다. 수십 년 전만 해도 사무실에서는 모든 문서가 종이로 작성되었기 때문에 종이 폐기물이 훨씬 더 많았다. 직장에서 종이를 디지털 문서, (디지털) 송장, 이메일로 전환한 것은 나무를 보호할 수 있는 유망한 조치였다. 하지만 인터넷과 전기가 환경에 입히는 손실은 간과되고 있다. 최근 Wired의 보고서에 따르면 대부분의 데이터 센터의 에너지원은 화석 연료이다. 클라우드에 더 많은 데이터를 저장할수록 탄소 배출량이 증가하여 녹색 구름을 회색으로 변하게 만든다. 이메일의 탄소 발자국은 우체국을 통해 보내는 우편물보다 적지만 여전히 4g의 이산화탄소를 유발하며 첨부 파일이 크면 50g에 달할 수 있다.

37.

Problems often [**arise / raise**]141) if an exotic species is suddenly introduced to an ecosystem. Britain's red and grey squirrels provide a clear example. When the grey arrived from America in the 1870s, both squirrel species competed for the same food and habitat, [**that / which**]142) put the native red squirrel populations under pressure. The grey had the edge [**because / because of**]143) it can [**adapt / adopt**]144) its diet; it is able, for instance, to eat green acorns, while the red can only digest [**mature / premature**]145) acorns. Within the same area of forest, grey squirrels can destroy the food supply before red squirrels even [**has / have**]146) a bite. Greys can also live more [**dense / densely**]147) and in varied habitats, so have survived more easily when woodland has [**destroyed / been destroyed**]148). As a result, the red squirrel has come close to [**distinction / extinction**]149) in England.

외래종이 갑자기 생태계에 유입되면 문제가 종종 발생한다. 영국의 붉은색 다람쥐와 회색 다람쥐가 명확한 예를 제공한다. 1870년대 미국에서 회색 다람쥐가 왔을 때, 두 다람쥐 종은 동일한 먹이와 서식지를 놓고 경쟁했고, 이것이 토종의 붉은 다람쥐 개체군을 압박했다. 회색 다람쥐는 먹이를 조절할 수 있기 때문에 우위를 점했다. 예를 들어 회색 다람쥐는 설익은 도토리를 먹을 수 있는 반면, 붉은 다람쥐는 다 익은 도토리만 소화할 수 있다. 숲의 같은 지역 내에서 회색 다람쥐는 붉은 다람쥐가 한 입 먹기도 전에 식량 공급을 파괴할 수 있다. 회색 다람쥐는 또한 더 밀집하며 다양한 서식지에서 살 수 있어서 삼림이 파괴되었을 때 더 쉽게 살아남았다. 그 결과, 붉은 다람쥐는 영국에서 거의 멸종 위기에 이르렀다.

38.

Growing crops forced people [**staying / to stay**]^150) in one place. Hunter-gatherers typically moved around frequently, and they had to be able to carry all their possessions with them every time they moved. In particular, mothers had to carry their young children. As a result, hunter-gatherer mothers [**could / should**]^151) have only one baby every four years or so, [**spaced / spacing**]^152) their births so that they never had to carry more than one child at a time. Farmers, on the other hand, could live in the same place year after year and did not have to worry about [**transport / transporting**]^153) young children long distances. Societies that settled down in one place [**was / were**]^154) able to shorten their birth intervals from four years to about two. This meant that each woman could have more children than her hunter-gatherer [**counterpart / counterparts**]^155), which in turn resulted in rapid population growth among farming communities. An [**increased / increasing**]^156) population was actually an advantage to agricultural societies, [**because / because of**]^157) farming required large amounts of human labor.

농작물 재배는 사람들이 한곳에 머무르게 했다. 수렵 채집인들은 일반적으로 자주 이동해야 했고, 이동할 때마다 모든 소유물을 가지고 다닐 수 있어야 했다. 특히, 어머니들은 어린아이를 업고 이동해야 했다. 그 결과, 수렵 채집인 어머니들은 대략 4년마다 한 명의 아이만 낳을 수 있었고, 한 번에 한 명 이상의 아이를 업고 다닐 필요가 없도록 출산 간격을 두었다. 반면, 농부들은 매년 같은 장소에서 살 수 있었고 어린아이를 장거리 이동시켜야 하는 걱정을 하지 않아도 되었다. 한곳에 정착하게 된 사회는 출산 간격을 4년에서 약 2년으로 단축할 수 있었다. 이는 여성 한 명이 수렵 채집인인 상대보다 더 많은 아이를 낳을 수 있다는 것을 의미했고, 그 결과 그것은 농경 사회에서 급격한 인구 증가를 야기했다. 인구 증가는 실제로 농경 사회에 유리했는데, 왜냐하면 농사는 많은 인간의 노동력을 필요로 했기 때문이다.

39.

Spending time as children allows animals [**learning / to learn**]^158) about their environment. Without childhood, animals must rely [**less / more**]^159) fully on hardware, and therefore be less flexible. Among migratory bird species, those that are born knowing how, when, and where to migrate — those that are migrating entirely with instructions they were born with — sometimes have very [**efficient / inefficient**]^160) migration routes. These birds, born knowing how to migrate, [**can / don't**]^161) adapt easily. So when lakes dry up, forest becomes farmland, or climate change pushes breeding grounds farther north, those birds that are born knowing how to migrate [**don't keep / keep**]^162) flying by the old rules and maps. By comparison, birds with the longest childhoods, and those that migrate with their parents, tend to [**have / having**]^163) the most efficient migration routes. Childhood facilitates the passing on of cultural information, and culture can [**evolve / involve**]^164) faster than genes. Childhood gives flexibility in a changing world.

동물은 유년기를 보내면서 환경에 대해 배울 수 있다. 유년기가 없으면, 동물은 하드웨어에 더 많이 의존해야 하므로 유연성이 떨어질 수밖에 없다. 철새 중에서도 언제, 어디로, 어떻게 이동해야 하는지를 알고 태어나는 새들, 즉 전적으로 태어날 때부터 주어진 지침에 따라 이동하는 새들은 때때로 매우 비효율적인 이동 경로를 가지고 있다. 이동 방법을 알고 태어난 새들은 쉽게 적응하지 못한다. 따라서 호수가 마르거나 숲이 농지로 바뀌거나 기후 변화로 번식지가 더 북쪽으로 밀려났을 때, 이동하는 방법을 알고 태어난 새들은 기존의 규칙과 지도를 따라 계속 날아간다. 이에 비해 유년기가 가장 길고 부모와 함께 이동하는 새는 가장 효율적인 이동 경로를 가지고 있는 경향이 있다. 유년기는 문화적 정보의 전달을 촉진하며, 문화는 유전자보다 더 빠르게 진화할 수 있다. 유년기는 변화하는 세상에서 유연성을 제공한다.

40.

Over the last several decades, scholars have developed standards for how best to create, organize, present, and preserve digital information for future generations. [**That / What**]^165) has remained [**neglected / neglecting**]^166) for the most part, however, are the needs of people with disabilities. As a result, many of the otherwise most valuable digital resources are [**useful / useless**]^167) for people who are deaf or hard of hearing, as well as for people who are blind, have low vision, or have difficulty [**distinguishing / to distinguish**]168) particular colors. While professionals working in educational technology and commercial web design [**has / have**]169) made significant progress in meeting the needs of such users, some scholars [**create / creating**]170) digital projects all too often fail to [**take / taking**]171) these needs into account. This situation would be much improved if more projects embraced the idea [**that / what**]172) we should always keep the largest possible audience in mind as we make design decisions, ensuring that our final product [**serve / serves**]173) the needs of those with disabilities as well as those without.

지난 수십 년 동안 학자들은 미래 세대를 위해 디지털 정보를 가장 잘 만들고, 정리하고, 제시하고, 보존하는 방법에 대한 표준을 개발해 왔다. 그러나 대부분의 경우 장애가 있는 사람들의 요구는 여전히 무시되어 왔다. 그 결과, 청각 장애가 있거나 듣는 것이 힘든 사람, 시각 장애가 있거나 시력이 낮거나 특정 색상을 구분하기 어려운 사람에게는 그렇지 않은 경우라면 가장 가치 있었을 디지털 자원 중 상당수가 무용지물이 되고 있다. 교육 기술 및 상업용 웹디자인에 종사하는 전문가들은 이러한 사용자의 요구를 충족시키는 데 상당한 진전을 이루었지만, 디지털 프로젝트를 만드는 일부 학자들은 이러한 요구를 고려하지 못하는 경우가 너무 많다. 더 많은 프로젝트에서 디자인을 결정할 때 최대한 많은 사용자를 항상 염두에 두고 최종 제품이 장애가 있는 사람들과 그렇지 않은 사람들 모두의 요구를 충족시킬 수 있도록 해야 한다는 생각을 받아들인다면 이러한 상황은 훨씬 개선될 것이다

41~42.

All humans, to an [**extent / intent**]174), seek activities that cause a degree of pain in order to experience pleasure, whether this is found in spicy food, strong massages, or stepping into a too-cold or too-hot bath. The key is [**that / what**]175) it is a 'safe threat'. The brain [**deceives / perceives**]176) the stimulus to be painful but ultimately nonthreatening. Interestingly, this could be [**different / similar**]177) to the way humor works: a 'safe threat' that causes pleasure by playfully [**observing / violating**]178) norms. We feel [**comfortable / uncomfortable**]179), but safe. In this context, [**where / which**]180) survival is clearly not in danger, the desire for pain is actually the desire for a reward, not suffering or punishment. This reward-like [**affect / effect**]181) comes from the feeling of mastery over the pain. The closer you look at your chilli-eating habit, the more [**remarkable / remarkably**]182) it seems. When the active ingredient of chillies — capsaicin — touches the tongue, it stimulates exactly the same receptor that [**activates / is activated**]183) when any of these tissues are burned. Knowing that our body is firing off danger signals, but that we are actually completely safe, [**produce / produces**]184) pleasure. All children start off hating chilli, but many learn to derive pleasure from it through [**repeated / repeating**]185) exposure and knowing that they will never experience any real harm. Interestingly, seeking pain for the pain itself [**appear / appears**]186) to be uniquely human. The only way scientists have trained animals to have a preference for chilli or to self-harm is to have the pain always [**directly / indirectly**]187) associated with a pleasurable reward.

모든 인간은 어느 정도는 쾌락을 경험하기 위해 약간의 고통을 유발하는 활동을 추구한다. 이것이 매운 음식 또는 강한 마사지, 너무 차갑거나 뜨거운 욕조에 들어가기 중 어디에서 발견되든지 간에 말이다. 핵심은 그것이 '안전한 위협'이라는 점이다. 뇌는 자극이 고통스럽지만 궁극적으로 위협적이지 않은 것으로 인식한다. 흥미롭게도 이것은 유머가 작동하는 방식, 즉 규범을 장난스럽게 위반함으로써 쾌락을 유발하는 '안전한 위협'과 유사할 수 있다. 우리는 불편하지만 안전하다고 느낀다. 생존이 위험하지 않은 이런 상황에서 고통에 대한 욕구는 실제로는 고통이나 처벌이 아닌 보상에 대한 욕구이다. 이러한 보상과 같은 효과는 고통에 대한 숙달된 느낌에서 비롯된다. 칠리를 먹는 습관을 자세히 들여다볼수록 이는 더욱 분명하게 드러난다. 칠리의 활성 성분인 캡사이신이 혀에 닿으면 피부 조직이 화상을 입었을 때 활성화되는 것과 똑같은 수용체를 자극한다. 우리 몸이 위험 신호를 보내고 있지만 실제로는 완전히 안전하다는 것을 알면 쾌감이 생긴다. 모든 아이들은 처음에는 칠리를 싫어하지만, 반복적인 노출과 실질적인 해를 경험하지 않는다는 것을 알게 됨을 통해 그것에서 쾌락을 얻는 방법을 배우게 된다. 흥미롭게도 고통 그 자체를 위해 고통을 추구하는 것은 인간만이 할 수 있는 행동으로 보인다. 동물이 칠리를 선호하게 하거나 스스로에게 해를 가하도록 과학자들이 훈련시키는 유일한 방법은 고통을 항상 즐거운 보상과 직접적으로 연관시키는 것이다.

43~45.

An airplane flew high above the deep blue seas far from any land. Flying the small plane was a student pilot who was sitting alongside an **[experienced / inexperienced]**188) flight instructor. As the student looked out the window, she was filled with **[wander / wonder]**189) and appreciation for the beauty of the world. Her instructor, meanwhile, waited **[patient / patiently]**190) for the right time to start a surprise flight emergency training exercise. When the plane hit a bit of turbulence, the instructor pushed a hidden button. Suddenly, all the monitors inside the plane flashed several times then went out **[complete / completely]**191)! Now the student was in control of an airplane **[that / what]**192) was flying well, but she had no **[implication / indication]**193) of where she was or where she should go. She did have a map, but no **[another / other]**194) instruments. She was at a loss and then the plane shook again. When the student began to panic, the instructor said, "Stay calm and steady. You can do it." Calm as ever, the instructor told her student, "Difficult times always happen **[during / while]**195) flight. The most important thing is to focus on your flight in those situations." Those words encouraged the student **[focusing / to focus]**196) on flying the aircraft first. "Thank you, I think I can make **[it / x]**197)," she said, "As I've been trained, I should search for visual markers." Then, the student carefully flew low enough **[seeing / to see]**198) if she could find any ships making their way across the surface of the ocean. Now the instructor and the student could see some ships. Although the ships were far apart, they were all **[sailed / sailing]**199) in a line. With the line of ships in view, the student could see the way to home and safety. The student looked at her in relief, **[who / whom]**200) smiled proudly back at her student.

비행기가 육지에서 멀리 떨어진 깊고 푸른 바다 위를 높이 날고 있었다. 소형 비행기를 조종하고 있는 것은 노련한 비행 교관과 나란히 앉아 있는 한 파일럿 교육생이었다. 교육생이 창문 밖을 바라볼 때, 그녀는 세상의 아름다움에 대한 경이로움과 감탄으로 가득 찼다. 한편, 비행 교관은 비행 중 돌발 비상 상황 대처 훈련을 시작할 적절한 때를 인내심을 가지고 기다리고 있었다. 비행기가 약간의 난기류를 만났을 때, 교관은 숨겨진 버튼을 눌렀다. 갑자기, 비행기 안의 모든 모니터가 여러 번 깜박이다가 완전히 꺼졌다! 이제 교육생은 잘 날고 있는 비행기를 조종하고 있었지만, 그녀는 자신이 어디에 있는지, 어디로 가야 하는지 알 방도가 없었다. 교육생은 지도는 가지고 있었지만, 다른 도구는 가지고 있지 않았다. 그녀는 어쩔 줄 몰라 했고 그때 비행기가 다시 흔들렸다. 교육생이 당황하기 시작하자 교관은 "침착하세요. 당신은 할 수 있습니다." 여느 때처럼 침착한 교관은 교육생에게 "비행 중에는 항상 어려운 상황이 발생합니다. 그러한 상황에서는 비행에 집중하는 것이 가장 중요합니다."라고 말했다. 그 말이 교육생이 먼저 비행에 집중할 수 있게끔 용기를 주었다. "감사합니다. 제가 해낼 수 있을 것 같아요."라고 그녀는 말했다. "훈련받은 대로, 저는 시각 표식을 찾아야겠어요." 그런 다음 교육생은 바다 표면을 가로지르는 배가 보이는지 확인할 수 있을 정도로 충분히 낮게 조심히 비행하였다. 이제 교관과 교육생은 배 몇 척을 볼 수 있었다. 배들은 멀리 떨어져 있었지만 모두 한 줄을 이루고 항해하고 있었다. 배들이 줄을 지어있는 것이 보이자, 교육생은 안전하게 복귀하는 길을 알 수 있었다. 교육생은 안도하며 그녀를 바라봤고, 그녀도 교육생을 향해 자랑스럽게 웃어보였다.

2024 고1 6월 모의고사　　❷ 회차 :　　점 / 200점

❶ voca　　❷ text　　❸ [/]　　❹ ___　　❺ quiz 1　　❻ quiz 2　　❼ quiz 3　　❽ quiz 4　　❾ quiz 5

18.

Dear Reader,

We always appreciate your support. As you know, our service is now available through an app. There [**have / has**]1) never been a better time to switch to an online membership of TourTide Magazine. At a 50% discount off your current print [**description / subscription**]2), you can [**access / assess**]3) a full year of online reading. Get new issues and daily web pieces at TourTide.com, read or listen to TourTide Magazine via the app, and [**get / to get**]4) our membersonly newsletter. You'll also gain access to our editors' selections of the best articles. Join today!

Yours, TourTide Team

19.

As I walked from the mailbox, my heart was beating [**rapid / rapidly**]5). In my hands, I held the letter from the university I had applied to. I thought my grades were good enough to [**cross / crossing**]6) the line and my application letter was well-written, but was it enough? I hadn't slept a wink for days. As I carefully tore into the paper of the envelope, the letter slowly emerged [**from / with**]7) the opening phrase, "It is our great pleasure..." I shouted with joy, "I am in!" As I held the letter, I began [**x / to**]8) make a fantasy about my college life in a faraway city.

20.

Having a [**mess / messy**]9) room can add up to [**negative / positive**]10) feelings and [**constructive / destructive**]11) thinking. Psychologists say that having a disorderly room can indicate a [**disorganized / disorganizing**]12) mental state. One of the professional tidying experts [**say / says**]13) that the moment you start cleaning your room, you also start changing your life and [**gain / gaining**]14) new perspective. When you clean your surroundings, positive and good atmosphere follows. You can do more things [**effective / efficiently**]15) and [**neat / neatly**]16). So, clean up your closets, organize your drawers, and [**arrange / arranging**]17) your things first, then peace of mind will follow.

21.

The soil of a farm field is forced to be the perfect environment for monoculture growth. This [**achieved / is achieved**]18) by adding nutrients in the form of fertilizer and water by way of irrigation. [**During / While**]19) the last fifty years, engineers and crop scientists have helped farmers [**become / becoming**]20) much more efficient at supplying [**exact / exactly**]21) the right amount of both. World usage of fertilizer has tripled since 1969, and the global capacity for irrigation has almost doubled; we are feeding and [**water / watering**]22) our fields more than ever, and our crops are loving it. [**Fortunately / Unfortunately**]23), these luxurious conditions have also excited the attention of certain agricultural undesirables. [**Because / Because of**]24) farm fields are loaded with nutrients and water [**relative / relatively**]25) to the natural land that surrounds them, they [**are desired / desired**]26) as luxury real estate by every random weed in the area.

22.

When it comes to [**help** / **helping**]27) out, you don't have to do much. All you have to do is come around and [**show** / **to show**]28) that you care. If you notice someone who is lonely, you could go and sit with [**them** / **themselves**]29). If you work with someone who eats lunch all by themselves, and you go and sit down with them, they will begin to be more [**social** / **sociable**]30) after a while, and they will owe [**it** / **them**]31) all to you. A person's happiness comes from attention. There are too many people out in the world [**who** / **whom**]32) feel like everyone [**has** / **have**]33) forgotten them or ignored them. Even if you say hi to someone passing by, they will begin to feel better about [**them** / **themselves**]34), like someone cares.

23.

We often try [**making** / **to make**]35) cuts in our challenges and take the easy route. When [**taking** / **took**]36) the quick exit, we fail to acquire the strength to compete. We often take the easy route to [**improve** / **involve**]37) our skills. Many of us never really work to achieve mastery in the key areas of life. These skills are key tools that can be useful to our career, health, and [**property** / **prosperity**]38). Highly successful athletes don't win [**because** / **because of**]39) better equipment; they win by facing hardship to gain strength and skill. They win through preparation. It's the [**mental** / **physical**]40) preparation, winning mindset, strategy, and skill that [**set** / **sets**]41) them apart. Strength comes from struggle, not from [**take** / **taking**]42) the path of least resistance. Hardship is not just a lesson for the next time in front of us. Hardship will be the greatest teacher we will ever [**had** / **have**]43) in life.

24.

Your behaviors are usually a reflection of your [**identify** / **identity**]44). What you do is an indication of the type of person you believe [**that** / **what**]45) you are — [**neither** / **either**]46) consciously [**nor** / **or**]47) nonconsciously. Research has shown that once a person believes in a particular aspect of their identity, they are [**less** / **more**]48) likely to act according to that belief. For example, people who [**identified** / **identify**]49) as "being a voter" were more likely to vote than those who simply claimed "voting" was an action they wanted [**performing** / **to perform**]50). Similarly, the person who accepts exercise as the part of their identity doesn't have to convince [**them** / **themselves**]51) to train. [**Do** / **Doing**]52) the right thing is easy. After all, when your behavior and your identity perfectly [**match** / **matches**]53), you are no longer pursuing behavior change. You are simply acting like the type of person you already believe [**you** / **yourself**]54) to be.

25.

The above graph shows the electronic waste collection and recycling rate by region in 2016 and 2019. In [**both** / **either**]55) years, Europe showed the highest electronic waste collection and recycling rates. The electronic waste collection and recycling [**rate** / **rates**]56) of Asia in 2019 was lower than in 2016. The Americas ranked second in 2016 and third in 2019, with 17 percent and 9 percent [**respectable** / **respectively**]57). In both years, the electronic waste collection and recycling rates in Oceania [**remained** / **remaining**]58) under 10 percent. Africa had the lowest electronic waste collection and recycling rates in both 2016 and 2019, [**showing** / **shown**]59) the smallest gap between 2016 and 2019.

26.

Fritz Zwicky, a memorable astrophysicist who coined the term 'supernova', [**born / was born**]60) in Varna, Bulgaria to a Swiss father and a Czech mother. At the age of six, he was sent to his grandparents who looked after him for [**almost / most**]61) of his childhood in Switzerland. There, he received an [**advanced / advancing**]62) education in mathematics and physics. In 1925, he emigrated to the United States and [**continued / continuing**]63) his physics research at California Institute of Technology (Caltech). He developed numerous theories that have had a profound influence on the understanding of our universe in the early 21st century. After [**be / being**]64) appointed as a professor of [**astrology / astronomy**]65) at Caltech in 1942, he developed some of the earliest jet engines and [**hold / holds**]66) more than 50 patents, many in jet propulsion.

29.

The hunter-gatherer lifestyle, which can [**be described / describe**]67) as "natural" to human beings, appears to have had much to recommend it. Examination of human remains from early hunter-gatherer societies [**has / have**]68) suggested that our ancestors enjoyed abundant food, obtainable without excessive effort, and [**suffer / suffered**]69) very few diseases. If this is true, it is not clear why so many humans settled in [**permanent / permanently**]70) villages and developed agriculture, growing crops and [**domesticated / domesticating**]71) animals: cultivating fields was hard work, and it was in farming villages that epidemic diseases first took root. [**However / Whatever**]72) its immediate effect on the lives of humans, the development of settlements and agriculture undoubtedly led to a high increase in population density. This period, known as the New Stone Age, was a major turning point in human development, opening the way to the growth of the first towns and cities, and eventually [**leading / led**]73) to settled "civilizations."

30.

[**Many / Much**]74) human and nonhuman animals save commodities or money for future consumption. This behavior seems to reveal a preference of a delayed reward over an immediate one: the agent gives up some immediate pleasure in exchange for a future [**one / ones**]75). Thus the discounted value of the future reward should be greater than the undiscounted value of the present one. However, in some cases the agent does not wait for the envisioned occasion but [**used / uses**]76) their savings [**premature / prematurely**]77). For example, early in the year an employee might set aside money to buy Christmas presents but then spend [**it / them**]78) on a summer vacation instead. Such cases could be examples of weakness of will. That is, the agents may judge or resolve to spend their savings in a certain way for the greatest benefit but then act [**different / differently**]79) when temptation for immediate pleasure [**appear / appears**]80).

31.

The costs of interruptions are well-documented. Martin Luther King Jr. lamented [**it / them**]81) when he described "that lovely poem that didn't get written because someone knocked on the door." Perhaps the most famous [**literary / literate**]82) example happened in 1797 when Samuel Taylor Coleridge started writing his poem Kubla Khan from a dream he had but then [**was visited / visited**]83) by an unexpected guest. For Coleridge, by [**coincidence / coincident**]84), the untimely visitor came at a particularly bad time. He forgot his inspiration and [**leave / left**]85) the work unfinished. While there are [**many / much**]86) documented cases of sudden disruptions that have had significant consequences for professionals in critical roles such as doctors, nurses, control room operators, stock traders, and pilots, they also impact most of us in our everyday lives, [**slowing / slows**]87) down work productivity and generally [**increases / increasing**]88) stress levels.

32.

There's a lot of scientific evidence demonstrating [**that** / **what**]89) focused attention leads to the reshaping of the brain. In animals [**rewarded** / **rewarding**]90) for noticing sound (to hunt or to avoid being hunted for example), we find much larger auditory centers in the brain. In animals [**rewarded** / **rewarding**]91) for sharp eyesight, the visual areas are larger. Brain scans of violinists [**provide** / **providing**]92) more evidence, showing dramatic growth and expansion in regions of the cortex that [**represent** / **represents**]93) the left hand, [**that** / **which**]94) has to finger the strings precisely, often at very high speed. [**Other** / **The other**]95) studies have shown that the hippocampus, which is vital for [**spacious** / **spatial**]96) memory, is enlarged in taxi drivers. The point is [**that** / **what**]97) the physical architecture of the brain changes according to [**where** / **which**]98) we direct our attention and [**that** / **what**]99) we practice doing.

33.

How did the human mind [**evolve** / **revolve**]100)? One possibility is that competition and conflicts with other human tribes caused our brains to evolve the way they [**did** / **had**]101). A human tribe that could out-think its enemies, even slightly, [**possess** / **possessed**]102) a vital advantage. The ability of your tribe to imagine and [**predict** / **predicting**]103) where and when a hostile enemy tribe might strike, and [**plan** / **planning**]104) accordingly, [**give** / **gives**]105) your tribe a significant military advantage. The human mind became a weapon in the struggle for survival, a weapon far more decisive than any before [**it** / **them**]106). And this mental advantage [**applied** / **was applied**]107), over and over, within each [**succeeding** / **successful**]108) generation. The tribe that could out-think [**its** / **their**]109) opponents [**was** / **were**]110) more likely to succeed in battle and would then pass on the genes responsible for this mental advantage to [**its** / **their**]111) offspring. You and I are the [**descendants** / **predecessors**]112) of the winners.

34.

To find the hidden potential in teams, instead of brainstorming, we're better off shifting to a [**process** / **progress**]113) called brainwriting. The [**initial** / **initiative**]114) steps are solo. You start by asking everyone to generate ideas [**separate** / **separately**]115). Next, you pool them and share them [**anonymously** / **unanimously**]116) among the group. To preserve [**dependent** / **independent**]117) judgment, each member evaluates them on their own. Only then does the team come together to select and [**define** / **refine**]118) the most promising options. By developing and assessing ideas individually before choosing and elaborating [**them** / **themselves**]119), teams can surface and advance possibilities that might not get attention otherwise. This brainwriting process makes sure [**that** / **what**]120) all ideas are brought to the table and all voices [**are brought** / **brought**]121) into the conversation. It is especially effective in groups that [**struggle** / **struggles**]122) to achieve collective intelligence.

35.

Simply [**give** / **giving**]123) employees a sense of agency — a feeling that they are in control, [**that** / **what**]124) they have genuine decision-making authority — can radically [**decrease** / **increase**]125) how much energy and focus they bring to their jobs. One 2010 study at a manufacturing plant in Ohio, for instance, carefully examined assembly-line workers who [**empowered** / **were empowered**]126) to make small decisions about their schedules and work environment. They designed their own uniforms and [**had**

/ **have**]127) authority over shifts while all the manufacturing processes and pay scales stayed the same. Within two months, productivity at the plant [**increasing / increased**]128) by 20 percent, with workers [**taken / taking**]129) shorter breaks and making fewer mistakes. Giving [**employees / employers**]130) a sense of control improved how much self-discipline they brought to their jobs.

36.

As businesses shift some core business activities to digital, such as sales, marketing, or archiving, it is assumed [**that / what**]131) the impact on the environment will be [**less / more**]132) negative. However, digital business activities can still [**threaten / threatens**]133) the environment. In some cases, the harm of digital businesses can be even [**less / more**]134) hazardous. A few decades ago, offices used to [**have / having**]135) much more paper waste since all documents were paper based. [**When / While**]136) workplaces shifted from paper to digital documents, invoices, and emails, it was a promising step to save trees. However, the cost of the Internet and electricity for the environment [**neglected / is neglected**]137). A recent Wired report declared [**that / what**]138) most data centers' energy source is fossil fuels. When we store bigger data on clouds, [**increased / increasing**]139) carbon emissions make our green clouds gray. The carbon footprint of an email is smaller than mail sent via a post office, but still, it causes four grams of CO_2, and it can be as much as 50 grams if the attachment [**is / was**]140) big.

37.

Problems often [**arise / raise**]141) if an exotic species is suddenly introduced to an ecosystem. Britain's red and grey squirrels provide a clear example. When the grey arrived from America in the 1870s, both squirrel species competed for the same food and habitat, [**that / which**]142) put the native red squirrel populations under pressure. The grey had the edge [**because / because of**]143) it can [**adapt / adopt**]144) its diet; it is able, for instance, to eat green acorns, while the red can only digest [**mature / premature**]145) acorns. Within the same area of forest, grey squirrels can destroy the food supply before red squirrels even [**has / have**]146) a bite. Greys can also live more [**dense / densely**]147) and in varied habitats, so have survived more easily when woodland has [**destroyed / been destroyed**]148). As a result, the red squirrel has come close to [**distinction / extinction**]149) in England.

38.

Growing crops forced people [**staying / to stay**]150) in one place. Hunter-gatherers typically moved around frequently, and they had to be able to carry all their possessions with them every time they moved. In particular, mothers had to carry their young children. As a result, hunter-gatherer mothers [**could / should**]151) have only one baby every four years or so, [**spaced / spacing**]152) their births so that they never had to carry more than one child at a time. Farmers, on the other hand, could live in the same place year after year and did not have to worry about [**transport / transporting**]153) young children long distances. Societies that settled down in one place [**was / were**]154) able to shorten their birth intervals from four years to about two. This meant that each woman could have more children than her hunter-gatherer [**counterpart / counterparts**]155), which in turn resulted in rapid population growth among farming communities. An [**increased / increasing**]156) population was actually an advantage to agricultural societies, [**because / because of**]157) farming required large amounts of human labor.

39.

Spending time as children allows animals [**learning / to learn**]158) about their environment. Without childhood, animals must rely [**less / more**]159) fully on hardware, and therefore be less flexible. Among migratory bird species, those that are born knowing how, when, and where to migrate — those that are migrating entirely with instructions they were born with — sometimes have very [**efficient / inefficient**]160) migration routes. These birds, born knowing how to migrate, [**can / don't**]161) adapt easily. So when lakes dry up, forest becomes farmland, or climate change pushes breeding grounds farther north, those birds that are born knowing how to migrate [**don't keep / keep**]162) flying by the old rules and maps. By comparison, birds with the longest childhoods, and those that migrate with their parents, tend to [**have / having**]163) the most efficient migration routes. Childhood facilitates the passing on of cultural information, and culture can [**evolve / involve**]164) faster than genes. Childhood gives flexibility in a changing world.

40.

Over the last several decades, scholars have developed standards for how best to create, organize, present, and preserve digital information for future generations. [**That / What**]165) has remained [**neglected / neglecting**]166) for the most part, however, are the needs of people with disabilities. As a result, many of the otherwise most valuable digital resources are [**useful / useless**]167) for people who are deaf or hard of hearing, as well as for people who are blind, have low vision, or have difficulty [**distinguishing / to distinguish**]168) particular colors. While professionals working in educational technology and commercial web design [**has / have**]169) made significant progress in meeting the needs of such users, some scholars [**create / creating**]170) digital projects all too often fail to [**take / taking**]171) these needs into account. This situation would be much improved if more projects embraced the idea [**that / what**]172) we should always keep the largest possible audience in mind as we make design decisions, ensuring that our final product [**serve / serves**]173) the needs of those with disabilities as well as those without.

41~42.

All humans, to an [**extent / intent**]174), seek activities that cause a degree of pain in order to experience pleasure, whether this is found in spicy food, strong massages, or stepping into a too-cold or too-hot bath. The key is [**that / what**]175) it is a 'safe threat'. The brain [**deceives / perceives**]176) the stimulus to be painful but ultimately nonthreatening. Interestingly, this could be [**different / similar**]177) to the way humor works: a 'safe threat' that causes pleasure by playfully [**observing / violating**]178) norms. We feel [**comfortable / uncomfortable**]179), but safe. In this context, [**where / which**]180) survival is clearly not in danger, the desire for pain is actually the desire for a reward, not suffering or punishment. This reward-like [**affect / effect**]181) comes from the feeling of mastery over the pain. The closer you look at your chilli-eating habit, the more [**remarkable / remarkably**]182) it seems. When the active ingredient of chillies — capsaicin — touches the tongue, it stimulates exactly the same receptor that [**activates / is activated**]183) when any of these tissues are burned. Knowing that our body is firing off danger signals, but that we are actually completely safe, [**produce / produces**]184) pleasure. All children start off hating chilli, but many learn to derive pleasure from it through [**repeated / repeating**]185) exposure and knowing that they will never experience any real harm. Interestingly, seeking pain for the pain itself **[appear / appears]**186) to be uniquely human. The only way scientists have trained animals to have a preference for chilli or to self-harm is to have the pain always **[directly / indirectly]**187) associated with a pleasurable reward.

43~45.

An airplane flew high above the deep blue seas far from any land. Flying the small plane was a student pilot who was sitting alongside an **[experienced / inexperienced]**188) flight instructor. As the student looked out the window, she was filled with **[wander / wonder]**189) and appreciation for the beauty of the world. Her instructor, meanwhile, waited **[patient / patiently]**190) for the right time to start a surprise flight emergency training exercise. When the plane hit a bit of turbulence, the instructor pushed a hidden button. Suddenly, all the monitors inside the plane flashed several times then went out **[complete / completely]**191)! Now the student was in control of an airplane **[that / what]**192) was flying well, but she had no **[implication / indication]**193) of where she was or where she should go. She did have a map, but no **[another / other]**194) instruments. She was at a loss and then the plane shook again. When the student began to panic, the instructor said, "Stay calm and steady. You can do it." Calm as ever, the instructor told her student, "Difficult times always happen **[during / while]**195) flight. The most important thing is to focus on your flight in those situations." Those words encouraged the student **[focusing / to focus]**196) on flying the aircraft first. "Thank you, I think I can make **[it / x]**197)," she said, "As I've been trained, I should search for visual markers." Then, the student carefully flew low enough **[seeing / to see]**198) if she could find any ships making their way across the surface of the ocean. Now the instructor and the student could see some ships. Although the ships were far apart, they were all **[sailed / sailing]**199) in a line. With the line of ships in view, the student could see the way to home and safety. The student looked at her in relief, **[who / whom]**200) smiled proudly back at her student.

2024 고1 6월 모의고사　❶ 회차 : 　점 / 320점

2024_1_6_18

Dear Reader,

We always a_____1) your support. As you know, our service is now a_____2) through an app. There has never been a better time to switch to an online m_____3) of TourTide Magazine. At a 50% discount off your current print s_____4) , you can access a full year of online reading. Get new issues and daily web pieces at TourTide.com, read or listen to TourTide Magazine via the app, and get our m_____5) newsletter. You'll also gain access to our editors' selections of the best articles. Join today! / Yours, TourTide Team

독자분께, 보내주신 성원에 항상 감사드립니다. 아시다시피, 이제 앱을 통해서도 저희 서비스를 이용하실 수 있습니다. TourTide Magazine의 온라인 회원으로 전환하기에 이보다 더 좋은 시기는 없습니다. 신의 현재 인쇄본 구독료에서 50% 할인된 가격으로 1년 치를 온라인으로 구독할 수 있습니다. TourTide.com에서 신간호와 일일 웹 기사를 받아보고, 앱을 통해 TourTide Magazine을 읽거나 청취해 보고, 회원 전용 뉴스레터 도 받아보세요. 편집자들이 선정한 최고의 기사도 받아 볼 수 있습니다. 오늘 가입하세요! / TourTide 팀 드림

2024_1_6_19

As I walked from the mailbox, my heart was b_____6) rapidly. In my hands, I held the letter from the university I had a_____7) to. I thought my grades were good enough to c_____8) the line and my a_____9) letter was well-written, but was it enough? I hadn't slept a wink for days. As I carefully t_____10) into the paper of the envelope, the letter slowly e_____11) with the opening phrase, "It is our great pleasure…" I shouted with joy, "I am in!" As I h_____12) the letter, I began to make a f_____13) about my college life in a f_____14) city.

우체통에서 걸어올 때 내 심장은 빠르게 뛰고 있었다. 내 손에는 지원했던 대학에서 보낸 편지가 들려있었다. 내 생각에는 합격할 만큼 성적이 좋았고 지원서도 잘 썼지만, 그것으로 충분했을까? 며칠 동안 한 숨도 잘 수 없었다. 봉투의 종이를 조심스럽게 찢자 "매우 기쁘게도…"라는 첫 문구와 함께 편지가 천천히 모습을 드러냈다. 나는 기뻐서 소리질렀다. "합격이야!" 나는 편지를 손에 쥐고 집에서 멀리 떨어진 도시에서의 대학 생활에 대해 상상하기 시작했다.

2024_1_6_20

Having a m_____15) room can add up to n_____16) feelings and d_____17) thinking. Psychologists say that having a d_____18) room can indicate a d_____19) mental state. One of the professional t_____20) experts says that the moment you start cleaning your room, you also start changing your life and gaining new p_____21) . When you clean your surroundings, p_____22) and good atmosphere follows. You can do more things e_____23) and neatly. So, clean up your closets, organize your drawers, and a_____24) your things first, then peace of mind will follow.

방이 지저분한 것은 결국 부정적인 감정과 파괴적인 사고로 이어질 수 있다. 심리학자들은 방이 무질서하다는 것은 정신 상태가 혼란스럽다는 것을 나타낼 수 있다고 말한다. 정리 전문가 중 한 명은 방청소를 시작하는 순간 당신은 인생을 변화시키고 새로운 관점을 얻기 시작한다고 말한다. 주변을 청소하면 긍정적이고 좋은 분위기가 따라온다. 당신은 더 많은 일을 효율적이고 깔끔하게 할 수 있다. 그러니 먼저 옷장을 청소하고, 서랍을 정리하고, 물건을 정돈한다면 마음의 평화가 따라올 것이다.

2024_1_6_21

The soil of a farm f_____25) is f_____26) to be the perfect environment for m_____27) growth. This is achieved by adding nutrients in the form of f_____28) and water by way of i_____29) . During the last fifty years, engineers and crop scientists have helped farmers become much more efficient at s_____30) exactly the right amount of both. World usage of fertilizer has t_____31) since 1969, and the global capacity for i_____32) has almost doubled; we are feeding and w_____33) our fields more than ever, and our c_____34) are loving it. Unfortunately, these l_____35) conditions have also excited the attention of certain a_____36) u_____37) . Because farm fields are loaded with nutrients and water r_____38) to the natural land that surrounds them, they are d_____39) as luxury real estate by every r_____40) weed in the area.

농지의 토양은 단일 작물 재배를 위한 완벽한 환경이어야 한다. 이것은 비료 형태로 양분을 더하고 관개로 물을 댐으로써 이루어진다. 지난 50년 동안 기술자와 농작물 연구자들은 농부들이 양쪽 모두의 정확한 적정량을 공급하는 데 훨씬 더 효율적일 수 있도록 도움을 주었다. 전 세계 비료 사용량은 1969년 이래로 세 배가 되었고, 전체 관개 능력은 거의 두 배가 되었다. 우리는 그 어느 때보다도 들판을 기름지게 하고 물을 대고 있으며, 우리의 농작물은 이를 좋아한다. 불행히도, 이러한 호사스러운 상황은 농업에서는 달갑지 않은 것들의 관심도 끌어들였다. 농지는 주위를 둘러싼 자연 지대에 비해 영양분과 물이 풍족히 채워져 있기 때문에 그 지역의 어떤 잡초라도 원하는 고급 부동산이 된다.

2024_1_6_22

When it comes to h_____41) out, you don't have to do much. All you have to do is come around and show that you c_____42) . If you notice someone who is l_____43) , you could go and sit with them. If you work with someone who eats lunch all by t_____44) , and you go and sit down with them, they will begin to be more s_____45) after a while, and they will o_____46) it all to you. A person's happiness comes from a_____47) . There are too many people out in the world who feel like everyone has f_____48) them or i_____49) them. Even if you say hi to someone p_____50) by, they will begin to feel better about themselves, like someone c_____51) .

도움을 주는 것에 관해서 당신은 많은 것을 할 필요는 없다. 그저 다가가서 관심을 갖고 있다는 것을 보여주기만 하면 된다. 외로운 사람을 발견하면 가서 함께 앉아 있으면 된다. 혼자서 점심을 먹는 사람과 함께 일한다면, 그리고 그 사람에게 다가가서 함께 앉는다면 얼마 지나지 않아 그 사람은 더 사교적으로 변하기 시작할 것이고, 이 모든 것을 당신 덕분이라고 할 것이다. 한 사람의 행복은 관심에서 비롯된다. 세상에는 모든 이가 자신을 잊었거나 무시한다고 느끼는 사람들이 너무 많다. 지나가는 사람들에게 인사만 건네도, 누군가 (그들에게) 관심을 가져주는 것처럼, 그들은 자기 자신에 대해 기분이 좋아지기 시작할 것이다.

2024_1_6_23

We often try to make c_____ 52) in our c_____ 53) and take the easy route. When taking the quick exit, we fail to a_____ 54) the strength to c_____ 55) . We often take the easy route to i_____ 56) our skills. Many of us never really work to achieve m_____ 57) in the key areas of life. These skills are key tools that can be useful to our career, health, and p_____ 58) . Highly successful athletes don't win because of better equipment; they win by facing h_____ 59) to gain strength and skill. They win through p_____ 60) . It's the mental preparation, winning mindset, strategy, and skill that set them a_____ 61) . Strength comes from s_____ 62) , not from taking the path of l_____ 63) r_____ 64) . Hardship is not just a lesson for the next time in front of us. H_____ 65) will be the greatest teacher we will ever have in life.

우리는 종종 우리의 도전을 멈추고, 쉬운 길을 택하려고 한다. 쉬운 길을 택하면 경쟁할 수 있는 힘을 얻지 못한다. 우리는 종종 실력을 향상하기 위해 쉬운 길을 택한다. 우리 중 다수가 인생의 핵심이 되는 영역에서 숙달을 위한 노력을 하지 않는다. 이러한 기술은 경력, 건강, 번영에 도움이 될 수 있는 핵심 도구이다. 성공한 운동선수들은 더 좋은 장비 때문에 승리하는 것이 아니다. 그들은 힘과 실력을 얻기 위해 고난에 맞섬으로써 승리한다. 그들은 준비를 통해 승리한다. 그들을 돋보이게 하는 것은 바로 정신적 준비, 승리하는 마음가짐, 전략, 그리고 기술이다. 힘은 저항이 가장 적은 길을 택하는 것이 아니라 맞서 싸우는 데서 나온다. 고난은 단지 우리 앞에 놓인 다음을 위한 교훈만은 아니다. 고난은 우리 인생에서 가장 위대한 스승이 될 것이다.

2024_1_6_24

Your behaviors are usually a r_____ 66) of your i_____ 67) . What you do is an i_____ 68) of the type of person you believe that you are — either consciously or nonconsciously. Research has shown that once a person believes in a particular a_____ 69) of their identity, they are more likely to act according to that b_____ 70) . For example, people who i_____ 71) as "being a voter" were more likely to vote than those who simply c_____ 72) "voting" was an action they wanted to p_____ 73) . Similarly, the person who accepts exercise as the part of their i_____ 74) doesn't have to c_____ 75) themselves to train. Doing the right thing is easy. After all, when your behavior and your identity perfectly m_____ 76) , you are no longer p_____ 77) behavior change. You are simply acting like the type of person you already believe yourself to be.

당신의 행동은 대개 당신의 정체성을 반영한다. 당신이 하는 행동은 의식적으로든 무의식적으로든 당신이 스스로를 어떤 사람이라고 믿고 있는지를 나타낸다. 연구에 따르면 자신의 정체성의 특정 측면을 믿는 사람은 그 믿음에 따라 행동할 가능성이 더 높다. 예를 들어, 자신을 "유권자"라고 느끼는 사람은 단순히 "투표"가 자신이 하고 싶은 행동이라고 주장하는 사람보다 투표할 가능성이 더 높았다. 마찬가지로, 운동을 자신의 정체성의 일부로 받아들이는 사람은 훈련하라고 스스로를 설득할 필요가 없다. 옳은 일을 하는 것은 쉽다. 결국, 자신의 행동과 정체성이 완벽하게 일치하면 더 이상 행동 변화를 추구하지 않아도 된다. 당신은 그저 당신 스스로가 그렇다고 이미 믿고 있는 유형의 사람처럼 행동하고 있을 뿐이다.

2024_1_6_26

Fritz Zwicky, a memorable **a_____**78) who **c_____**79) the **t_____**80) 'supernova', was born in Varna, Bulgaria to a Swiss father and a Czech mother. At the age of six, he was sent to his grandparents who looked **a_____**81) him for most of his childhood in Switzerland. There, he received an advanced education in mathematics and physics. In 1925, he **e_____**82) to the United States and continued his physics research at California Institute of Technology (Caltech). He developed numerous **t_____**83) that have had a **p_____**84) influence on the understanding of our **u_____**85) in the early 21st century. After being **a_____**86) as a professor of **a_____**87) at Caltech in 1942, he developed some of the earliest jet engines and holds more than 50 **p_____**88) , many in jet **p_____**89) .

'초신성'이라는 용어를 만든 유명한 천체 물리학자 Fritz Zwicky는 불가리아의 Varna에서 스위스인 아버지와 체코인 어머니 사이에서 태어났다. 여섯 살이 되던 해, 그는 스위스에서 보낸 어린 시절의 대부분 동안 그를 돌봐준 조부모에게 보내졌다. 그곳에서, 그는 수학과 물리학에 대한 고급 교육을 받았다. 1925년 미국으로 이주하여 California Institute of Technology(Caltech)에서 물리학 연구를 이어갔다. 그는 21세기 초 우주에 대한 이해에 지대한 영향을 미친 수많은 이론을 발전시켰다. 1942년 Caltech의 천문학 교수로 임용된 후 그는 초창기 제트 엔진을 개발했고, 50개 이상의 특허를 보유하고 있으며, 이 중 많은 부분이 제트 추진 분야의 특허이다.

2024_1_6_29

The **h_____**90) lifestyle, which can be described as "natural" to human beings, appears to have **h_____**91) much to recommend it. **E_____**92) of human **r_____**93) from early hunter-gatherer societies **h_____**94) suggested that our ancestors enjoyed abundant food, **o_____**95) without **e_____**96) effort, and suffered very **f_____**97) diseases. If this is true, it is not clear why so many humans settled in **p_____**98) villages and developed agriculture, growing crops and **d_____**99) animals: **c_____**100) fields was hard work, and it was in farming villages that **e_____**101) diseases first took root. Whatever its immediate effect on the lives of humans, the development of **s_____**102) and **a_____**103) undoubtedly led to a high increase in **p_____**104) **d_____**105) . This period, known as the New Stone Age, was a major turning point in human development, opening the way to the growth of the first towns and cities, and eventually leading to settled " **c_____**106) ."

수렵 채집 생활 방식은 인류에게 "자연스러운" 것으로 묘사될 수 있으며, 그것을 추천할 만한 많은 것(장점)이 있는 것으로 보인다. 초기 수렵 채집 사회의 유적 조사는 인류의 조상들이 과도한 노력 없이도 구할 수 있는 풍족한 식량을 누릴 수 있었고 질병에 걸리는 일도 거의 없었다는 것을 알려준다. 이것이 사실이라면, 왜 그렇게 많은 인류가 영구적으로 마을에 정착하여 농작물을 재배하고 동물을 기르면서 농업을 발달시켰는지는 분명하지 않다. 밭을 경작하는 것은 힘든 일이었고, 전염병이 처음 뿌리를 내린 곳은 농경 마을이었다. 인간의 삶에 미치는 즉각적인 영향이 무엇이든, 정착지와 농업의 발전은 의심의 여지 없이 인구 밀도의 높은 증가로 이어졌다. 신석기 시대로 알려진 이 시기는 인류 발전의 중요한 전환점으로, 최초의 마을과 도시가 성장하는 길을 열었고, 결국 정착된 "문명"으로 이어졌다.

2024_1_6_30

Many human and nonhuman animals save **c**_____107) or money for future **c**_____108) . This behavior seems to reveal a **p**_____109) of a **d**_____110) reward over an **i**_____111) one: the agent gives up some immediate **p**_____112) in exchange for a **f**_____113) one. Thus the **d**_____114) value of the future reward should be **g**_____115) than the **u**_____116) value of the **p**_____117) one. However, in some cases the agent does not wait for the **e**_____118) occasion but uses their savings **p**_____119) . For example, early in the year an employee might set **a**_____120) money to buy Christmas presents but then spend it on a summer vacation instead. Such cases could be examples of **w**_____121) of will. That is, the agents may judge or **r**_____122) to spend their savings in a certain way for the greatest **b**_____123) but then act differently when **t**_____124) for immediate pleasure appears.

많은 인간과 인간이 아닌 동물은 물건이나 돈을 미래의 소비를 위해 저축한다. 이러한 행동은 즉각적인 보상보다 지연된 보상을 선호하는 것을 드러내는 듯하다. 즉, 행위자는 미래의 보상을 위해 당장의 쾌락을 포기하는 것이다. 그러므로 미래 보상의 하락된 가치는 하락되지 않은 현재의 가치보다 더 커야만 한다. 그러나, 어떤 경우 행위자가 계획한 일을 기다리지 않고 그들의 저축을 조기에 사용하는 경우도 있다. 예를 들어, 연초에 한 직원이 자기 돈을 크리스마스 선물을 사기 위해 모아두었지만 대신 여름 휴가에 사용할 수 있다. 이러한 사례는 의지의 약함의 예시가 될 수 있다. 즉, 행위자는 그들의 저축을 가장 큰 이익을 위해 특정 방식으로 사용하기로 판단하거나 결심했으나 즉각적인 즐거움에 대한 유혹이 생기면 다르게 행동할 수도 있다.

2024_1_6_31

The costs of **i**_____125) are well-documented. Martin Luther King Jr. **l**_____126) them when he described "that lovely poem that didn't get **w**_____127) because someone **k**_____128) on the door." Perhaps the most famous **l**_____129) example happened in 1797 when Samuel Taylor Coleridge started writing his poem Kubla Khan from a dream he had but then was **v**_____130) by an unexpected guest. For Coleridge, by **c**_____131) , the untimely visitor came at a particularly bad time. He forgot his **i**_____132) and left the work **u**_____133) . While there are many **d**_____134) cases of sudden disruptions that have had significant consequences for **p**_____135) in critical roles such as doctors, nurses, control room operators, stock traders, and pilots, they also impact most of us in our everyday lives, slowing down work **p**_____136) and generally increasing stress levels.

방해로 인한 대가는 잘 기록되어 있다. Martin Luther King Jr.는 "누군가 문을 두드리는 바람에 쓰여지지 못한 사랑스러운 시"를 묘사하며 이를 슬퍼했다. 아마도 가장 유명한 문학적 사례는 1797년 Samuel Taylor Coleridge가 꿈을 꾸고 Kubla Khan이 라는 시를 쓰기 시작했는데 뜻밖의 손님이 찾아왔을 때 일어났던 일일 것이다. 공교롭게도 Coleridge에게 이 불청객은 특히 좋지 않은 시기에 찾아왔다. 그는 영감을 잊고 작품을 미완성으로 남겼다. 의사, 간호사, 관제실 운영자, 주식 거래자, 조종사와 같은 중요한 역할을 담당하는 전문가들에게 심각한 결과를 초래한 갑작스러운 방해의 사례가 많이 기록되어 있지만, 갑작스러운 방해는 일상 생활에서 대부분의 사람들에게도 영향을 미쳐 업무 생산성을 떨어뜨리며 일반적으로 스트레스 수준을 높인다.

2024_1_6_32

There's a lot of scientific evidence d_____137) that focused a_____138) leads to the r_____139) of the brain. In animals r_____140) for noticing sound (to hunt or to avoid being hunted for example), we find much larger a_____141) centers in the brain. In animals rewarded for sharp eyesight, the v_____142) areas are larger. Brain scans of violinists provide more evidence, showing dramatic growth and expansion in regions of the c_____143) that represent the left hand, which has to finger the strings p_____144), often at very high speed. Other studies have shown that the h_____145), which is vital for s_____146) memory, is e_____147) in taxi drivers. The point is that the physical architecture of the brain changes according to where we d_____148) our attention and what we practice doing.

주의 집중이 뇌의 재구조화로 이어진다는 과학적 증거는 많이 있다. (예를 들어 사냥하거나 사냥감이 되는 것을 피하기 위해) 소리를 알아채는 것에 대한 보상을 받은 동물에서 우리는 뇌의 청각 중추가 훨씬 더 큰 것을 발견한다. 예리한 시력에 대한 보상을 받은 동물은 시각 영역이 더 크다. 바이올린 연주자의 뇌 스캔 결과는 더 많은 증거를 제공해서 종종 매우 빠른 속도로 현을 정확하게 켜야 하는 왼손을 나타내는 피질 영역의 극적인 성장과 확장을 보여준다. 다른 연구는 공간 기억에 필수적인 해마가 택시 운전사에게서 확대되는 것을 보여준다. 요점은 우리가 어디에 주의를 기울이고 무엇을 연습하느냐에 따라 뇌의 물리적 구조가 달라진다는 것이다.

2024_1_6_33

How did the human mind e_____149) ? One possibility is that c_____150) and c_____151) with other human tribes caused our brains to e_____152) the way they did. A human tribe that could o_____153) its enemies, even slightly, p_____154) a vital advantage. The ability of your tribe to imagine and p_____155) where and when a h_____156) enemy tribe might s_____157), and plan accordingly, gives your tribe a significant m_____158) advantage. The human mind became a w_____159) in the struggle for survival, a weapon far more d_____160) than any before it. And this m_____161) advantage was applied, over and over, within each s_____162) generation. The tribe that could out-think its o_____163) was more likely to s_____164) in battle and would then pass on the genes responsible for this mental advantage to its o_____165). You and I are the descendants of the winners.

인간의 생각은 어떻게 진화했을까? 한 가지 가능성은 다른 인간 부족과의 경쟁과 갈등이 우리 두뇌가 그렇게 진화하도록 했다는 것이다. 적보다 조금이라도 더 우수한 생각을 할 수 있는 인간 부족은 중요한 우위를 점했다. 적대적인 적 부족이 언제 어디서 공격할지 상상하고 예측하며 그에 따라 계획을 세울 수 있는 능력은 부족에게 상당한 군사적 우위를 가져다준다. 인간의 생각은 생존을 위한 투쟁에서 그 이전의 어떤 무기보다 훨씬 더 결정적인 무기가 되었다. 그리고 이러한 정신적 우위는 다음 세대에 걸쳐 계속해서 적용되었다. 상대보다 더 우수한 생각을 할 수 있는 부족은 전투에서 승리할 확률이 높았고, 이러한 정신적 우위를 담당하는 유전자를 자손에게 물려주었다. 당신과 나는 승자의 후손이다.

2024_1_6_34

To find the hidden potential in teams, instead of b_____ 166) , we're better off s_____ 167) to a process called b_____ 168) . The initial steps are solo. You start by asking everyone to generate ideas s_____ 169) . Next, you pool them and share them a_____ 170) among the group. To preserve i_____ 171) judgment, each member e_____ 172) them on their own. Only then d_____ 173) the team come together to select and refine the most p_____ 174) options. By developing and a_____ 175) ideas individually before choosing and e_____ 176) them, teams can s_____ 177) and a_____ 178) possibilities that might not get attention otherwise. This brainwriting process makes sure that all ideas are b_____ 179) to the table and all voices are brought into the conversation. It is especially e_____ 180) in groups that struggle to achieve c_____ 181) intelligence.

팀의 숨겨진 잠재력을 찾으려면 브레인스토밍 대신 브레인라이팅이라는 과정으로 전환하는 것이 좋다. 초기 단계는 혼자서 진행한다. 먼저 모든 사람에게 개별적으로 아이디어를 내도록 요청한다. 그런 다음, 아이디어를 모아 익명으로 그룹에 공유한다. 독립적인 판단을 유지하기 위해 각 구성원이 스스로 그 아이디어를 평가한다. 그리고 나서야 팀이 함께 모여 가장 유망한 옵션을 선택하고 다듬는다. 아이디어를 선택하고 구체화하기 전에 개별적으로 아이디어를 전개하고 평가함으로써 팀은 다른 방법으로는 주목받지 못했을 가능성을 드러내고 발전시킬 수 있다. 이 브레인라이팅 과정은 모든 아이디어를 테이블에 올려놓고 모든 의견을 대화에 반영할 수 있도록 한다. 특히 집단 지성을 달성하는 데 어려움을 겪는 그룹에서 효과적이다.

2024_1_6_35

Simply giving employees a sense of a_____ 182) — a feeling that they are in c_____ 183) , that they have g_____ 184) decision-making a_____ 185) — can radically i_____ 186) how much energy and focus they bring to their jobs. One 2010 study at a m_____ 187) plant in Ohio, for instance, carefully e_____ 188) assembly-line workers who were e_____ 189) to make small decisions about their schedules and work environment. They designed their own u_____ 190) and had a_____ 191) over shifts while all the manufacturing processes and pay scales s_____ 192) the same. Within two months, p_____ 193) at the plant increased by 20 percent, with workers t_____ 194) shorter breaks and making fewer m_____ 195) . Giving employees a sense of c_____ 196) improved how much s_____ 197) they brought to their jobs.

단순히 직원들에게 주인의식(그들이 통제하고 있는 느낌, 진정한 의사 결정 권한이 있다는 느낌)을 주는 것만으로도 그들이 자신의 업무에 쏟는 에너지와 집중력을 급격하게 높일 수 있다. 예를 들어, 오하이오주의 한 제조 공장에서 진행된 2010년의 한 연구는 그들의 일정과 작업 환경에 대한 작은 결정 권한을 부여받은 조립 라인 근로자를 주의 깊게 살펴보았다. 그들은 그들 자신의 유니폼을 디자인했고, 근무 교대에 대한 권한을 가진 반면에, 모든 생산 과정과 임금규모는 동일하게 유지되었다. 두 달 만에 직원들은 휴식 시간을 더 짧게 가졌고, 실수를 더 적게 하였으며, 그 공장의 생산성은 20퍼센트 증가했다. 자신들이 통제권을 쥐고 있다는 느낌을 직원들에게 부여한 것이 그들이 업무에 끌어들이는 자기 통제력을 향상시켰다.

2024_1_6_36

As businesses s_____198) some core business activities to d_____199) , such as sales, marketing, or archiving, it is assumed that the impact on the environment will be less n_____200) . However, digital business activities can still t_____201) the environment. In some cases, the harm of digital businesses can be even more h_____202) . A few decades ago, offices used to have much more paper waste since all documents were paper b_____203) . When workplaces shifted from paper to digital documents, invoices, and emails, it was a p_____204) step to save trees. However, the cost of the Internet and electricity for the environment is n_____205) . A recent Wired report declared that most data centers' energy source is f_____206) fuels. When we store bigger data on clouds, increased carbon e_____207) make our green clouds g_____208) . The carbon footprint of an email is smaller than mail s_____209) via a post office, but still, it causes four grams of CO_2, and it can be as much as 50 grams if the a_____210) is big.

기업이 영업, 마케팅, 파일 보관 등 일부 핵심 비즈니스 활동을 디지털로 전환함에 따라 환경에 미치는 영향이 덜 부정적일 것으로 예상된다. 그러나 디지털 비즈니스 활동은 여전히 환경을 위협할 수 있다. 경우에 따라서는 디지털 비즈니스가 끼치는 해악이 훨씬 더 위험할 수 있다. 수십 년 전만 해도 사무실에서는 모든 문서가 종이로 작성되었기 때문에 종이 폐기물이 훨씬 더 많았다. 직장에서 종이를 디지털 문서, (디지털) 송장, 이메일로 전환한 것은 나무를 보호할 수 있는 유망한 조치였다 하지만 인터넷과 전기가 환경에 입히는 손실은 간과되고 있다. 최근 Wired의 보고서에 따르면 대부분이 데이터 센터의 에너지원은 화석 연료이다. 클라우드에 더 많은 데이터를 저장할수록 탄소 배출량이 증가하여 녹색 구름을 회색으로 변하게 만든다. 이메일의 탄소 발자국은 우체국을 통해 보내는 우편물보다 적지만 여전히 4g의 이산화탄소를 유발하며 첨부 파일이 크면 50g에 달할 수 있다.

2024_1_6_37

Problems often a_____211) if an e_____212) species is suddenly introduced to an ecosystem. Britain's red and grey squirrels provide a clear example. When the grey a_____213) from America in the 1870s, both squirrel species c_____214) for the same food and h_____215) , which put the native red squirrel populations under p_____216) . The grey had the edge because it can a_____217) its diet; it is able, for instance, to eat green acorns, while the red can only digest m_____218) acorns. Within the same area of forest, grey squirrels can destroy the food supply before red squirrels even have a bite. Greys can also live more d_____219) and in v_____220) habitats, so h_____221) survived more easily when woodland has been d_____222) . As a result, the red squirrel has come close to e_____223) in England.

외래종이 갑자기 생태계에 유입되면 문제가 종종 발생한다. 영국의 붉은색 다람쥐와 회색 다람쥐가 명확한 예를 제공한다. 1870년대 미국에서 회색 다람쥐가 왔을 때, 두 다람쥐 종은 동일한 먹이와 서식지를 놓고 경쟁했고, 이것이 토종의 붉은 다람쥐 개체군을 압박했다. 회색 다람쥐는 먹이를 조절할 수 있기 때문에 우위를 점했다. 예를 들어 회색 다람쥐는 설익은 도토리를 먹을 수 있는 반면, 붉은 다람쥐는 다 익은 도토리만 소화할 수 있다. 숲의 같은 지역 내에서 회색 다람쥐는 붉은 다람쥐가 한 입 먹기도 전에 식량 공급을 파괴할 수 있다. 회색 다람쥐는 또한 더 밀집하며 다양한 서식지에서 살 수 있어서 삼림이 파괴되었을 때 더 쉽게 살아남았다. 그 결과, 붉은 다람쥐는 영국에서 거의 멸종 위기에 이르렀다.

2024_1_6_38

G_____224) crops forced people to s_____225) in one place. H_____226) typically moved around frequently, and they had to be able to carry all their p_____227) with them every t_____228) they moved. In particular, mothers had to carry their young children. As a result, hunter-gatherer mothers could have only one baby every four y_____229) or so, s_____230) their births so that they never had to carry more than one child at a time. Farmers, on the other hand, could live in the same place year after year and did not have to worry about t_____231) young children long distances. Societies that s_____232) down in one place were able to s_____233) their birth i_____234) from four years to about two. This meant that each woman could have more children than her hunter-gatherer c_____235) , which in turn resulted in r_____236) population growth among f_____237) communities. An increased population was actually an a_____238) to a_____239) societies, because farming required large amounts of human l_____240) .

농작물 재배는 사람들이 한곳에 머무르게 했다. 수렵 채집인들은 일반적으로 자주 이동해야 했고, 이동할 때마다 모든 소유물을 가지고 다닐 수 있어야 했다. 특히, 어머니들은 어린아이를 업고 이동해야 했다. 그 결과, 수렵 채집인 어머니들은 대략 4년마다 한 명의 아이만 낳을 수 있었고, 한 번에 한 명 이상의 아이를 업고 다닐 필요가 없도록 출산 간격을 두었다. 반면, 농부들은 매년 같은 장소에서 살 수 있었고 어린아이를 장거리 이동시켜야 하는 걱정을 하지 않아도 되었다. 한곳에 정착하게 된 사회는 출산 간격을 4년에서 약 2년으로 단축할 수 있었다. 이는 여성 한 명이 수렵 채집인인 상대보다 더 많은 아이를 낳을 수 있다는 것을 의미했고, 그 결과 그것은 농경 사회에서 급격한 인구 증가를 야기했다. 인구 증가는 실제로 농경 사회에 유리했는데, 왜냐하면 농사는 많은 인간의 노동력을 필요로 했기 때문이다.

2024_1_6_39

Spending time as c_____241) allows animals to l_____242) about their environment. Without childhood, animals must rely more fully on h_____243) , and therefore be less f_____244) . Among m_____245) bird species, those that are born knowing how, when, and where to migrate — those that are migrating entirely with i_____246) they were born with — sometimes have very i_____247) migration routes. These birds, b_____248) knowing how to migrate, don't a_____249) easily. So when lakes dry up, forest becomes farmland, or climate change pushes breeding grounds f_____250) north, those birds that are born knowing how to migrate keep flying by the old rules and maps. By c_____251) , birds with the longest childhoods, and those that migrate with their parents, tend to have the most efficient migration routes. Childhood f_____252) the p_____253) on of cultural information, and c_____254) can e_____255) faster than g_____256) . Childhood gives f_____257) in a changing world.

동물은 유년기를 보내면서 환경에 대해 배울 수 있다. 유년기가 없으면, 동물은 하드웨어에 더 많이 의존해야 하므로 유연성이 떨어질 수밖에 없다. 철새 중에서도 언제, 어디로, 어떻게 이동해야 하는지를 알고 태어나는 새들, 즉 전적으로 태어날 때부터 주어진 지침에 따라 이동하는 새들은 때때로 매우 비효율적인 이동 경로를 가지고 있다. 이동 방법을 알고 태어난 새들은 쉽게 적응하지 못한다. 따라서 호수가 마르거나 숲이 농지로 바뀌거나 기후 변화로 번식지가 더 북쪽으로 밀려났을 때, 이동하는 방법을 알고 태어난 새들은 기존의 규칙과 지도를 따라 계속 날아간다. 이에 비해 유년기가 가장 길고 부모와 함께 이동하는 새는 가장 효율적인 이동 경로를 가지고 있는 경향이 있다. 유년기는 문화적 정보의 전달을 촉진하며, 문화는 유전자보다 더 빠르게 진화할 수 있다. 유년기는 변화하는 세상에서 유연성을 제공한다.

2024_1_6_40

Over the last several decades, scholars have developed standards for how best to create, organize, present, and preserve d_____258) information for f_____259) generations. What has remained n_____260) for the most part, however, are the needs of people with d_____261) . As a result, many of the otherwise most v_____262) digital resources are u_____263) for people who are deaf or hard of hearing, as well as for people who are blind, have low vision, or have difficulty d_____264) particular colors. While p_____265) working in educational technology and commercial web design have made significant p_____266) in m_____267) the needs of such users, some scholars c_____268) digital projects all too often f_____269) to take these needs into a_____270) . This situation would be much i_____271) if more projects e_____272) the idea that we should always keep the l_____273) possible audience in mind as we make design decisions, ensuring that our final product serves the n_____274) of those with d_____275) as well as those w_____276) .

지난 수십 년 동안 학자들은 미래 세대를 위해 디지털 정보를 가장 잘 만들고, 정리하고, 제시하고, 보존하는 방법에 대한 표준을 개발해 왔다. 그러나 대부분의 경우 장애가 있는 사람들의 요구는 여전히 무시되어 왔다. 그 결과, 청각 장애가 있거나 듣는 것이 힘든 사람, 시각 장애가 있거나 시력이 낮거나 특정 색상을 구분하기 어려운 사람에게는 그렇지 않은 경우라면 가장 가치 있었을 디지털 자원 중 상당수가 무용지물이 되고 있다. 교육 기술 및 상업용 웹디자인에 종사하는 전문가들은 이러한 사용자의 요구를 충족시키는 데 상당한 진전을 이루었지만, 디지털 프로젝트를 만드는 일부 학자들은 이러한 요구를 고려하지 못하는 경우가 너무 많다. 더 많은 프로젝트에서 디자인을 결정할 때 최대한 많은 사용자를 항상 염두에 두고 최종 제품이 장애가 있는 사람들과 그렇지 않은 사람들 모두의 요구를 충족시킬 수 있도록 해야 한다는 생각을 받아들인다면 이러한 상황은 훨씬 개선될 것이다.

2024_1_6_41-42

All humans, to an extent, seek activities that cause a degree of p_____277) in order to experience p_____278) , whether this is found in s_____279) food, strong m_____280) , or stepping into a too-cold or too-hot bath. The key is that it is a 'safe t_____281) '. The brain perceives the s_____282) to be painful but ultimately n_____283) . Interestingly, this could be similar to the way h_____284) works: a 'safe threat' that causes pleasure by playfully v_____285) n_____286) . We feel uncomfortable, but safe. In this context, w_____287) survival is clearly not in danger, the desire for pain is actually the desire for a r_____288) , not suffering or p_____289) . This reward-like effect comes from the feeling of m_____290) over the pain. The closer you look at your chilli-eating habit, the more r_____291) it seems. When the active ingredient of chillies — capsaicin — touches the tongue, it s_____292) exactly the same receptor that is a_____293) when any of these tissues are b_____294) . Knowing that our body is firing off d_____295) signals, but that we are actually completely safe, produces pleasure. All children start off hating chilli, but many learn to d_____296) pleasure from it through r_____297) exposure and knowing that they will never experience any real harm. Interestingly, s_____298) pain for the pain itself appears to be uniquely h_____299) . The only way scientists have trained animals to have a p_____300) for chilli or to self-harm is to have the pain always d_____301) a_____302) with a p_____303) reward.

모든 인간은 어느 정도는 쾌락을 경험하기 위해 약간의 고통을 유발하는 활동을 추구한다. 이것이 매운 음식 또는 강한 마사지, 너무 차갑거나 뜨거운 욕조에 들어가기 중 어디에서 발견되든지 간에 말이다. 핵심은 그것이 '안전한 위협'이라는 점이다. 뇌는 자극이 고통스럽지만 궁극적으로 위협적이지 않은 것으로 인식한다. 흥미롭게도 이것은 유머가 작동하는 방식, 즉 규범을 장난스럽게 위반함으로써 쾌락을 유발하는 '안전한 위협'과 유사할 수 있다. 우리는 불편하지만 안전하다고 느낀다. 생존이 위험하지 않은 이런 상황에서 고통에 대한 욕구는 실제로는 고통이나 처벌이 아닌 보상에 대한 욕구이다. 이러한 보상과 같은 효과는 고통에 대한 숙달된 느낌에서 비롯된다. 칠리를 먹는 습관을 자세히 들여다볼수록 이는 더욱 분명하게 드러난다. 칠리의 활성 성분인 캡사이신이 혀에 닿으면 피부 조직이 화상을 입었을 때 활성화되는 것과 똑같은 수용체를 자극한다. 우리 몸이 위험 신호를 보내고 있지만 실제로는 완전히 안전하다는 것을 알면 쾌감이 생긴다. 모든 아이들은 처음에는 칠리를 싫어하지 만, 반복적인 노출과 실질적인 해를 경험하지 않는다는 것을 알게 됨을 통해 그것에서 쾌락을 얻는 방법을 배우게 된다. 흥미롭게도 고통 그 자체를 위해 고통을 추구하는 것은 인간만이 할 수 있는 행동으로 보인다. 동물이 칠리를 선호하게 하거나 스스로에게 해를 가하도록 과학자들이 훈련시키는 유일한 방법은 고통을 항상 즐거운 보상과 직접적으로 연관시키는 것이다.

2024_1_6_43-45

An airplane f_____304) high above the deep blue seas far from any land. Flying the small plane was a s_____305) pilot who was sitting alongside an e_____306) flight instructor. As the student looked out the window, she was filled with wonder and a_____307) for the beauty of the world. Her instructor, meanwhile, waited patiently for the right time to start a s_____308) flight e_____309) training exercise. When the plane hit a bit of t_____310) , the instructor pushed a hidden button. Suddenly, all the monitors inside the plane flashed several times then went out completely! Now the student was in control of an airplane that was flying well, but she had no i_____311) of where she was or where she should go. She did have a map, but no other instruments. She was at a l_____312) and then the plane shook again. When the student began to p_____313) , the instructor said, "Stay calm and s_____314) . You can do it." C_____315) as ever, the instructor told her student, "Difficult times always happen during flight. The most important thing is to focus on your flight in those situations." Those words e_____316) the student to focus on flying the aircraft first. "Thank you, I think I can make it," she said, "As I've been trained, I should search for visual m_____317) ." Then, the student carefully flew l_____318) enough to see if she could find any ships making their way across the surface of the ocean. Now the instructor and the student could see some ships. Although the ships were far apart, they were all sailing in a line. With the line of ships in view, the student could see the way to home and s_____319) . The student looked at her in r_____320) , who smiled proudly back at her student.

비행기가 육지에서 멀리 떨어진 깊고 푸른 바다 위를 높이 날고 있었다. 소형 비행기를 조종하고 있는 것은 노련한 비행 교관과 나란히 앉아 있는 한 파일럿 교육생이었다. 교육생이 창문 밖을 바라볼 때, 그녀는 세상의 아름다움에 대한 경이로움과 감탄으로 가득 찼다. 한편, 비행 교관은 비행 중 돌발 비상 상황 대처 훈련을 시작할 적절한 때를 인내심을 가지고 기다리고 있었다. 비행기가 약간의 난기류를 만났을 때, 교관은 숨겨진 버튼을 눌렀다. 갑자기, 비행기 안의 모든 모니터가 여러 번 깜박이다가 완전히 꺼졌다! 이제 교육생은 잘 날고 있는 비행기를 조종하고 있었지만, 그녀는 자신이 어디에 있는지, 어디로 가야 하는지 알 방도가 없었다. 교육생은 지도는 가지고 있었지만, 다른 도구는 가지고 있지 않았다. 그녀는 어쩔 줄 몰라 했고 그때 비행기가 다시 흔들렸다. 교육생이 당황하기 시작하자 교관은 "침착하세요. 당신은 할 수 있습니다." 여느 때처럼 침착한 교관은 교육생에게 "비행 중에는 항상 어려운 상황이 발생합니다. 그러한 상황에서는 비행에 집중하는 것이 가장 중요합니다."라고 말했다. 그 말이 교육생이 먼저 비행에 집중할 수 있게끔 용기를 주었다. "감사합니다. 제가 해낼 수 있을 것 같아요."라고 그녀는 말했다. "훈련받은 대로, 저는 시각 표식을 찾아야겠어요." 그런 다음 교육생은 바다 표면을 가로지르는 배가 보이는지 확인할 수 있을 정도로 충분히 낮게 조심히 비행하였다. 이제 교관과 교육생은 배 몇 척을 볼 수 있었다. 배들은 멀리 떨어져 있었지만 모두 한 줄을 이루고 항해하고 있었다. 배들이 줄을 지어있는 것이 보이자, 교육생은 안전하게 복귀하는 길을 알 수 있었다. 교육생은 안도하며 그녀를 바라봤고, 그녀도 교육생을 향해 자랑스럽게 웃어보였다.

2024 고1 6월 모의고사 ❷ 회차 : 점 / 320점

❶ voca ❷ text ❸ [/] ❹ ____ ❺ quiz 1 ❻ quiz 2 ❼ quiz 3 ❽ quiz 4 ❾ quiz 5

2024_1_6_18

Dear Reader, / We always a_____ 1) your support. As you know, our service is now a_____ 2) through an app. There has never been a better time to switch to an online m_____ 3) of TourTide Magazine. At a 50% discount off your current print s_____ 4) , you can access a full year of online reading. Get new issues and daily web pieces at TourTide.com, read or listen to TourTide Magazine via the app, and get our m_____ 5) newsletter. You'll also gain access to our editors' selections of the best articles. Join today! / Yours, TourTide Team

2024_1_6_19

As I walked from the mailbox, my heart was b_____ 6) rapidly. In my hands, I held the letter from the university I had a_____ 7) to. I thought my grades were good enough to c_____ 8) the line and my a_____ 9) letter was well-written, but was it enough? I hadn't slept a wink for days. As I carefully t_____ 10) into the paper of the envelope, the letter slowly e_____ 11) with the opening phrase, "It is our great pleasure…" I shouted with joy, "I am in!" As I h_____ 12) the letter, I began to make a f_____ 13) about my college life in a f_____ 14) city.

2024_1_6_20

Having a m_____ 15) room can add up to n_____ 16) feelings and d_____ 17) thinking. Psychologists say that having a d_____ 18) room can indicate a d_____ 19) mental state. One of the professional t_____ 20) experts says that the moment you start cleaning your room, you also start changing your life and gaining new p_____ 21) . When you clean your surroundings, p_____ 22) and good atmosphere follows. You can do more things e_____ 23) and neatly. So, clean up your closets, organize your drawers, and a_____ 24) your things first, then peace of mind will follow.

2024_1_6_21

The soil of a farm f_____ 25) is f_____ 26) to be the perfect environment for m_____ 27) growth. This is achieved by adding nutrients in the form of f_____ 28) and water by way of i_____ 29) . During the last fifty years, engineers and crop scientists have helped farmers become much more efficient at s_____ 30) exactly the right amount of both. World usage of fertilizer has t_____ 31) since 1969, and the global capacity for i_____ 32) has almost doubled; we are feeding and w_____ 33) our fields more than ever, and our c_____ 34) are loving it. Unfortunately, these l_____ 35) conditions have also excited the attention of certain a_____ 36) u_____ 37) . Because farm fields are loaded with nutrients and water r_____ 38) to the natural land that surrounds them, they are d_____ 39) as luxury real estate by every r_____ 40) weed in the area.

2024_1_6_22

When it comes to **h**_____ **41)** out, you don't have to do much. All you have to do is come around and show that you **c**_____ **42)** . If you notice someone who is **l**_____ **43)** , you could go and sit with them. If you work with someone who eats lunch all by **t**_____ **44)** , and you go and sit down with them, they will begin to be more **s**_____ **45)** after a while, and they will **o**_____ **46)** it all to you. A person's happiness comes from **a**_____ **47)** . There are too many people out in the world who feel like everyone has **f**_____ **48)** them or **i**_____ **49)** them. Even if you say hi to someone **p**_____ **50)** by, they will begin to feel better about themselves, like someone **c**_____ **_51)** .

2024_1_6_23

We often try to make **c**_____ **52)** in our **c**_____ **53)** and take the easy route. When taking the quick exit, we fail to **a**_____ **54)** the strength to **c**_____ **55)** . We often take the easy route to **i**_____ **56)** our skills. Many of us never really work to achieve **m**_____ **57)** in the key areas of life. These skills are key tools that can be useful to our career, health, and **p**_____ **58)** . Highly successful athletes don't win because of better equipment; they win by facing **h**_____ **59)** to gain strength and skill. They win through **p**_____ **60)** . It's the mental preparation, winning mindset, strategy, and skill that set them **a**_____ **61)** . Strength comes from **s**_____ **62)** , not from taking the path of **l**_____ **63)** **r**_____ **64)** . Hardship is not just a lesson for the next time in front of us. **H**_____ **65)** will be the greatest teacher we will ever have in life.

2024_1_6_24

Your behaviors are usually a **r**_____ **66)** of your **i**_____ **67)** . What you do is an **i**_____ **68)** of the type of person you believe that you are — either consciously or nonconsciously. Research has shown that once a person believes in a particular **a**_____ **69)** of their identity, they are more likely to act according to that **b**_____ **70)** . For example, people who **i**_____ **71)** as "being a voter" were more likely to vote than those who simply **c**_____ **72)** "voting" was an action they wanted to **p**_____ **73)** . Similarly, the person who accepts exercise as the part of their **i**_____ **74)** doesn't have to **c**_____ **75)** themselves to train. Doing the right thing is easy. After all, when your behavior and your identity perfectly **m**_____ **76)** , you are no longer **p**_____ **77)** behavior change. You are simply acting like the type of person you already believe yourself to be.

2024_1_6_26

Fritz Zwicky, a memorable **a**_____78) who **c**_____79) the **t**_____80) 'supernova', was born in Varna, Bulgaria to a Swiss father and a Czech mother. At the age of six, he was sent to his grandparents who looked **a**_____81) him for most of his childhood in Switzerland. There, he received an advanced education in mathematics and physics. In 1925, he **e**_____82) to the United States and continued his physics research at California Institute of Technology (Caltech). He developed numerous **t**_____83) that have had a **p**_____84) influence on the understanding of our **u**_____85) in the early 21st century. After being **a**_____86) as a professor of **a**_____87) at Caltech in 1942, he developed some of the earliest jet engines and holds more than 50 **p**_____88), many in jet **p**_____89).

2024_1_6_29

The **h**_____90) lifestyle, which can be described as "natural" to human beings, appears to have **h**_____91) much to recommend it. **E**_____92) of human **r**_____93) from early hunter-gatherer societies **h**_____94) suggested that our ancestors enjoyed abundant food, **o**_____95) without **e**_____96) effort, and suffered very **f**_____97) diseases. If this is true, it is not clear why so many humans settled in **p**_____98) villages and developed agriculture, growing crops and **d**_____99) animals: **c**_____100) fields was hard work, and it was in farming villages that **e**_____101) diseases first took root. Whatever its immediate effect on the lives of humans, the development of **s**_____102) and **a**_____103) undoubtedly led to a high increase in **p**_____104) **d**_____105). This period, known as the New Stone Age, was a major turning point in human development, opening the way to the growth of the first towns and cities, and eventually leading to settled " **c**_____106) ."

2024_1_6_30

Many human and nonhuman animals save **c**_____107) or money for future **c**_____108). This behavior seems to reveal a **p**_____109) of a **d**_____110) reward over an **i**_____111) one: the agent gives up some immediate **p**_____112) in exchange for a **f**_____113) one. Thus the **d**_____114) value of the future reward should be **g**_____115) than the **u**_____116) value of the **p**_____117) one. However, in some cases the agent does not wait for the **e**_____118) occasion but uses their savings **p**_____119). For example, early in the year an employee might set **a**_____120) money to buy Christmas presents but then spend it on a summer vacation instead. Such cases could be examples of **w**_____121) of will. That is, the agents may judge or **r**_____122) to spend their savings in a certain way for the greatest **b**_____123) but then act differently when **t**_____124) for immediate pleasure appears.

2024_1_6_31

The costs of i_____125) are well-documented. Martin Luther King Jr. l_____126) them when he described "that lovely poem that didn't get w_____127) because someone k_____128) on the door." Perhaps the most famous l_____129) example happened in 1797 when Samuel Taylor Coleridge started writing his poem Kubla Khan from a dream he had but then was v_____130) by an unexpected guest. For Coleridge, by c_____131) , the untimely visitor came at a particularly bad time. He forgot his i_____132) and left the work u_____133) . While there are many d_____134) cases of sudden disruptions that have had significant consequences for p_____135) in critical roles such as doctors, nurses, control room operators, stock traders, and pilots, they also impact most of us in our everyday lives, slowing down work p_____136) and generally increasing stress levels.

2024_1_6_32

There's a lot of scientific evidence d_____137) that focused a_____138) leads to the r_____139) of the brain. In animals r_____140) for noticing sound (to hunt or to avoid being hunted for example), we find much larger a_____141) centers in the brain. In animals rewarded for sharp eyesight, the v_____142) areas are larger. Brain scans of violinists provide more evidence, showing dramatic growth and expansion in regions of the c_____143) that represent the left hand, which has to finger the strings p_____144) , often at very high speed. Other studies have shown that the h_____145) , which is vital for s_____146) memory, is e_____147) in taxi drivers. The point is that the physical architecture of the brain changes according to where we d_____148) our attention and what we practice doing.

2024_1_6_33

How did the human mind e_____149) ? One possibility is that c_____150) and c_____151) with other human tribes caused our brains to e_____152) the way they did. A human tribe that could o_____153) its enemies, even slightly, p_____154) a vital advantage. The ability of your tribe to imagine and p_____155) where and when a h_____156) enemy tribe might s_____157) , and plan accordingly, gives your tribe a significant m_____158) advantage. The human mind became a w_____159) in the struggle for survival, a weapon far more d_____160) than any before it. And this m_____161) advantage was applied, over and over, within each s_____162) generation. The tribe that could out-think its o_____163) was more likely to s_____164) in battle and would then pass on the genes responsible for this mental advantage to its o_____165) . You and I are the descendants of the winners.

2024_1_6_34

To find the hidden potential in teams, instead of **b**_____ 166) , we're better off **s**_____ 167) to a process called **b**_____ 168) . The initial steps are solo. You start by asking everyone to generate ideas **s**_____ 169) . Next, you pool them and share them **a**_____ 170) among the group. To preserve **i**_____ 171) judgment, each member **e**_____ 172) them on their own. Only then **d**_____ 173) the team come together to select and refine the most **p**_____ 174) options. By developing and **a**_____ 175) ideas individually before choosing and **e**_____ 176) them, teams can **s**_____ 177) and **a**_____ 178) possibilities that might not get attention otherwise. This brainwriting process makes sure that all ideas are **b**_____ 179) to the table and all voices are brought into the conversation. It is especially **e**_____ 180) in groups that struggle to achieve **c**_____ 181) intelligence.

2024_1_6_35

Simply giving employees a sense of **a**_____ 182) — a feeling that they are in **c**_____ 183) , that they have **g**_____ 184) decision-making **a**_____ 185) — can radically **i**_____ 186) how much energy and focus they bring to their jobs. One 2010 study at a **m**_____ 187) plant in Ohio, for instance, carefully **e**_____ 188) assembly-line workers who were **e**_____ 189) to make small decisions about their schedules and work environment. They designed their own **u**_____ 190) and had **a**_____ 191) over shifts while all the manufacturing processes and pay scales **s**_____ 192) the same. Within two months, **p**_____ 193) at the plant increased by 20 percent, with workers **t**_____ 194) shorter breaks and making fewer **m**_____ 195) . Giving employees a sense of **c**_____ 196) improved how much **s**_____ 197) they brought to their jobs.

2024_1_6_36

As businesses **s**_____ 198) some core business activities to **d**_____ 199) , such as sales, marketing, or archiving, it is assumed that the impact on the environment will be less **n**_____ 200) . However, digital business activities can still **t**_____ 201) the environment. In some cases, the harm of digital businesses can be even more **h**_____ 202) . A few decades ago, offices used to have much more paper waste since all documents were paper **b**_____ 203) . When workplaces shifted from paper to digital documents, invoices, and emails, it was a **p**_____ 204) step to save trees. However, the cost of the Internet and electricity for the environment is **n**_____ 205) . A recent Wired report declared that most data centers' energy source is **f**_____ 206) fuels. When we store bigger data on clouds, increased carbon **e**_____ 207) make our green clouds **g**_____ 208) . The carbon footprint of an email is smaller than mail **s**_____ 209) via a post office, but still, it causes four grams of CO_2, and it can be as much as 50 grams if the **a**_____ 210) is big.

2024_1_6_37

Problems often a_____211) if an e_____212) species is suddenly introduced to an ecosystem. Britain's red and grey squirrels provide a clear example. When the grey a_____213) from America in the 1870s, both squirrel species c_____214) for the same food and h_____215) , which put the native red squirrel populations under p_____216) . The grey had the edge because it can a_____217) its diet; it is able, for instance, to eat green acorns, while the red can only digest m_____218) acorns. Within the same area of forest, grey squirrels can destroy the food supply before red squirrels even have a bite. Greys can also live more d_____219) and in v_____220) habitats, so h_____221) survived more easily when woodland has been d_____222) . As a result, the red squirrel has come close to e_____223) in England.

2024_1_6_38

G_____224) crops forced people to s_____225) in one place. H_____226) typically moved around frequently, and they had to be able to carry all their p_____227) with them every t_____228) they moved. In particular, mothers had to carry their young children. As a result, hunter-gatherer mothers could have only one baby every four y_____229) or so, s_____230) their births so that they never had to carry more than one child at a time. Farmers, on the other hand, could live in the same place year after year and did not have to worry about t_____231) young children long distances. Societies that s_____232) down in one place were able to s_____233) their birth i_____234) from four years to about two. This meant that each woman could have more children than her hunter-gatherer c_____235) , which in turn resulted in r_____236) population growth among f_____237) communities. An increased population was actually an a_____238) to a_____239) societies, because farming required large amounts of human l_____240) .

2024_1_6_39

Spending time as c_____241) allows animals to l_____242) about their environment. Without childhood, animals must rely more fully on h_____243) , and therefore be less f_____244) . Among m_____245) bird species, those that are born knowing how, when, and where to migrate — those that are migrating entirely with i_____246) they were born with — sometimes have very i_____247) migration routes. These birds, b_____248) knowing how to migrate, don't a_____249) easily. So when lakes dry up, forest becomes farmland, or climate change pushes breeding grounds f_____250) north, those birds that are born knowing how to migrate keep flying by the old rules and maps. By c_____251) , birds with the longest childhoods, and those that migrate with their parents, tend to have the most efficient migration routes. Childhood f_____252) the p_____253) on of cultural information, and c_____254) can e_____255) faster than g_____256) . Childhood gives f_____257) in a changing world.

2024_1_6_40

Over the last several decades, scholars have developed standards for how best to create, organize, present, and preserve **d**_____258) information for **f**_____259) generations. What has remained **n**_____260) for the most part, however, are the needs of people with **d**_____261) . As a result, many of the otherwise most **v**_____262) digital resources are **u**_____263) for people who are deaf or hard of hearing, as well as for people who are blind, have low vision, or have difficulty **d**_____264) particular colors. While **p**_____265) working in educational technology and commercial web design have made significant **p**_____266) in **m**_____267) the needs of such users, some scholars **c**_____268) digital projects all too often **f**_____269) to take these needs into **a**_____270) . This situation would be much **i**_____271) if more projects **e**_____272) the idea that we should always keep the **l**_____273) possible audience in mind as we make design decisions, ensuring that our final product serves the **n**_____274) of those with **d**_____275) as well as those **w**_____276) .

2024_1_6_41-42

All humans, to an extent, seek activities that cause a degree of **p**_____277) in order to experience **p**_____278) , whether this is found in **s**_____279) food, strong **m**_____280) , or stepping into a too-cold or too-hot bath. The key is that it is a 'safe **t**_____281) '. The brain perceives the **s**_____282) to be painful but ultimately **n**_____283) . Interestingly, this could be similar to the way **h**_____284) works: a 'safe threat' that causes pleasure by playfully **v**_____285) **n**_____286) . We feel uncomfortable, but safe. In this context, **w**_____287) survival is clearly not in danger, the desire for pain is actually the desire for a **r**_____288) , not suffering or **p**_____289) . This reward-like effect comes from the feeling of **m**_____290) over the pain. The closer you look at your chilli-eating habit, the more **r**_____291) it seems. When the active ingredient of chillies — capsaicin — touches the tongue, it **s**_____292) exactly the same receptor that is **a**_____293) when any of these tissues are **b**_____294) . Knowing that our body is firing off **d**_____295) signals, but that we are actually completely safe, produces pleasure. All children start off hating chilli, but many learn to **d**_____296) pleasure from it through **r**_____297) exposure and knowing that they will never experience any real harm. Interestingly, **s**_____298) pain for the pain itself appears to be uniquely **h**_____299) . The only way scientists have trained animals to have a **p**_____300) for chilli or to self-harm is to have the pain always **d**_____301) **a**_____302) with a **p**_____303) reward.

2024_1_6_43-45

An airplane **f**_____ **304)** high above the deep blue seas far from any land. Flying the small plane was a **s**_____ **305)** pilot who was sitting alongside an **e**_____ **306)** flight instructor. As the student looked out the window, she was filled with wonder and **a**_____ **307)** for the beauty of the world. Her instructor, meanwhile, waited patiently for the right time to start a **s**_____ **308)** flight **e**_____ **309)** training exercise. When the plane hit a bit of **t**_____ **310)** , the instructor pushed a hidden button. Suddenly, all the monitors inside the plane flashed several times then went out completely! Now the student was in control of an airplane that was flying well, but she had no **i**_____ **311)** of where she was or where she should go. She did have a map, but no other instruments. She was at a **l**_____ **312)** and then the plane shook again. When the student began to **p**_____ **313)** , the instructor said, "Stay calm and **s**_____ **314)** . You can do it." **C**_____ **315)** as ever, the instructor told her student, "Difficult times always happen during flight. The most important thing is to focus on your flight in those situations." Those words **e**_____ **316)** the student to focus on flying the aircraft first. "Thank you, I think I can make it," she said, "As I've been trained, I should search for visual **m**_____ **317)** ." Then, the student carefully flew **l**_____ **318)** enough to see if she could find any ships making their way across the surface of the ocean. Now the instructor and the student could see some ships. Although the ships were far apart, they were all sailing in a line. With the line of ships in view, the student could see the way to home and **s**_____ **319)** . The student looked at her in **r**_____ **320)** , who smiled proudly back at her student.

2024 고1 6월 모의고사

❶ voca   ❷ text   ❸ [/]   ❹ _____   ❺ quiz 1   ❻ quiz 2   ❼ quiz 3   ❽ quiz 4   ❾ quiz 5

1. 1) 2024_1_6_18

Dear Reader, We always appreciate your support.

(A) You'll also gain access to our editors' selections of the best articles. Join today!

(B) Yours, TourTide Team

(C) At a 50% discount off your current print subscription, you can access a full year of online reading. Get new issues and daily web pieces at TourTide.com, read or listen to TourTide Magazine via the app, and get our membersonly newsletter.

(D) As you know, our service is now available through an app. There has never been a better time to switch to an online membership of TourTide Magazine.

2. 2) 2024_1_6_19

As I walked from the mailbox, my heart was beating rapidly.

(A) I shouted with joy, "I am in!"

(B) As I held the letter, I began to make a fantasy about my college life in a faraway city.

(C) In my hands, I held the letter from the university I had applied to. I thought my grades were good enough to cross the line and my application letter was well-written, but was it enough?

(D) I hadn't slept a wink for days. As I carefully tore into the paper of the envelope, the letter slowly emerged with the opening phrase, "It is our great pleasure..."

3. 3) 2024_1_6_20

Having a messy room can add up to negative feelings and destructive thinking.

(A) You can do more things efficiently and neatly.

(B) So, clean up your closets, organize your drawers, and arrange your things first, then peace of mind will follow.

(C) Psychologists say that having a disorderly room can indicate a disorganized mental state. One of the professional tidying experts says that the moment you start cleaning your room, you also start changing your life and gaining new perspective.

(D) When you clean your surroundings, positive and good atmosphere follows.

4. 4) 2024_1_6_21

The soil of a farm field is forced to be the perfect environment for monoculture growth.

(A) World usage of fertilizer has tripled since 1969, and the global capacity for irrigation has almost doubled; we are feeding and watering our fields more than ever, and our crops are loving it.

(B) This is achieved by adding nutrients in the form of fertilizer and water by way of irrigation. During the last fifty years, engineers and crop scientists have helped farmers become much more efficient at supplying exactly the right amount of both.

(C) Unfortunately, these luxurious conditions have also excited the attention of certain agricultural undesirables.

(D) Because farm fields are loaded with nutrients and water relative to the natural land that surrounds them, they are desired as luxury real estate by every random weed in the area.

5. 5) 2024_1_6_22

When it comes to helping out, you don't have to do much.

(A) All you have to do is come around and show that you care. If you notice someone who is lonely, you could go and sit with them.

(B) There are too many people out in the world who feel like everyone has forgotten them or ignored them.

(C) If you work with someone who eats lunch all by themselves, and you go and sit down with them, they will begin to be more social after a while, and they will owe it all to you. A person's happiness comes from attention.

(D) Even if you say hi to someone passing by, they will begin to feel better about themselves, like someone cares.

6. 6) 2024_1_6_23

We often try to make cuts in our challenges and take the easy route.

(A) Strength comes from struggle, not from taking the path of least resistance. Hardship is not just a lesson for the next time in front of us. Hardship will be the greatest teacher we will ever have in life.

(B) When taking the quick exit, we fail to acquire the strength to compete. We often take the easy route to improve our skills. Many of us never really work to achieve mastery in the key areas of life. These skills are key tools that can be useful to our career, health, and prosperity.

(C) Highly successful athletes don't win because of better equipment; they win by facing hardship to gain strength and skill. They win through preparation. It's the mental preparation, winning mindset, strategy, and skill that set them apart.

7. 7) 2024_1_6_24

Your behaviors are usually a reflection of your identity.

(A) What you do is an indication of the type of person you believe that you are — either consciously or nonconsciously. Research has shown that once a person believes in a particular aspect of their identity, they are more likely to act according to that belief. For example, people who identified as "being a voter" were more likely to vote than those who simply claimed "voting" was an action they wanted to perform.

(B) After all, when your behavior and your identity perfectly match, you are no longer pursuing behavior change. You are simply acting like the type of person you already believe yourself to be.

(C) Similarly, the person who accepts exercise as the part of their identity doesn't have to convince themselves to train. Doing the right thing is easy.

8. 8) 2024_1_6_25

The above graph shows the electronic waste collection and recycling rate by region in 2016 and 2019.

(A) In both years, the electronic waste collection and recycling rates in Oceania remained under 10 percent.

(B) Africa had the lowest electronic waste collection and recycling rates in both 2016 and 2019, showing the smallest gap between 2016 and 2019.

(C) The electronic waste collection and recycling rate of Asia in 2019 was lower than in 2016.

(D) In both years, Europe showed the highest electronic waste collection and recycling rates.

(E) The Americas ranked second in 2016 and third in 2019, with 17 percent and 9 percent respectively.

9. 9) 2024_1_6_26

Fritz Zwicky, a memorable astrophysicist who coined the term 'supernova', was born in Varna, Bulgaria to a Swiss father and a Czech mother.

(A) In 1925, he emigrated to the United States and continued his physics research at California Institute of Technology (Caltech).

(B) At the age of six, he was sent to his grandparents who looked after him for most of his childhood in Switzerland. There, he received an advanced education in mathematics and physics.

(C) He developed numerous theories that have had a profound influence on the understanding of our universe in the early 21st century.

(D) After being appointed as a professor of astronomy at Caltech in 1942, he developed some of the earliest jet engines and holds more than 50 patents, many in jet propulsion.

10. 10) 2024_1_6_29

The hunter-gatherer lifestyle, which can be described as "natural" to human beings, appears to have had much to recommend it.

(A) Whatever its immediate effect on the lives of humans, the development of settlements and agriculture undoubtedly led to a high increase in population density.

(B) Examination of human remains from early hunter-gatherer societies has suggested that our ancestors enjoyed abundant food, obtainable without excessive effort, and suffered very few diseases. If this is true, it is not clear why so many humans settled in permanent villages and developed agriculture, growing crops and domesticating animals: cultivating fields was hard work, and it was in farming villages that epidemic diseases first took root.

(C) This period, known as the New Stone Age, was a major turning point in human development, opening the way to the growth of the first towns and cities, and eventually leading to settled "civilizations."

11. 11) 2024_1_6_30

Many human and nonhuman animals save commodities or money for future consumption.

(A) However, in some cases the agent does not wait for the envisioned occasion but uses their savings prematurely. For example, early in the year an employee might set aside money to buy Christmas presents but then spend it on a summer vacation instead.

(B) Such cases could be examples of weakness of will.

(C) This behavior seems to reveal a preference of a delayed reward over an immediate one: the agent gives up some immediate pleasure in exchange for a future one. Thus the discounted value of the future reward should be greater than the undiscounted value of the present one.

(D) That is, the agents may judge or resolve to spend their savings in a certain way for the greatest benefit but then act differently when temptation for immediate pleasure appears.

12. 12) 2024_1_6_31

The costs of interruptions are well-documented.

(A) While there are many documented cases of sudden disruptions that have had significant consequences for professionals in critical roles such as doctors, nurses, control room operators, stock traders, and pilots, they also impact most of us in our everyday lives, slowing down work productivity and generally increasing stress levels.

(B) Martin Luther King Jr. lamented them when he described "that lovely poem that didn't get written because someone knocked on the door."

(C) He forgot his inspiration and left the work unfinished.

(D) Perhaps the most famous literary example happened in 1797 when Samuel Taylor Coleridge started writing his poem Kubla Khan from a dream he had but then was visited by an unexpected guest. For Coleridge, by coincidence, the untimely visitor came at a particularly bad time.

13. 13) 2024_1_6_32

There's a lot of scientific evidence demonstrating that focused attention leads to the reshaping of the brain.

(A) The point is that the physical architecture of the brain changes according to where we direct our attention and what we practice doing.

(B) Other studies have shown that the hippocampus, which is vital for spatial memory, is enlarged in taxi drivers.

(C) In animals rewarded for sharp eyesight, the visual areas are larger.

(D) Brain scans of violinists provide more evidence, showing dramatic growth and expansion in regions of the cortex that represent the left hand, which has to finger the strings precisely, often at very high speed.

(E) In animals rewarded for noticing sound (to hunt or to avoid being hunted for example), we find much larger auditory centers in the brain.

14. 14) 2024_1_6_33

How did the human mind evolve?

(A) And this mental advantage was applied, over and over, within each succeeding generation.

(B) The ability of your tribe to imagine and predict where and when a hostile enemy tribe might strike, and plan accordingly, gives your tribe a significant military advantage. The human mind became a weapon in the struggle for survival, a weapon far more decisive than any before it.

(C) The tribe that could out-think its opponents was more likely to succeed in battle and would then pass on the genes responsible for this mental advantage to its offspring.

(D) One possibility is that competition and conflicts with other human tribes caused our brains to evolve the way they did. A human tribe that could out-think its enemies, even slightly, possessed a vital advantage.

(E) You and I are the descendants of the winners.

15. 15) 2024_1_6_34

To find the hidden potential in teams, instead of brainstorming, we're better off shifting to a process called brainwriting.

(A) To preserve independent judgment, each member evaluates them on their own. Only then does the team come together to select and refine the most promising options. By developing and assessing ideas individually before choosing and elaborating them, teams can surface and advance possibilities that might not get attention otherwise.

(B) The initial steps are solo. You start by asking everyone to generate ideas separately. Next, you pool them and share them anonymously among the group.

(C) This brainwriting process makes sure that all ideas are brought to the table and all voices are brought into the conversation. It is especially effective in groups that struggle to achieve collective intelligence.

16. 16) 2024_1_6_35

Simply giving employees a sense of agency — a feeling that they are in control, that they have genuine decision-making authority — can radically increase how much energy and focus they bring to their jobs.

(A) Giving employees a sense of control improved how much self-discipline they brought to their jobs.

(B) One 2010 study at a manufacturing plant in Ohio, for instance, carefully examined assembly-line workers who were empowered to make small decisions about their schedules and work environment. They designed their own uniforms and had authority over shifts while all the manufacturing processes and pay scales stayed the same.

(C) Within two months, productivity at the plant increased by 20 percent, with workers taking shorter breaks and making fewer mistakes.

17. 17) 2024_1_6_36

As businesses shift some core business activities to digital, such as sales, marketing, or archiving, it is assumed that the impact on the environment will be less negative.

(A) When workplaces shifted from paper to digital documents, invoices, and emails, it was a promising step to save trees. However, the cost of the Internet and electricity for the environment is neglected. A recent Wired report declared that most data centers' energy source is fossil fuels.

(B) When we store bigger data on clouds, increased carbon emissions make our green clouds gray. The carbon footprint of an email is smaller than mail sent via a post office, but still, it causes four grams of CO_2, and it can be as much as 50 grams if the attachment is big.

(C) However, digital business activities can still threaten the environment. In some cases, the harm of digital businesses can be even more hazardous. A few decades ago, offices used to have much more paper waste since all documents were paper based.

18. 18) 2024_1_6_37

Problems often arise if an exotic species is suddenly introduced to an ecosystem.

(A) As a result, the red squirrel has come close to extinction in England.

(B) The grey had the edge because it can adapt its diet; it is able, for instance, to eat green acorns, while the red can only digest mature acorns. Within the same area of forest, grey squirrels can destroy the food supply before red squirrels even have a bite.

(C) Greys can also live more densely and in varied habitats, so have survived more easily when woodland has been destroyed.

(D) Britain's red and grey squirrels provide a clear example. When the grey arrived from America in the 1870s, both squirrel species competed for the same food and habitat, which put the native red squirrel populations under pressure.

19. 19) 2024_1_6_38

Growing crops forced people to stay in one place.

(A) An increased population was actually an advantage to agricultural societies, because farming required large amounts of human labor.

(B) Hunter-gatherers typically moved around frequently, and they had to be able to carry all their possessions with them every time they moved. In particular, mothers had to carry their young children.

(C) Societies that settled down in one place were able to shorten their birth intervals from four years to about two. This meant that each woman could have more children than her hunter-gatherer counterpart, which in turn resulted in rapid population growth among farming communities.

(D) As a result, hunter-gatherer mothers could have only one baby every four years or so, spacing their births so that they never had to carry more than one child at a time. Farmers, on the other hand, could live in the same place year after year and did not have to worry about transporting young children long distances.

20. 20) 2024_1_6_39

Spending time as children allows animals to learn about their environment.

(A) Childhood facilitates the passing on of cultural information, and culture can evolve faster than genes.

(B) These birds, born knowing how to migrate, don't adapt easily. So when lakes dry up, forest becomes farmland, or climate change pushes breeding grounds farther north, those birds that are born knowing how to migrate keep flying by the old rules and maps.

(C) By comparison, birds with the longest childhoods, and those that migrate with their parents, tend to have the most efficient migration routes.

(D) Childhood gives flexibility in a changing world.

(E) Without childhood, animals must rely more fully on hardware, and therefore be less flexible. Among migratory bird species, those that are born knowing how, when, and where to migrate — those that are migrating entirely with instructions they were born with — sometimes have very inefficient migration routes.

21. 21) 2024_1_6_40

Over the last several decades, scholars have developed standards for how best to create, organize, present, and preserve digital information for future generations.

(A) What has remained neglected for the most part, however, are the needs of people with disabilities.

(B) As a result, many of the otherwise most valuable digital resources are useless for people who are deaf or hard of hearing, as well as for people who are blind, have low vision, or have difficulty distinguishing particular colors.

(C) This situation would be much improved if more projects embraced the idea that we should always keep the largest possible audience in mind as we make design decisions, ensuring that our final product serves the needs of those with disabilities as well as those without.

(D) While professionals working in educational technology and commercial web design have made significant progress in meeting the needs of such users, some scholars creating digital projects all too often fail to take these needs into account.

22. 22) ²⁰²⁴_¹_⁶_⁴¹⁻⁴²

All humans, to an extent, seek activities that cause a degree of pain in order to experience pleasure, whether this is found in spicy food, strong massages, or stepping into a too-cold or too-hot bath.

(A) The closer you look at your chilli-eating habit, the more remarkable it seems. When the active ingredient of chillies — capsaicin — touches the tongue, it stimulates exactly the same receptor that is activated when any of these tissues are burned. Knowing that our body is firing off danger signals, but that we are actually completely safe, produces pleasure.

(B) We feel uncomfortable, but safe. In this context, where survival is clearly not in danger, the desire for pain is actually the desire for a reward, not suffering or punishment. This reward-like effect comes from the feeling of mastery over the pain.

(C) The key is that it is a 'safe threat'. The brain perceives the stimulus to be painful but ultimately nonthreatening. Interestingly, this could be similar to the way humor works: a 'safe threat' that causes pleasure by playfully violating norms.

(D) All children start off hating chilli, but many learn to derive pleasure from it through repeated exposure and knowing that they will never experience any real harm. Interestingly, seeking pain for the pain itself appears to be uniquely human. The only way scientists have trained animals to have a preference for chilli or to self-harm is to have the pain always directly associated with a pleasurable reward.

23. 23) ²⁰²⁴_¹_⁶_⁴³⁻⁴⁵

An airplane flew high above the deep blue seas far from any land.

(A) Now the instructor and the student could see some ships. Although the ships were far apart, they were all sailing in a line. With the line of ships in view, the student could see the way to home and safety. The student looked at her in relief, who smiled proudly back at her student.

(B) Calm as ever, the instructor told her student, "Difficult times always happen during flight. The most important thing is to focus on your flight in those situations." Those words encouraged the student to focus on flying the aircraft first. "Thank you, I think I can make it," she said, "As I've been trained, I should search for visual markers." Then, the student carefully flew low enough to see if she could find any ships making their way across the surface of the ocean.

(C) Flying the small plane was a student pilot who was sitting alongside an experienced flight instructor. As the student looked out the window, she was filled with wonder and appreciation for the beauty of the world. Her instructor, meanwhile, waited patiently for the right time to start a surprise flight emergency training exercise. When the plane hit a bit of turbulence, the instructor pushed a hidden button. Suddenly, all the monitors inside the plane flashed several times then went out completely!

(D) Now the student was in control of an airplane that was flying well, but she had no indication of where she was or where she should go. She did have a map, but no other instruments. She was at a loss and then the plane shook again. When the student began to panic, the instructor said, "Stay calm and steady. You can do it."

2024 고1 6월 모의고사

❶ voca ❷ text ❸ [/] ❹ _____ ❺ quiz 1 ⑥ quiz 2 ❼ quiz 3 ❽ quiz 4 ❾ quiz 5

1. 1)밑줄 친 ⓐ~ⓖ 중 어법, 혹은 문맥상 어휘의 사용이 어색한 것끼리 짝지어진 것을 고르시오.

2024_1_6_18

Dear Reader,

We always ⓐ **appreciate** your support. As you know, our service is now ⓑ **available** through an app. There ⓒ **has** never been a better time to switch to an online membership of TourTide Magazine. At a 50% discount off your current print ⓓ **prescription** , you can ⓔ **assess** a full year of online reading. Get new issues and daily web pieces at TourTide.com, read or ⓕ **listen to** TourTide Magazine via the app, and get our membersonly newsletter. You'll also gain ⓖ **access** to our editors' selections of the best articles. Join today!

Yours, TourTide Team

① ⓐ, ⓓ ② ⓐ, ⓔ ③ ⓒ, ⓕ ④ ⓓ, ⓔ ⑤ ⓔ, ⓕ

2. 2)밑줄 친 ⓐ~ⓖ 중 어법, 혹은 문맥상 어휘의 사용이 어색한 것끼리 짝지어진 것을 고르시오.

2024_1_6_19

As I walked from the mailbox, my heart was beating ⓐ **rapidly**. In my hands, I held the letter from the university I had ⓑ **applied**. I thought my grades were good enough to cross the line and my ⓒ **application** letter was well-written, but ⓓ **does** it enough? I hadn't ⓔ **slept** a wink for days. As I carefully tore into the paper of the envelope, the letter slowly ⓕ **emerged** with the opening phrase, "It is our great pleasure..". I shouted with joy, "I am in"! As I held the letter, I began to ⓖ **make** a fantasy about my college life in a faraway city.

① ⓑ, ⓓ ② ⓓ, ⓔ ③ ⓓ, ⓕ
④ ⓔ, ⓕ ⑤ ⓓ, ⓔ, ⓕ, ⓖ

3. 3)밑줄 친 ⓐ~ⓖ 중 어법, 혹은 문맥상 어휘의 사용이 어색한 것끼리 짝지어진 것을 고르시오.

2024_1_6_20

Having a messy room can add up to ⓐ **positive** feelings and ⓑ **destructive** thinking. Psychologists say that having a ⓒ **disorderly** room can indicate a ⓓ **organized** mental state. One of the professional tidying experts ⓔ **say** that the moment you start cleaning your room, you also start changing your life and gaining new perspective. When you clean your surroundings, positive and good atmosphere follows. You can do ⓕ **more** things efficiently and ⓖ **neat** . So, clean up your closets, organize your drawers, and arrange your things first, then peace of mind will follow.

① ⓐ, ⓒ   ② ⓐ, ⓑ, ⓕ   ③ ⓐ, ⓒ, ⓕ
④ ⓐ, ⓑ, ⓔ, ⓕ   ⑤ ⓐ, ⓓ, ⓔ, ⓖ

4. 4)밑줄 친 ⓐ~ⓚ 중 어법, 혹은 문맥상 어휘의 사용이 어색한 것끼리 짝지어진 것을 고르시오.

2024_1_6_21

The soil of a farm field is forced to be the ⓐ **flawed** environment for ⓑ **monoculture** growth. This is achieved by adding nutrients in the form of ⓒ **fertilization** and water by way of irrigation. ⓓ **During** the last fifty years, engineers and crop scientists have helped farmers ⓔ **becoming** much ⓕ **more** efficient at supplying exactly the right amount of both. World usage of fertilizer has tripled since 1969, and the global capacity for irrigation has almost doubled; we are feeding and watering our fields ⓖ **more** than ever, and our crops are loving it. Unfortunately, these ⓗ **luxurious** conditions have also excited the attention of certain agricultural ⓘ **undesirables** . Because farm fields are loaded with nutrients and water relative to the ⓙ **natural** land that surrounds them, they are ⓚ **desired** as luxury real estate by every random weed in the area.

① ⓑ, ⓒ   ② ⓐ, ⓒ, ⓔ   ③ ⓐ, ⓘ, ⓙ
④ ⓑ, ⓔ, ⓘ   ⑤ ⓐ, ⓒ, ⓕ, ⓙ

5. 5)밑줄 친 ⓐ~ⓗ 중 어법, 혹은 문맥상 어휘의 사용이 어색한 것끼리 짝지어진 것을 고르시오.

2024_1_6_22

When it comes to ⓐ **help** out, you don't have to do much. All you have to do is come around and show that you care. If you notice someone who is lonely, you could go and sit with them. If you work with someone who ⓑ **eats** lunch all by themselves, and you go and sit down with them, they will begin to be ⓒ **less** social after a while, and they will ⓓ **owe** it all to you. A person's happiness comes from ⓔ **attention** . There are too many people out in the world who feel like everyone has forgotten them or ⓕ **ignored** them. Even if you say hi to someone ⓖ **passes** by, they will begin to feel better about themselves, like someone ⓗ **care** .

① ⓐ, ⓑ, ⓓ   ② ⓐ, ⓑ, ⓖ   ③ ⓑ, ⓒ, ⓗ
④ ⓒ, ⓔ, ⓗ   ⑤ ⓐ, ⓒ, ⓖ, ⓗ

6. 6)밑줄 친 ⓐ~ⓘ 중 어법, 혹은 문맥상 어휘의 사용이 어색한 것끼리 짝지어진 것을 고르시오.

2024_1_6_23

We often try to make ⓐ **cuts** in our challenges and take the easy route. When taking the quick exit, we fail to ⓑ **acquire** the strength to compete. We often take the easy route to improve our skills. Many of us never really work to achieve ⓒ **shortcut** in the key areas of life. These skills are key tools that can be ⓓ **useful** to our career, health, and prosperity. ⓔ **Highly** ⓕ **successful** athletes don't win because of better equipment; they win by facing ⓖ **hardship** to gain strength and skill. They win through preparation. It's the mental preparation, winning mindset, strategy, and skill that set them apart. Strength comes from ⓗ **struggle** , not from taking the path of ⓘ **most** resistance. Hardship is not just a lesson for the next time in front of us. Hardship will be the greatest teacher we will ever have in life.

① ⓐ, ⓔ   ② ⓒ, ⓘ   ③ ⓔ, ⓘ
④ ⓐ, ⓒ, ⓓ, ⓖ   ⑤ ⓐ, ⓓ, ⓕ, ⓘ

7. 7)밑줄 친 ⓐ~ⓛ 중 어법, 혹은 문맥상 어휘의 사용이 어색한 것끼리 짝지어진 것을 고르시오.

2024_1_6_24

Your behaviors are usually a reflection of your identity. ⓐ **What** you do is an indication of the type of person you believe that you ⓑ **are** — either consciously or nonconsciously. Research has shown that once a person believes in a ⓒ **particular** aspect of their identity, they are ⓓ **more** likely to act according to that belief. For example, people who identified as "being a voter" ⓔ **were** ⓕ **more** likely to vote than those who simply claimed "voting" was an action they wanted to perform. ⓖ **Similarly**, the person who accepts exercise as the part of their identity ⓗ **doesn't** have to convince themselves ⓘ **to train**. Doing the right thing is easy. After all, when your behavior and your identity perfectly ⓙ **mismatch**, you are no longer pursuing behavior ⓚ **promise**. You are simply acting like the type of person you already believe yourself to ⓛ **be**.

① ⓑ, ⓒ   ② ⓓ, ⓚ   ③ ⓘ, ⓚ
④ ⓙ, ⓚ   ⑤ ⓕ, ⓘ, ⓚ, ⓛ

8. 8)밑줄 친 ⓐ~ⓖ 중 어법, 혹은 문맥상 어휘의 사용이 어색한 것끼리 짝지어진 것을 고르시오.

2024_1_6_26

Fritz Zwicky, a ⓐ **memorable** astrophysicist who ⓑ **coins** the term 'supernova', ⓒ **born** in Varna, Bulgaria to a Swiss father and a Czech mother. At the age of six, he was sent to his grandparents who looked after him for most of his childhood in Switzerland. There, he ⓓ **received** an advanced education in mathematics and physics. In 1925, he emigrated to the United States and continued his physics research at California Institute of Technology (Caltech). He developed numerous theories that ⓔ **had** had a profound influence on

the understanding of our universe in the early 21st century. After ⓕ **being appointed** as a professor of astronomy at Caltech in 1942, he developed some of the earliest jet engines and holds ⓖ **more** than 50 patents, many in jet propulsion.

① ⓑ, ⓒ, ⓓ   ② ⓑ, ⓒ, ⓔ   ③ ⓑ, ⓔ, ⓖ
④ ⓒ, ⓔ, ⓖ   ⑤ ⓐ, ⓑ, ⓕ, ⓖ

9. 9)밑줄 친 ⓐ~ⓚ 중 어법, 혹은 문맥상 어휘의 사용이 어색한 것끼리 짝지어진 것을 고르시오.

2024_1_6_29

The hunter-gatherer lifestyle, which can be described as "ⓐ **natural**" to human beings, appears to ⓑ **have** much to recommend it. Examination of human ⓒ **remains from** early hunter-gatherer societies ⓓ **has** suggested that our ancestors enjoyed ⓔ **abundant** food, obtainable without excessive effort, and suffered very few ⓕ **disease**. If this is true, it is not clear why so many humans settled in ⓖ **permanent** villages and developed agriculture, growing crops and domesticating animals: cultivating fields ⓗ **were** ⓘ **hard** work, and it was in farming villages ⓙ **what** epidemic diseases first took root. Whatever its immediate effect on the lives of humans, the development of settlements and agriculture undoubtedly led to a high ⓚ **increase** in population density. This period, known as the New Stone Age, was a major turning point in human development, opening the way to the growth of the first towns and cities, and eventually leading to settled "civilizations".

① ⓒ, ⓕ   ② ⓐ, ⓒ, ⓗ   ③ ⓑ, ⓒ, ⓚ
④ ⓕ, ⓗ, ⓚ   ⑤ ⓑ, ⓕ, ⓗ, ⓙ

10. 10)**밑줄 친 ⓐ~ⓙ 중 어법, 혹은 문맥상 어휘의 사용이 어색한 것끼리 짝지어진 것을 고르시오.**

2024_1_6_30

Many human and nonhuman animals save commodities or money for future ⓐ **consumption**. This behavior seems ⓑ **to release** a preference of a ⓒ **delayed** reward over an immediate one: the agent gives up some ⓓ **immediate** pleasure in exchange for a ⓔ **future** one. Thus the ⓕ **discounted** value of the future reward should be greater than the ⓖ **undiscounted** value of the present one. However, in some cases the agent does not wait for the envisioned occasion but uses their savings prematurely. For example, early in the year an employee might set aside money to buy Christmas presents but then spend it on a summer vacation instead. Such cases could be examples of ⓗ **weakness** of will. That is, the agents may judge or resolve to spend their savings in a certain way for the greatest benefit but then act ⓘ **differently** when temptation for ⓙ **delayed** pleasure appears.

① ⓑ, ⓓ   ② ⓑ, ⓙ   ③ ⓖ, ⓙ
④ ⓗ, ⓙ   ⑤ ⓐ, ⓑ, ⓖ

11. 11)**밑줄 친 ⓐ~ⓘ 중 어법, 혹은 문맥상 어휘의 사용이 어색한 것끼리 짝지어진 것을 고르시오.**

2024_1_6_31

The costs of interruptions are well-documented. Martin Luther King Jr. ⓐ **lamented** them when he described "that lovely poem that didn't get ⓑ **written** because someone knocked on the door". Perhaps the most famous ⓒ **literary** example happened in 1797 when Samuel Taylor Coleridge started writing his poem Kubla Khan from a dream he ⓓ **had** but then was visited by an unexpected guest. For Coleridge, by coincidence, the ⓔ **untimely** visitor came at a particularly bad time. He forgot his ⓕ **inspiration** and left the work ⓖ **unfinished** . While there are many ⓗ **documents** cases of sudden disruptions that have had significant consequences for professionals in critical roles such as doctors, nurses, control room operators, stock traders, and pilots, they also impact most of us in our everyday lives, slowing down work ⓘ **produce** and generally increasing stress levels.

① ⓓ, ⓗ   ② ⓔ, ⓖ   ③ ⓔ, ⓘ
④ ⓗ, ⓘ   ⑤ ⓓ, ⓔ, ⓕ

12. 12)**밑줄 친 ⓐ~ⓙ 중 어법, 혹은 문맥상 어휘의 사용이 어색한 것끼리 짝지어진 것을 고르시오.**

2024_1_6_32

There's a lot of scientific evidence ⓐ **demonstrating** that focused attention leads to the reshaping of the brain. In animals ⓑ **rewarded** for noticing sound (to hunt or to avoid ⓒ **being hunted** for example), we find much larger auditory centers in the brain. In animals ⓓ **are rewarded** for sharp eyesight, the visual areas are larger. Brain scans of violinists provide ⓔ **more** evidence, showing dramatic growth and expansion in regions of the cortex that represent the left hand, ⓕ **which** has to finger the strings precisely, often at very high speed. Other studies have shown that the hippocampus, which is vital for ⓖ **auditory** memory, is enlarged in taxi drivers. The point is that the physical architecture of the brain changes according to where we ⓗ **direct** our attention and ⓘ **that** we practice ⓙ **to do** .

① ⓑ, ⓓ, ⓔ   ② ⓒ, ⓓ, ⓘ   ③ ⓒ, ⓖ, ⓘ
④ ⓔ, ⓗ, ⓙ   ⑤ ⓓ, ⓖ, ⓘ, ⓙ

13. 13)**밑줄 친 ⓐ~ⓚ 중 어법, 혹은 문맥상 어휘의 사용이 어색한 것끼리 짝지어진 것을 고르시오.**
2024_1_6_33

How did the human mind evolve? One possibility is that ⓐ **competition** and conflicts with other human tribes caused our brains ⓑ **to evolve** the way they ⓒ **did** . A human tribe that could out-think its enemies, even ⓓ **slightly**, possessed a vital advantage. The ability of your tribe to imagine and predict where and when a ⓔ **romantic** enemy tribe might strike, and plan accordingly, ⓕ **gives** your tribe a significant military advantage. The human mind became a weapon in the struggle for survival, a weapon far ⓖ **less** decisive than any before it. And this ⓗ **mental** advantage was applied, over and over, within each succeeding generation. The tribe that could out-think its opponents was ⓘ **more** likely to succeed in battle and would then pass on the genes responsible for this mental advantage to its ⓙ **offspring** . You and I are the ⓚ **ascendants** of the winners.

① ⓓ, ⓖ   ② ⓕ, ⓚ   ③ ⓑ, ⓔ, ⓖ
④ ⓔ, ⓖ, ⓚ   ⑤ ⓔ, ⓘ, ⓚ

14. 14)**밑줄 친 ⓐ~ⓙ 중 어법, 혹은 문맥상 어휘의 사용이 어색한 것끼리 짝지어진 것을 고르시오.**
2024_1_6_34

To find the hidden potential in teams, instead of brainstorming, we're better ⓐ **off** shifting to a process called brainwriting. The initial steps are ⓑ **solo** . You start by asking everyone to generate ideas ⓒ **collaboratively** . Next, you pool them and share them ⓓ **unanimously** among the group. To preserve ⓔ **independent** judgment, each member evaluates them on their own. Only then does the team come together to select and refine the most promising ⓕ **options**. By developing and assessing ideas ⓖ **interdependently** before choosing and elaborating them, teams can surface and advance possibilities that might not get attention otherwise. This ⓗ **brainwriting** process makes sure that all ideas are brought to the table and all voices are brought into the conversation. It is especially ⓘ **effective** in groups that struggle to achieve ⓙ **collective** intelligence.

① ⓐ, ⓕ, ⓙ   ② ⓑ, ⓖ, ⓗ   ③ ⓒ, ⓓ, ⓖ
④ ⓒ, ⓗ, ⓘ   ⑤ ⓕ, ⓗ, ⓘ

15. 15)**밑줄 친 ⓐ~ⓚ 중 어법, 혹은 문맥상 어휘의 사용이 어색한 것끼리 짝지어진 것을 고르시오.**
2024_1_6_35

Simply ⓐ **given** employees a sense of agency — a feeling that they are ⓑ **in** control, ⓒ **that** they have genuine decision-making authority — can radically ⓓ **decrease** how much energy and focus they bring to their jobs. One 2010 study at a manufacturing plant in Ohio, for instance, carefully examined assembly-line workers who were ⓔ **empowered** to make small decisions about their schedules and work environment. They designed their own uniforms and had authority over shifts ⓕ **while** all the manufacturing processes and pay scales stayed the ⓖ **same**. Within two months, productivity at the plant ⓗ **increased** by 20 percent, with workers ⓘ **taken** shorter breaks and ⓙ **making** fewer mistakes. ⓚ **Giving** employees a sense of control improved how much self-discipline they brought to their jobs.

① ⓐ, ⓓ, ⓔ   ② ⓐ, ⓓ, ⓘ   ③ ⓑ, ⓒ, ⓔ
④ ⓐ, ⓔ, ⓗ, ⓘ   ⑤ ⓒ, ⓔ, ⓕ, ⓚ

16. 16)밑줄 친 ⓐ~ⓜ 중 어법, 혹은 문맥상 어휘의 사용이 어색한 것끼리 짝지어진 것을 고르시오.

2024_1_6_36

As businesses shift some core business activities to digital, such as sales, marketing, or archiving, it is assumed ⓐ **which** the impact on the environment will be ⓑ **less** ⓒ **negative**. However, digital business activities can still threaten the environment. In some cases, the ⓓ **harm** of digital businesses can be even ⓔ **less** hazardous. A few decades ago, offices ⓕ **used** to have much ⓖ **less** paper waste since all documents were paper based. When workplaces shifted from paper to digital documents, invoices, and emails, it was a ⓗ **promising** step to save trees. However, the cost of the Internet and electricity for the environment is ⓘ **neglected** . A recent Wired report declared that most data centers' energy source is ⓙ **fossil** fuels. When we store bigger data on clouds, ⓚ **dwindled** carbon ⓛ **emissions** make our green clouds gray. The carbon footprint of an email is smaller than mail sent via a post office, but still, it causes four grams of CO_2, and it can be as much as 50 grams if the ⓜ **attachment** is big.

① ⓑ, ⓔ, ⓖ   ② ⓒ, ⓔ, ⓜ   ③ ⓐ, ⓔ, ⓖ, ⓚ
④ ⓒ, ⓖ, ⓙ, ⓜ   ⑤ ⓔ, ⓘ, ⓚ, ⓜ

17. 17)밑줄 친 ⓐ~ⓙ 중 어법, 혹은 문맥상 어휘의 사용이 어색한 것끼리 짝지어진 것을 고르시오.

2024_1_6_37

Problems often arise if an exotic species ⓐ **is** suddenly introduced to an ecosystem. Britain's red and grey squirrels provide a clear example. When the grey ⓑ **arrive** America in the 1870s, both squirrel species competed for the ⓒ **different** food and habitat, which put the native red squirrel populations under pressure. The grey had the ⓓ **edge** because it can ⓔ **adapt** its diet; it is able, for instance, to eat green acorns, while the red can only digest mature acorns. Within the ⓕ **same** area of forest, grey squirrels can destroy the food supply before red squirrels even have a bite. Greys can also live ⓖ **less** densely and in varied habitats, so ⓗ **have** survived ⓘ **more** easily when woodland has been destroyed. As a result, the red squirrel has come close to ⓙ **prosperity** in England.

① ⓐ, ⓑ   ② ⓐ, ⓒ, ⓖ   ③ ⓑ, ⓘ, ⓙ
④ ⓐ, ⓒ, ⓓ, ⓗ   ⑤ ⓑ, ⓒ, ⓖ, ⓙ

18. 18)밑줄 친 ⓐ~ⓜ 중 어법, 혹은 문맥상 어휘의 사용이 어색한 것끼리 짝지어진 것을 고르시오.

2024_1_6_38

Growing crops forced people to stay in one place. Hunter-gatherers typically moved around ⓐ **frequently**, and they had to be able to carry all their ⓑ **assessions** with them every time they moved. In ⓒ **particular**, mothers had to carry their young children. As a result, hunter-gatherer mothers could have only one baby every four ⓓ **years** or so, ⓔ **space** their births so that they never had to carry ⓕ **more** than one child at a time. Farmers, on the other hand, could live in the ⓖ **same** place year after year and did not have to worry about ⓗ **transporting** young children long distances. Societies that settled down in one place were able to ⓘ **shorten** their birth intervals from four years to about two. This meant that each woman could have ⓙ **less** children than her hunter-gatherer counterpart, which in turn resulted in ⓚ **rapid** population growth among farming communities. An ⓛ **increased** population was actually an advantage to agricultural societies, because farming required ⓜ **small** amounts of human labor.

① ⓑ, ⓕ, ⓜ   ② ⓗ, ⓘ, ⓜ   ③ ⓑ, ⓔ, ⓗ, ⓘ
④ ⓑ, ⓔ, ⓙ, ⓜ   ⑤ ⓔ, ⓗ, ⓙ, ⓜ

19. 19)**밑줄 친 ⓐ~ⓚ 중 어법, 혹은 문맥상 어휘의 사용이 어색한 것끼리 짝지어진 것을 고르시오.**

2024_1_6_39

ⓐ **Spending** time as children allows animals to learn about their environment. Without childhood, animals must rely ⓑ **more** fully on ⓒ **hardware** , and therefore be ⓓ **less** flexible. Among migratory bird species, those that are born knowing how, when, and where to migrate — those that are migrating entirely with instructions they were born with — sometimes have very ⓔ **efficient** migration routes. These birds, born knowing how to migrate, don't ⓕ **adapt** easily. So when lakes dry up, forest becomes farmland, or climate change pushes breeding grounds farther north, those birds that are born knowing ⓖ **how** to migrate keep flying by the old rules and maps. By comparison, birds with the ⓗ **shortest** childhoods, and those that migrate with their parents, tend to have the most efficient migration routes. Childhood ⓘ **facilitates** the passing on of cultural information, and culture can evolve ⓙ **faster** than genes. Childhood gives ⓚ **flexibility** in a changing world.

① ⓒ, ⓔ   ② ⓔ, ⓗ   ③ ⓔ, ⓘ
④ ⓗ, ⓘ   ⑤ ⓒ, ⓘ, ⓙ

20. 20)**밑줄 친 ⓐ~ⓘ 중 어법, 혹은 문맥상 어휘의 사용이 어색한 것끼리 짝지어진 것을 고르시오.**

2024_1_6_40

Over the last several decades, scholars have developed standards for how best to create, organize, present, and preserve digital information for future generations. ⓐ **That** has remained ⓑ **neglected** for the most part, however, are the needs of people with ⓒ **disabilities** . As a result, many of the otherwise most ⓓ **valuable** digital resources are useless for people who are deaf or hard of hearing, as well as for people who are blind, have low vision, or have difficulty ⓔ **distinguishing** particular colors. While professionals working in educational technology and commercial web design have made significant ⓕ **procedures** in meeting the needs of such users, some scholars creating digital projects all too often fail to take these needs into account. This situation would be much improved if more projects ⓖ **embraced** the idea that we should always keep the ⓗ **smallest** possible audience in mind as we make design decisions, ensuring that our final product serves the needs of those with disabilities as well as those ⓘ **with** .

① ⓐ, ⓓ, ⓖ   ② ⓑ, ⓒ, ⓗ   ③ ⓑ, ⓗ, ⓘ
④ ⓐ, ⓕ, ⓗ, ⓘ   ⑤ ⓒ, ⓕ, ⓖ, ⓗ

21. 21)밑줄 친 ⓐ~ⓜ 중 어법, 혹은 문맥상 어휘의 사용이 어색한 것끼리 짝지어진 것을 고르시오.

2024_1_6_41-42

All humans, to an extent, ⓐ **seek** activities that cause a degree of pain in order to experience pleasure, ⓑ **whether** this is found in spicy food, strong massages, or stepping into a too-cold or too-hot bath. The key is that it is a 'safe threat'. The brain perceives the stimulus to be painful but ultimately ⓒ **nonthreatening** . Interestingly, this could be similar to the way humor works: a 'safe threat' that causes pleasure by playfully violating ⓓ **norms** . We feel uncomfortable, but ⓔ **safe** . In this context, where survival is clearly not in danger, the desire for pain is actually the desire for a ⓕ **reward** , not suffering or ⓖ **punishment**. This reward-like effect comes from the feeling of mastery over the pain. The closer you look at your chilli-eating habit, the ⓗ **more** remarkable it seems. When the active ingredient of chillies — capsaicin — touches the tongue, it stimulates exactly the ⓘ **same** receptor that is activated when any of these tissues are burned. Knowing that our body is firing off danger signals, but that we are actually completely ⓙ **dangerous** , produces ⓚ **pleasure** . All children start off hating chilli, but many learn to ⓛ **derive** pleasure from it through repeated exposure and knowing that they will never experience any real harm. Interestingly, seeking pain for the pain itself appears to be uniquely human. The only way scientists have trained animals to have a ⓜ **inference** for chilli or to self-harm is to have the pain always directly associated with a pleasurable reward.

① ⓑ, ⓘ   ② ⓕ, ⓘ   ③ ⓖ, ⓙ
④ ⓗ, ⓙ   ⑤ ⓙ, ⓜ

22. 22)밑줄 친 ⓐ~ⓗ 중 어법, 혹은 문맥상 어휘의 사용이 어색한 것끼리 짝지어진 것을 고르시오.

2024_1_6_43-45

An airplane flew ⓐ **high** above the deep blue seas far from any land. Flying the small plane was a student pilot who was sitting alongside an experienced flight instructor. As the student looked out the window, she was filled with ⓑ **wonder** and appreciation for the beauty of the world. Her instructor, meanwhile, waited patiently for the right time to start a surprise flight ⓒ **emergence** training exercise. When the plane hit a bit of turbulence, the instructor pushed a hidden button. Suddenly, all the monitors inside the plane flashed several times then went out completely! Now the student was in control of an airplane that was flying well, but she had no indication of where she was or where she should go. She did have a map, but no other instruments. She was at a loss and then the plane shook again. When the student began to panic, the instructor said, "Stay ⓓ **calm** and steady. You can do it". Calm as ever, the instructor told her student, "Difficult times always happen during flight. The most important thing is to ⓔ **focus on** your flight in those situations". Those words encouraged the student to ⓕ **neglect** flying the aircraft first. "Thank you, I think I can make it", she said, "As I've been ⓖ **training** , I should search for visual markers". Then, the student carefully flew low enough to see if she could find any ships making their way across the surface of the ocean. Now the instructor and the student could see some ships. Although the ships were far apart, they were all sailing in a line. With the line of ships in view, the student could see the way to home and safety. The student looked at her in ⓗ **relief** , who smiled proudly back at her student.

① ⓑ, ⓕ   ② ⓐ, ⓑ, ⓖ   ③ ⓐ, ⓕ, ⓗ
④ ⓒ, ⓕ, ⓖ   ⑤ ⓑ, ⓔ, ⓖ, ⓗ

2024 고1 6월 모의고사

❶ voca ❷ text ❸ [/] ❹ _____ ❺ quiz 1 ❻ quiz 2 ❼ quiz 3 ❽ quiz 4 ❾ quiz 5

☑ 밑줄 친 부분 중 어법, 혹은 문맥상 어휘의 사용이 어색한 것은 모두 몇 개인가?

23. 1) 2024_1_6_18

Dear Reader,
We always ① **appreciate** your support. As you know, our service is now ② **available** through an app. There ③ **has** never been a better time to switch to an online membership of TourTide Magazine. At a 50% discount off your current print ④ **subscription** , you can ⑤ **access** a full year of online reading. Get new issues and daily web pieces at TourTide.com, read or ⑥ **listen to** TourTide Magazine via the app, and get our membersonly newsletter. You'll also gain ⑦ **assess** to our editors' selections of the best articles. Join today!
Yours,
TourTide Team

① 1개   ② 2개   ③ 3개   ④ 5개   ⑤ 6개

24. 2) 2024_1_6_19

As I walked from the mailbox, my heart was beating ① **rapidly**. In my hands, I held the letter from the university I had ② **applied**. I thought my grades were good enough to cross the line and my ③ **appliance** letter was well-written, but ④ **was** it enough? I hadn't ⑤ **been slept** a wink for days. As I carefully tore into the paper of the envelope, the letter slowly ⑥ **emerged** with the opening phrase, "It is our great pleasure..". I shouted with joy, "I am in"! As I held the letter, I began to ⑦ **making** a fantasy about my college life in a faraway city.

① 없음   ② 1개   ③ 3개   ④ 4개   ⑤ 6개

25. 3) 2024_1_6_20

Having a messy room can add up to ① **positive** feelings and ② **destructive** thinking. Psychologists say that having a ③ **disorderly** room can indicate a ④ **disorganized** mental state. One of the professional tidying experts ⑤ **say** that the moment you start cleaning your room, you also start changing your life and gaining new perspective. When you clean your surroundings, positive and good atmosphere follows. You can do ⑥ **more** things efficiently and ⑦ **neat** . So, clean up your closets, organize your drawers, and arrange your things first, then peace of mind will follow.

① 없음   ② 1개   ③ 3개   ④ 4개   ⑤ 7개

26. 4) 2024_1_6_21

The soil of a farm field is forced to be the ① **flawed** environment for ② **monoculture** growth. This is achieved by adding nutrients in the form of ③ **fertilizer** and water by way of irrigation. ④ **While** the last fifty years, engineers and crop scientists have helped farmers ⑤ **become** much ⑥ **less** efficient at supplying exactly the right amount of both. World usage of fertilizer has tripled since 1969, and the global capacity for irrigation has almost doubled; we are feeding and watering our fields ⑦ **less** than ever, and our crops are loving it. Unfortunately, these ⑧ **luxurious** conditions have also excited the attention of certain agricultural ⑨ **desirables** . Because farm fields are loaded with nutrients and water relative to the ⑩ **natural** land that surrounds them, they are ⑪ **desired** as luxury real estate by every random weed in the area.

① 없음   ② 1개   ③ 4개   ④ 5개   ⑤ 9개

27. 5) 2024_1_6_22

When it comes to ① **helping** out, you don't have to do much. All you have to do is come around and show that you care. If you notice someone who is lonely, you could go and sit with them. If you work with someone who ② **eat** lunch all by themselves, and you go and sit down with them, they will begin to be ③ **less** social after a while, and they will ④ **owe** it all to you. A person's happiness comes from ⑤ **separation** . There are too many people out in the world who feel like everyone has forgotten them or ⑥ **ignored** them. Even if you say hi to someone ⑦ **passes** by, they will begin to feel better about themselves, like someone ⑧ **care** .

① 1개　　② 4개　　③ 5개　　④ 7개　　⑤ 8개

28. 6) 2024_1_6_23

We often try to make ① **cuts** in our challenges and take the easy route. When taking the quick exit, we fail to ② **acquire** the strength to compete. We often take the easy route to improve our skills. Many of us never really work to achieve ③ **mastery** in the key areas of life. These skills are key tools that can be ④ **useless** to our career, health, and prosperity. ⑤ **Highly** ⑥ **successive** athletes don't win because of better equipment; they win by facing ⑦ **luck** to gain strength and skill. They win through preparation. It's the mental preparation, winning mindset, strategy, and skill that set them apart. Strength comes from ⑧ **winning** , not from taking the path of ⑨ **least** resistance. Hardship is not just a lesson for the next time in front of us. Hardship will be the greatest teacher we will ever have in life.

① 없음　　② 1개　　③ 4개　　④ 7개　　⑤ 9개

29. 7) 2024_1_6_24

Your behaviors are usually a reflection of your identity. ① **What** you do is an indication of the type of person you believe that you ② **be** — either consciously or nonconsciously. Research has shown that once a person believes in a ③ **general** aspect of their identity, they are ④ **more** likely to act according to that belief. For example, people who identified as "being a voter" ⑤ **was** ⑥ **less** likely to vote than those who simply claimed "voting" was an action they wanted to perform. ⑦ **Similarly** , the person who accepts exercise as the part of their identity ⑧ **doesn't** have to convince themselves ⑨ **training** . Doing the right thing is easy. After all, when your behavior and your identity perfectly ⑩ **match** , you are no longer pursuing behavior ⑪ **change** . You are simply acting like the type of person you already believe yourself to ⑫ **be** .

① 1개　　② 4개　　③ 5개　　④ 6개　　⑤ 9개

30. 8) 2024_1_6_26

Fritz Zwicky, a ① **memorable** astrophysicist who ② **coined** the term 'supernova', ③ **born** in Varna, Bulgaria to a Swiss father and a Czech mother. At the age of six, he was sent to his grandparents who looked after him for most of his childhood in Switzerland. There, he ④ **received** an advanced education in mathematics and physics. In 1925, he emigrated to the United States and continued his physics research at California Institute of Technology (Caltech). He developed numerous theories that ⑤ **had** had a profound influence on the understanding of our universe in the early 21st century. After ⑥ **appointing** as a professor of astronomy at Caltech in 1942, he developed some of the earliest jet engines and holds ⑦ **more** than 50 patents, many in jet propulsion.

① 2개　　② 3개　　③ 4개　　④ 5개　　⑤ 7개

31. 9) 2024_1_6_29

The hunter-gatherer lifestyle, which can be described as "① **artificial**" to human beings, appears to ② **have** much to recommend it. Examination of human ③ **remains** early hunter-gatherer societies ④ **has** suggested that our ancestors enjoyed ⑤ **abundant** food, obtainable without excessive effort, and suffered very few ⑥ **diseases** . If this is true, it is not clear why so many humans settled in ⑦ **permanent** villages and developed agriculture, growing crops and domesticating animals: cultivating fields ⑧ **were** ⑨ **hardly** work, and it was in farming villages ⑩ **what** epidemic diseases first took root. Whatever its immediate effect on the lives of humans, the development of settlements and agriculture undoubtedly led to a high ⑪ **increase** in population density. This period, known as the New Stone Age, was a major turning point in human development, opening the way to the growth of the first towns and cities, and eventually leading to settled "civilizations".

① 5개　　② 6개　　③ 7개　　④ 9개　　⑤ 10개

32. 10) 2024_1_6_30

Many human and nonhuman animals save commodities or money for future ① **assumption**. This behavior seems ② **to release** a preference of a ③ **delayed** reward over an immediate one: the agent gives up some ④ **immediate** pleasure in exchange for a ⑤ **past** one. Thus the ⑥ **discounted** value of the future reward should be greater than the ⑦ **discounted** value of the present one. However, in some cases the agent does not wait for the envisioned occasion but uses their savings prematurely. For example, early

in the year an employee might set aside money to buy Christmas presents but then spend it on a summer vacation instead. Such cases could be examples of ⑧ **weakness** of will. That is, the agents may judge or resolve to spend their savings in a certain way for the greatest benefit but then act ⑨ **differently** when temptation for ⑩ **immediate** pleasure appears.

① 1개　　② 2개　　③ 4개　　④ 5개　　⑤ 9개

33. 11) 2024_1_6_31

The costs of interruptions are well-documented. Martin Luther King Jr. ① **appreciated** them when he described "that lovely poem that didn't get ② **written** because someone knocked on the door". Perhaps the most famous ③ **literary** example happened in 1797 when Samuel Taylor Coleridge started writing his poem Kubla Khan from a dream he ④ **had** but then was visited by an unexpected guest. For Coleridge, by coincidence, the ⑤ **untimely** visitor came at a particularly bad time. He forgot his ⑥ **inspiration** and left the work ⑦ **finished** . While there are many ⑧ **documents** cases of sudden disruptions that have had significant consequences for professionals in critical roles such as doctors, nurses, control room operators, stock traders, and pilots, they also impact most of us in our everyday lives, slowing down work ⑨ **productivity** and generally increasing stress levels.

① 2개　　② 3개　　③ 5개　　④ 8개　　⑤ 9개

34. 12) 2024_1_6_32

There's a lot of scientific evidence ① **demonstrated** that focused attention leads to the reshaping of the brain. In animals ② **rewarding** for noticing sound (to hunt or to avoid ③ **being hunted** for example), we find much larger auditory centers in the brain. In animals ④ **rewarded** for sharp eyesight, the visual areas are larger. Brain scans of violinists provide ⑤ **more** evidence, showing dramatic growth and expansion in regions of the cortex that represent the left hand, ⑥ **that** has to finger the strings precisely, often at very high speed. Other studies have shown that the hippocampus, which is vital for ⑦ **auditory** memory, is enlarged in taxi drivers. The point is that the physical architecture of the brain changes according to where we ⑧ **indirect** our attention and ⑨ **what** we practice ⑩ **to do** .

① 1개   ② 3개   ③ 4개   ④ 6개   ⑤ 8개

35. 13) 2024_1_6_33

How did the human mind evolve? One possibility is that ① **collaboration** and conflicts with other human tribes caused our brains ② **evolving** the way they ③ **did** . A human tribe that could out-think its enemies, even ④ **highly**, possessed a vital advantage. The ability of your tribe to imagine and predict where and when a ⑤ **hostile** enemy tribe might strike, and plan accordingly, ⑥ **to give** your tribe a significant military advantage. The human mind became a weapon in the struggle for survival, a weapon far ⑦ **more** decisive than any before it. And this ⑧ **mental** advantage was applied, over and over, within each succeeding generation. The tribe that could out-think its opponents was ⑨ **more** likely to succeed in battle and would then pass on the genes responsible for this mental advantage to its ⑩ **offspring** . You and I are the ⑪ **descendants** of the winners.

① 없음   ② 1개   ③ 3개   ④ 4개   ⑤ 6개

36. 14) 2024_1_6_34

To find the hidden potential in teams, instead of brainstorming, we're better ① **off** shifting to a process called brainwriting. The initial steps are ② **solo** . You start by asking everyone to generate ideas ③ **separately** . Next, you pool them and share them ④ **unanimously** among the group. To preserve ⑤ **independent** judgment, each member evaluates them on their own. Only then does the team come together to select and refine the most promising ⑥ **options**. By developing and assessing ideas ⑦ **interdependently** before choosing and elaborating them, teams can surface and advance possibilities that might not get attention otherwise. This ⑧ **brainstorming** process makes sure that all ideas are brought to the table and all voices are brought into the conversation. It is especially ⑨ **affective** in groups that struggle to achieve ⑩ **collective** intelligence.

① 없음   ② 4개   ③ 5개   ④ 6개   ⑤ 9개

37. 15) 2024_1_6_35

Simply ① **giving** employees a sense of agency — a feeling that they are ② **in** control, ③ **which** they have genuine decision-making authority — can radically ④ **increase** how much energy and focus they bring to their jobs. One 2010 study at a manufacturing plant in Ohio, for instance, carefully examined assembly-line workers who were ⑤ **empowered** to make small decisions about their schedules and work environment. They designed their own uniforms and had authority over shifts ⑥ **while** all the manufacturing processes and pay scales stayed the ⑦ **same**. Within two months, productivity at the plant ⑧ **increased** by 20 percent, with workers ⑨ **taken** shorter breaks and ⑩ **making** fewer mistakes. ⑪ **Giving** employees a sense of control improved how much self-discipline they brought to their jobs.

① 2개   ② 3개   ③ 4개   ④ 5개   ⑤ 11개

38. 16) 2024_1_6_36

As businesses shift some core business activities to digital, such as sales, marketing, or archiving, it is assumed ① **which** the impact on the environment will be ② **less** ③ **negative**. However, digital business activities can still threaten the environment. In some cases, the ④ **harm** of digital businesses can be even ⑤ **less** hazardous. A few decades ago, offices ⑥ **were used** to have much ⑦ **less** paper waste since all documents were paper based. When workplaces shifted from paper to digital documents, invoices, and emails, it was a ⑧ **promising** step to save trees. However, the cost of the Internet and electricity for the environment is ⑨ **neglected** . A recent Wired report declared that most data centers' energy source is ⑩ **fossil** fuels. When we store bigger data on clouds, ⑪ **dwindled** carbon ⑫ **emissions** make our green clouds gray. The carbon footprint of an email is smaller than mail sent via a post office, but still, it causes four grams of CO_2, and it can be as much as 50 grams if the ⑬ **detachment** is big.

① 2개　　② 3개　　③ 6개　　④ 7개　　⑤ 13개

39. 17) 2024_1_6_37

Problems often arise if an exotic species ① **are** suddenly introduced to an ecosystem. Britain's red and grey squirrels provide a clear example. When the grey ② **arrived from** America in the 1870s, both squirrel species competed for the ③ **same** food and habitat, which put the native red squirrel populations under pressure. The grey had the ④ **edge** because it can ⑤ **adopt** its diet; it is able, for instance, to eat green acorns, while the red can only digest mature acorns. Within the ⑥ **same** area of forest, grey squirrels can destroy the food supply before red squirrels even have a bite. Greys can also live ⑦ **less** densely and in varied habitats, so ⑧ **have** survived ⑨ **less** easily when woodland has been destroyed. As a result, the red squirrel has come close to ⑩ **prosperity** in England.

① 없음　　② 2개　　③ 5개　　④ 8개　　⑤ 9개

40. 18) 2024_1_6_38

Growing crops forced people to stay in one place. Hunter-gatherers typically moved around ① **frequently**, and they had to be able to carry all their ② **possessions** with them every time they moved. In ③ **general**, mothers had to carry their young children. As a result, hunter-gatherer mothers could have only one baby every four ④ **years** or so, ⑤ **space** their births so that they never had to carry ⑥ **less** than one child at a time. Farmers, on the other hand, could live in the ⑦ **different** place year after year and did not have to worry about ⑧ **settling** young children long distances. Societies that settled down in one place were able to ⑨ **shorten** their birth intervals from four years to about two. This meant that each woman could have ⑩ **more** children than her hunter-gatherer counterpart, which in turn resulted in ⑪ **rapid** population growth among farming communities. An ⑫ **dwindled** population was actually an advantage to agricultural societies, because farming required ⑬ **large** amounts of human labor.

① 1개　　② 5개　　③ 6개　　④ 7개　　⑤ 10개

41. 19) 2024_1_6_39

① **Spend** time as children allows animals to learn about their environment. Without childhood, animals must rely ② **more** fully on ③ **hardware** , and therefore be ④ **less** flexible. Among migratory bird species, those that are born knowing how, when, and where to migrate — those that are migrating entirely with instructions they were born with — sometimes have very ⑤ **inefficient** migration routes. These birds, born knowing how to migrate, don't ⑥ **adopt** easily. So when lakes dry up, forest becomes farmland, or climate change pushes breeding grounds farther north, those birds that are born knowing ⑦ **how** to migrate keep flying by the old rules and maps. By comparison, birds with the ⑧ **shortest** childhoods, and those that migrate with their parents, tend to have the most efficient migration routes. Childhood ⑨ **facilitates** the passing on of cultural information, and culture can evolve ⑩ **faster** than genes. Childhood gives ⑪ **inefficiency** in a changing world.

① 없음　　② 4개　　③ 5개　　④ 8개　　⑤ 9개

42. 20) 2024_1_6_40

Over the last several decades, scholars have developed standards for how best to create, organize, present, and preserve digital information for future generations. ① **What** has remained ② **neglected** for the most part, however, are the needs of people with ③ **disabilities** . As a result, many of the otherwise most ④ **worthless** digital resources are useless for people who are deaf or hard of hearing, as well as for people who are blind, have low vision, or have difficulty ⑤ **distinguishing** particular colors. While professionals working in educational technology and commercial web design have made significant ⑥ **procedures** in meeting the needs of such users, some scholars creating digital projects all too often fail to take these needs into account. This situation would be much improved if more projects ⑦ **neglected** the idea that we should always keep the ⑧ **largest** possible audience in mind as we make design decisions, ensuring that our final product serves the needs of those with disabilities as well as those ⑨ **with** .

① 없음　　② 3개　　③ 4개　　④ 6개　　⑤ 8개

43. 21) 2024_1_6_41-42

All humans, to an extent, ① **seek** activities that cause a degree of pain in order to experience pleasure, ② **whether** this is found in spicy food, strong massages, or stepping into a too-cold or too-hot bath. The key is that it is a 'safe threat'. The brain perceives the stimulus to be painful but ultimately ③ **nonthreatening** . Interestingly, this could be similar to the way humor works: a 'safe threat' that causes pleasure by playfully violating ④ **norms** . We feel uncomfortable, but ⑤ **risky** . In this context, where survival is clearly not in danger, the desire for pain is actually the desire for a ⑥ **reward** , not suffering or ⑦ **reward**. This reward-like effect comes from the feeling of mastery over the pain. The closer you look at your chilli-eating habit, the ⑧ **less** remarkable it seems. When the active ingredient of chillies — capsaicin — touches the tongue, it stimulates exactly the ⑨ **same** receptor that is activated when any of these tissues are burned. Knowing that our body is firing off danger signals, but that we are actually completely ⑩ **dangerous** , produces ⑪ **pleasure** . All children start off hating chilli, but many learn to ⑫ **derive** pleasure from it through repeated exposure and knowing that they will never experience any real harm. Interestingly, seeking pain for the pain itself appears to be uniquely human. The only way scientists have trained animals to have a ⑬ **inference** for chilli or to self-harm is to have the pain always directly associated with a pleasurable reward.

① 2개　　② 5개　　③ 7개　　④ 9개　　⑤ 13개

44. 22) 2024_1_6_43-45

An airplane flew ① **highly** above the deep blue seas far from any land. Flying the small plane was a student pilot who was sitting alongside an experienced flight instructor. As the student looked out the window, she was filled with ② **wander** and appreciation for the beauty of the world. Her instructor, meanwhile, waited patiently for the right time to start a surprise flight ③ **emergence** training exercise. When the plane hit a bit of turbulence, the instructor pushed a hidden button. Suddenly, all the monitors inside the plane flashed several times then went out completely! Now the student was in control of an airplane that was flying well, but she had no indication of where she was or where she should go. She did have a map, but no other instruments. She was at a loss and then the plane shook again. When the student began to panic, the instructor said, "Stay ④ **calmly** and steady. You can do it". Calm as ever, the instructor told her student, "Difficult times always happen during flight. The most important thing is to ⑤ **neglect** your flight in those situations". Those words encouraged the student to ⑥ **neglect** flying the aircraft first. "Thank you, I think I can make it", she said, "As I've been ⑦ **trained** , I should search for visual markers". Then, the student carefully flew low enough to see if she could find any ships making their way across the surface of the ocean. Now the instructor and the student could see some ships. Although the ships were far apart, they were all sailing in a line. With the line of ships in view, the student could see the way to home and safety. The student looked at her in ⑧ **relief** , who smiled proudly back at her student.

① 없음　　② 1개　　③ 5개　　④ 6개　　⑤ 8개

2024 고1 6월 모의고사

❶ voca   ❷ text   ❸ [/]   ❹ ____   ❺ quiz 1   ❻ quiz 2   ❼ quiz 3   ❽ quiz 4   ❾ quiz 5

45. ¹⁾**밑줄 부분 중 어법, 혹은 문맥상 어휘의 쓰임이 어색한 것을 올바르게 고쳐 쓰시오. (4개)**

2024_1_6_18

Dear Reader,
We always ① **aggravate** your support. As you know, our service is now ② **unavailable** through an app. There ③ **has** never been a better time to switch to an online membership of TourTide Magazine. At a 50% discount off your current print ④ **prescription** , you can ⑤ **access** a full year of online reading. Get new issues and daily web pieces at TourTide.com, read or ⑥ **listen** TourTide Magazine via the app, and get our membersonly newsletter. You'll also gain ⑦ **access** to our editors' selections of the best articles. Join today!
Yours,
TourTide Team

기호	어색한 표현		올바른 표현
(　　)	_____	⇨	_____
(　　)	_____	⇨	_____
(　　)	_____	⇨	_____
(　　)	_____	⇨	_____

46. ²⁾**밑줄 부분 중 어법, 혹은 문맥상 어휘의 쓰임이 어색한 것을 올바르게 고쳐 쓰시오. (4개)**

2024_1_6_19

As I walked from the mailbox, my heart was beating ① **slowly**. In my hands, I held the letter from the university I had ② **applied**. I thought my grades were good enough to cross the line and my ③ **application** letter was well-written, but ④ **does** it enough? I hadn't ⑤ **slept** a wink for days. As I carefully tore into the paper of the envelope, the letter slowly ⑥ **was emerged** with the opening phrase, "It is our great pleasure..". I shouted with joy, "I am in"! As I held the letter, I began to ⑦ **make** a fantasy about my college life in a faraway city.

기호	어색한 표현		올바른 표현
(　　)	_____	⇨	_____
(　　)	_____	⇨	_____
(　　)	_____	⇨	_____
(　　)	_____	⇨	_____

47. 3)밑줄 부분 중 어법, 혹은 문맥상 어휘의 쓰임이 어색한 것을 올바르게 고쳐 쓰시오. (7개)

2024_1_6_20

Having a messy room can add up to ① **positive** feelings and ② **constructive** thinking. Psychologists say that having a ③ **disorder** room can indicate a ④ **organized** mental state. One of the professional tidying experts ⑤ **say** that the moment you start cleaning your room, you also start changing your life and gaining new perspective. When you clean your surroundings, positive and good atmosphere follows. You can do ⑥ **less** things efficiently and ⑦ **neat** . So, clean up your closets, organize your drawers, and arrange your things first, then peace of mind will follow.

기호	어색한 표현		올바른 표현
( )	_____	⇨	_____
( )	_____	⇨	_____
( )	_____	⇨	_____
( )	_____	⇨	_____
( )	_____	⇨	_____
( )	_____	⇨	_____
( )	_____	⇨	_____

48. 4)밑줄 부분 중 어법, 혹은 문맥상 어휘의 쓰임이 어색한 것을 올바르게 고쳐 쓰시오. (9개)

2024_1_6_21

The soil of a farm field is forced to be the ① **flawed** environment for ② **multiculture** growth. This is achieved by adding nutrients in the form of ③ **fertilizer** and water by way of irrigation. ④ **While** the last fifty years, engineers and crop scientists have helped farmers ⑤ **become** much ⑥ **less** efficient at supplying exactly the right amount of both. World usage of fertilizer has tripled since 1969, and the global capacity for irrigation has almost doubled; we are feeding and watering our fields ⑦ **less** than ever, and our crops are loving it. Unfortunately, these ⑧ **barren** conditions have also excited the attention of certain agricultural ⑨ **desirables** . Because farm fields are loaded with

nutrients and water relative to the ⑩ **artificial** land that surrounds them, they are ⑪ **undesired** as luxury real estate by every random weed in the area.

기호	어색한 표현		올바른 표현
( )	_____	⇨	_____
( )	_____	⇨	_____
( )	_____	⇨	_____
( )	_____	⇨	_____
( )	_____	⇨	_____
( )	_____	⇨	_____
( )	_____	⇨	_____
( )	_____	⇨	_____
( )	_____	⇨	_____

49. 5)밑줄 부분 중 어법, 혹은 문맥상 어휘의 쓰임이 어색한 것을 올바르게 고쳐 쓰시오. (2개)

2024_1_6_22

When it comes to ① **helping** out, you don't have to do much. All you have to do is come around and show that you care. If you notice someone who is lonely, you could go and sit with them. If you work with someone who ② **eats** lunch all by themselves, and you go and sit down with them, they will begin to be ③ **more** social after a while, and they will ④ **doubt** it all to you. A person's happiness comes from ⑤ **separation** . There are too many people out in the world who feel like everyone has forgotten them or ⑥ **ignored** them. Even if you say hi to someone ⑦ **passing** by, they will begin to feel better about themselves, like someone ⑧ **cares** .

기호	어색한 표현		올바른 표현
( )	_____	⇨	_____
( )	_____	⇨	_____

50. 6)밑줄 부분 중 어법, 혹은 문맥상 어휘의 쓰임이 어색한 것을 올바르게 고쳐 쓰시오. (8개)

2024_1_6_23

We often try to make ① **detours** in our challenges and take the easy route. When taking the quick exit, we fail to ② **inquire** the strength to compete. We often take the easy route to improve our skills. Many of us never really work to achieve ③ **shortcut** in the key areas of life. These skills are key tools that can be ④ **useless** to our career, health, and prosperity. ⑤ **High** ⑥ **successive** athletes don't win because of better equipment; they win by facing ⑦ **luck** to gain strength and skill. They win through preparation. It's the mental preparation, winning mindset, strategy, and skill that set them apart. Strength comes from ⑧ **winning** , not from taking the path of ⑨ **least** resistance. Hardship is not just a lesson for the next time in front of us. Hardship will be the greatest teacher we will ever have in life.

기호	어색한 표현		올바른 표현
( )	_____	⇨	_____
( )	_____	⇨	_____
( )	_____	⇨	_____
( )	_____	⇨	_____
( )	_____	⇨	_____
( )	_____	⇨	_____
( )	_____	⇨	_____
( )	_____	⇨	_____

51. 7)밑줄 부분 중 어법, 혹은 문맥상 어휘의 쓰임이 어색한 것을 올바르게 고쳐 쓰시오. (7개)

2024_1_6_24

Your behaviors are usually a reflection of your identity. ① **What** you do is an indication of the type of person you believe that you ② **are** — either consciously or nonconsciously. Research has shown that once a person believes in a ③ **particular** aspect of their identity, they are ④ **less** likely to act according to that belief. For example, people who identified as "being a voter" ⑤ **were** ⑥ **less** likely to vote than those who simply claimed "voting" was an action they wanted to perform. ⑦ **Conversely** , the person who accepts exercise as the part of their identity ⑧ **isn't** have to convince themselves ⑨ **training** . Doing the right thing is easy. After all, when your behavior and your identity perfectly ⑩ **mismatch** , you are no longer pursuing behavior ⑪ **promise** . You are simply acting like the type of person you already believe yourself to ⑫ **be** .

기호	어색한 표현		올바른 표현
( )	_____	⇨	_____
( )	_____	⇨	_____
( )	_____	⇨	_____
( )	_____	⇨	_____
( )	_____	⇨	_____
( )	_____	⇨	_____
( )	_____	⇨	_____

52. 8)밑줄 부분 중 어법, 혹은 문맥상 어휘의 쓰임이 어색한 것을 올바르게 고쳐 쓰시오. (1개)

2024_1_6_26

Fritz Zwicky, a ① **memorial** astrophysicist who ② **coined** the term 'supernova', ③ **was born** in Varna, Bulgaria to a Swiss father and a Czech mother. At the age of six, he was sent to his grandparents who looked after him for most of his childhood in Switzerland. There, he ④ **received** an advanced education in mathematics and physics. In 1925, he emigrated to the United States and continued his physics research at California Institute of Technology (Caltech). He developed numerous theories that ⑤ **have** had a profound influence on the understanding of our universe in the early 21st century. After ⑥ **being appointed** as a professor of astronomy at Caltech in 1942, he developed some of the earliest jet engines and holds ⑦ **more** than 50 patents, many in jet propulsion.

기호	어색한 표현		올바른 표현
( )	_____	⇨	_____

53. 9)밑줄 부분 중 어법, 혹은 문맥상 어휘의 쓰임이 어색한 것을 올바르게 고쳐 쓰시오. (8개)

2024_1_6_29

The hunter-gatherer lifestyle, which can be described as "① **artificial**" to human beings, appears to ② **have** much to recommend it. Examination of human ③ **remains** early hunter-gatherer societies ④ **has** suggested that our ancestors enjoyed ⑤ **limited** food, obtainable without excessive effort, and suffered very few ⑥ **disease** . If this is true, it is not clear why so many humans settled in ⑦ **temporary** villages and developed agriculture, growing crops and domesticating animals: cultivating fields ⑧ **was** ⑨ **hardly** work, and it was in farming villages ⑩ **what** epidemic diseases first took root. Whatever its immediate effect on the lives of humans, the development of settlements and agriculture undoubtedly led to a high ⑪ **increase** in population density. This period, known as the New Stone Age, was a major turning point in human development, opening the way to the growth of the first towns and cities, and eventually leading to settled "civilizations".

기호	어색한 표현		올바른 표현
( )	_____	⇒	_____
( )	_____	⇒	_____
( )	_____	⇒	_____
( )	_____	⇒	_____
( )	_____	⇒	_____
( )	_____	⇒	_____
( )	_____	⇒	_____
( )	_____	⇒	_____

54. 10)밑줄 부분 중 어법, 혹은 문맥상 어휘의 쓰임이 어색한 것을 올바르게 고쳐 쓰시오. (9개)

2024_1_6_30

Many human and nonhuman animals save commodities or money for future ① **assumption**. This behavior seems ② **to release** a preference of a ③ **immediate** reward over an immediate one: the agent gives up some ④ **immediate** pleasure in exchange for a ⑤ **past** one. Thus the ⑥ **inflated** value of the future reward should be greater than the ⑦ **discounted** value of the present one. However, in some cases the agent does not wait for the envisioned occasion but uses their savings prematurely. For example, early in the year an employee might set aside money to buy Christmas presents but then spend it on a summer vacation instead. Such cases could be examples of ⑧ **determination** of will. That is, the agents may judge or resolve to spend their savings in a certain way for the greatest benefit but then act ⑨ **consistently** when temptation for ⑩ **delayed** pleasure appears.

기호	어색한 표현		올바른 표현
( )	_____	⇒	_____
( )	_____	⇒	_____
( )	_____	⇒	_____
( )	_____	⇒	_____
( )	_____	⇒	_____
( )	_____	⇒	_____
( )	_____	⇒	_____
( )	_____	⇒	_____

55. 11)밑줄 부분 중 어법, 혹은 문맥상 어휘의 쓰임이 어색한 것을 올바르게 고쳐 쓰시오. (4개)

2024_1_6_31

The costs of interruptions are well-documented. Martin Luther King Jr. ① **lamented** them when he described "that lovely poem that didn't get ② **written** because someone knocked on the door". Perhaps the most famous ③ **literal** example happened in 1797 when Samuel Taylor Coleridge started writing his poem Kubla Khan from a dream he ④ **had** but then was visited by an unexpected guest. For Coleridge, by coincidence, the ⑤ **untime** visitor came at a particularly bad time. He forgot his ⑥ **perspiration** and left the work ⑦ **finished** . While there are many ⑧ **documented** cases of sudden disruptions that have had significant consequences for professionals in critical roles such as doctors, nurses, control room operators, stock traders, and pilots, they also impact most of us in our everyday lives, slowing down work ⑨ **productivity** and generally increasing stress levels.

기호	어색한 표현		올바른 표현
( )	_____	⇒	_____
( )	_____	⇒	_____
( )	_____	⇒	_____
( )	_____	⇒	_____

56. 12)밑줄 부분 중 어법, 혹은 문맥상 어휘의 쓰임이 어색한 것을 올바르게 고쳐 쓰시오. (4개)

2024_1_6_32

There's a lot of scientific evidence ① **demonstrating** that focused attention leads to the reshaping of the brain. In animals ② **rewarded** for noticing sound (to hunt or to avoid ③ **being hunted** for example), we find much larger auditory centers in the brain. In animals ④ **are rewarded** for sharp eyesight, the visual areas are larger. Brain scans of violinists provide ⑤ **less** evidence, showing dramatic growth and expansion in regions of the cortex that represent the left hand,

⑥ **which** has to finger the strings precisely, often at very high speed. Other studies have shown that the hippocampus, which is vital for ⑦ **auditory** memory, is enlarged in taxi drivers. The point is that the physical architecture of the brain changes according to where we ⑧ **direct** our attention and ⑨ **what** we practice ⑩ **to do** .

기호	어색한 표현		올바른 표현
( )	_____	⇒	_____
( )	_____	⇒	_____
( )	_____	⇒	_____
( )	_____	⇒	_____

57. 13)밑줄 부분 중 어법, 혹은 문맥상 어휘의 쓰임이 어색한 것을 올바르게 고쳐 쓰시오. (4개)

2024_1_6_33

How did the human mind evolve? One possibility is that ① **collaboration** and conflicts with other human tribes caused our brains ② **to evolve** the way they ③ **were** . A human tribe that could out-think its enemies, even ④ **highly**, possessed a vital advantage. The ability of your tribe to imagine and predict where and when a ⑤ **hostile** enemy tribe might strike, and plan accordingly, ⑥ **gives** your tribe a significant military advantage. The human mind became a weapon in the struggle for survival, a weapon far ⑦ **less** decisive than any before it. And this ⑧ **mental** advantage was applied, over and over, within each succeeding generation. The tribe that could out-think its opponents was ⑨ **more** likely to succeed in battle and would then pass on the genes responsible for this mental advantage to its ⑩ **offspring** . You and I are the ⑪ **descendants** of the winners.

기호	어색한 표현		올바른 표현
( )	_____	⇒	_____
( )	_____	⇒	_____
( )	_____	⇒	_____
( )	_____	⇒	_____

58. 14)**밑줄 부분 중 어법, 혹은 문맥상 어휘의 쓰임이 어색한 것을 올바르게 고쳐 쓰시오. (8개)**

2024_1_6_34

To find the hidden potential in teams, instead of brainstorming, we're better ① **on** shifting to a process called brainwriting. The initial steps are ② **together** . You start by asking everyone to generate ideas ③ **collaboratively** . Next, you pool them and share them ④ **anonymously** among the group. To preserve ⑤ **independent** judgment, each member evaluates them on their own. Only then does the team come together to select and refine the most promising ⑥ **requirements**. By developing and assessing ideas ⑦ **interdependently** before choosing and elaborating them, teams can surface and advance possibilities that might not get attention otherwise. This ⑧ **brainstorming** process makes sure that all ideas are brought to the table and all voices are brought into the conversation. It is especially ⑨ **affective** in groups that struggle to achieve ⑩ **independent** intelligence.

기호	어색한 표현		올바른 표현
( )	_____	⇒	_____
( )	_____	⇒	_____
( )	_____	⇒	_____
( )	_____	⇒	_____
( )	_____	⇒	_____
( )	_____	⇒	_____
( )	_____	⇒	_____
( )	_____	⇒	_____

59. 15)**밑줄 부분 중 어법, 혹은 문맥상 어휘의 쓰임이 어색한 것을 올바르게 고쳐 쓰시오. (3개)**

2024_1_6_35

Simply ① **giving** employees a sense of agency — a feeling that they are ② **in** control, ③ **that** they have genuine decision-making authority — can radically ④ **increase** how much energy and focus they bring to their jobs. One 2010 study at a manufacturing plant in Ohio, for instance, carefully examined assembly-line workers who were ⑤ **empowered** to make small decisions about their schedules and work environment. They designed their own uniforms and had authority over shifts ⑥ **during** all the manufacturing processes and pay scales stayed the ⑦ **same**. Within two months, productivity at the plant ⑧ **dwindled** by 20 percent, with workers ⑨ **taking** shorter breaks and ⑩ **making** fewer mistakes. ⑪ **Given** employees a sense of control improved how much self-discipline they brought to their jobs.

기호	어색한 표현		올바른 표현
( )	_____	⇒	_____
( )	_____	⇒	_____
( )	_____	⇒	_____

60. 16)**밑줄 부분 중 어법, 혹은 문맥상 어휘의 쓰임이 어색한 것을 올바르게 고쳐 쓰시오. (12개)**

2024_1_6_36

As businesses shift some core business activities to digital, such as sales, marketing, or archiving, it is assumed ① **which** the impact on the environment will be ② **more** ③ **positive**. However, digital business activities can still threaten the environment. In some cases, the ④ **benefit** of digital businesses can be even ⑤ **less** hazardous. A few decades ago, offices ⑥ **were used** to have much ⑦ **more** paper waste since all documents were paper based. When workplaces shifted from paper to digital documents, invoices, and emails, it was a ⑧ **promised** step to save trees. However, the cost of the Internet and electricity for the environment is ⑨ **overestimated** . A recent Wired report declared that most data centers' energy source is ⑩ **green** fuels. When we store bigger data on clouds, ⑪ **dwindled** carbon ⑫ **transmissions** make our green clouds gray. The carbon footprint of an email is smaller than mail sent via a post office, but still, it causes four grams of CO_2, and it can be as much as 50 grams if the ⑬ **detachment** is big.

기호	어색한 표현		올바른 표현
( )	_____	⇨	_____
( )	_____	⇨	_____
( )	_____	⇨	_____
( )	_____	⇨	_____
( )	_____	⇨	_____
( )	_____	⇨	_____
( )	_____	⇨	_____
( )	_____	⇨	_____
( )	_____	⇨	_____
( )	_____	⇨	_____
( )	_____	⇨	_____
( )	_____	⇨	_____

61. 17)밑줄 부분 중 어법, 혹은 문맥상 어휘의 쓰임 이 어색한 것을 올바르게 고쳐 쓰시오. (4개)

2024_1_6_37

Problems often arise if an exotic species ① **is** suddenly introduced to an ecosystem. Britain's red and grey squirrels provide a clear example. When the grey ② **arrive** America in the 1870s, both squirrel species competed for the ③ **different** food and habitat, which put the native red squirrel populations under pressure. The grey had the ④ **edge** because it can ⑤ **adopt** its diet; it is able, for instance, to eat green acorns, while the red can only digest mature acorns. Within the ⑥ **same** area of forest, grey squirrels can destroy the food supply before red squirrels even have a bite. Greys can also live ⑦ **more** densely and in varied habitats, so ⑧ **have** survived ⑨ **less** easily when woodland has been destroyed. As a result, the red squirrel has come close to ⑩ **extinction** in England.

기호	어색한 표현		올바른 표현
( )	_____	⇨	_____
( )	_____	⇨	_____
( )	_____	⇨	_____
( )	_____	⇨	_____

62. 18)밑줄 부분 중 어법, 혹은 문맥상 어휘의 쓰임 이 어색한 것을 올바르게 고쳐 쓰시오. (6개)

2024_1_6_38

Growing crops forced people to stay in one place. Hunter-gatherers typically moved around ① **frequently**, and they had to be able to carry all their ② **possessions** with them every time they moved. In ③ **general**, mothers had to carry their young children. As a result, hunter-gatherer mothers could have only one baby every four ④ **year** or so, ⑤ **spacing** their births so that they never had to carry ⑥ **more** than one child at a time. Farmers, on the other hand, could live in the ⑦ **same** place year after year and did not have to worry about ⑧ **settling** young children long distances. Societies that settled down in one place were able to ⑨ **lengthen** their birth intervals from four years to about two. This meant that each woman could have ⑩ **more** children than her hunter-gatherer counterpart, which in turn resulted in ⑪ **steady** population growth among farming communities. An ⑫ **dwindled** population was actually an advantage to agricultural societies, because farming required ⑬ **large** amounts of human labor.

기호	어색한 표현		올바른 표현
( )	_____	⇨	_____
( )	_____	⇨	_____
( )	_____	⇨	_____
( )	_____	⇨	_____
( )	_____	⇨	_____
( )	_____	⇨	_____

63. [19)]**밑줄 부분 중 어법, 혹은 문맥상 어휘의 쓰임이 어색한 것을 올바르게 고쳐 쓰시오. (10개)**

2024_1_6_39

① **Spend** time as children allows animals to learn about their environment. Without childhood, animals must rely ② **less** fully on ③ **software** , and therefore be ④ **more** flexible. Among migratory bird species, those that are born knowing how, when, and where to migrate — those that are migrating entirely with instructions they were born with — sometimes have very ⑤ **efficient** migration routes. These birds, born knowing how to migrate, don't ⑥ **adopt** easily. So when lakes dry up, forest becomes farmland, or climate change pushes breeding grounds farther north, those birds that are born knowing ⑦ **what** to migrate keep flying by the old rules and maps. By comparison, birds with the ⑧ **shortest** childhoods, and those that migrate with their parents, tend to have the most efficient migration routes. Childhood ⑨ **facilitates** the passing on of cultural information, and culture can evolve ⑩ **slower** than genes. Childhood gives ⑪ **inefficiency** in a changing world.

기호	어색한 표현		올바른 표현
( )	_____	⇨	_____
( )	_____	⇨	_____
( )	_____	⇨	_____
( )	_____	⇨	_____
( )	_____	⇨	_____
( )	_____	⇨	_____
( )	_____	⇨	_____
( )	_____	⇨	_____
( )	_____	⇨	_____
( )	_____	⇨	_____

64. [20)]**밑줄 부분 중 어법, 혹은 문맥상 어휘의 쓰임이 어색한 것을 올바르게 고쳐 쓰시오. (5개)**

2024_1_6_40

Over the last several decades, scholars have developed standards for how best to create, organize, present, and preserve digital information for future generations. ① **What** has remained ② **neglected** for the most part, however, are the needs of people with ③ **disabilities** . As a result, many of the otherwise most ④ **worthless** digital resources are useless for people who are deaf or hard of hearing, as well as for people who are blind, have low vision, or have difficulty ⑤ **distinguishes** particular colors. While professionals working in educational technology and commercial web design have made significant ⑥ **procedures** in meeting the needs of such users, some scholars creating digital projects all too often fail to take these needs into account. This situation would be much improved if more projects ⑦ **neglected** the idea that we should always keep the ⑧ **smallest** possible audience in mind as we make design decisions, ensuring that our final product serves the needs of those with disabilities as well as those ⑨ **without** .

기호	어색한 표현		올바른 표현
( )	_____	⇨	_____
( )	_____	⇨	_____
( )	_____	⇨	_____
( )	_____	⇨	_____
( )	_____	⇨	_____

65. 21)밑줄 부분 중 어법, 혹은 문맥상 어휘의 쓰임이 어색한 것을 올바르게 고쳐 쓰시오. (10개)

2024_1_6_41-42

All humans, to an extent, ① **seeks** activities that cause a degree of pain in order to experience pleasure, ② **if** this is found in spicy food, strong massages, or stepping into a too-cold or too-hot bath. The key is that it is a 'safe threat'. The brain perceives the stimulus to be painful but ultimately ③ **nonthreatening** . Interestingly, this could be similar to the way humor works: a 'safe threat' that causes pleasure by playfully violating ④ **norms** . We feel uncomfortable, but ⑤ **risky** . In this context, where survival is clearly not in danger, the desire for pain is actually the desire for a ⑥ **regret** , not suffering or ⑦ **reward**. This reward-like effect comes from the feeling of mastery over the pain. The closer you look at your chilli-eating habit, the ⑧ **more** remarkable it seems. When the active ingredient of chillies — capsaicin — touches the tongue, it stimulates exactly the ⑨ **different** receptor that is activated when any of these tissues are burned. Knowing that our body is firing off danger signals, but that we are actually completely ⑩ **dangerous** , produces ⑪ **hatred** . All children start off hating chilli, but many learn to ⑫ **deprive** pleasure from it through repeated exposure and knowing that they will never experience any real harm. Interestingly, seeking pain for the pain itself appears to be uniquely human. The only way scientists have trained animals to have a ⑬ **inference** for chilli or to self-harm is to have the pain always directly associated with a pleasurable reward.

기호	어색한 표현		올바른 표현
(　　)	＿＿＿＿＿	⇨	＿＿＿＿＿
(　　)	＿＿＿＿＿	⇨	＿＿＿＿＿
(　　)	＿＿＿＿＿	⇨	＿＿＿＿＿
(　　)	＿＿＿＿＿	⇨	＿＿＿＿＿
(　　)	＿＿＿＿＿	⇨	＿＿＿＿＿
(　　)	＿＿＿＿＿	⇨	＿＿＿＿＿
(　　)	＿＿＿＿＿	⇨	＿＿＿＿＿
(　　)	＿＿＿＿＿	⇨	＿＿＿＿＿
(　　)	＿＿＿＿＿	⇨	＿＿＿＿＿
(　　)	＿＿＿＿＿	⇨	＿＿＿＿＿

66. 22)밑줄 부분 중 어법, 혹은 문맥상 어휘의 쓰임이 어색한 것을 올바르게 고쳐 쓰시오. (1개)

2024_1_6_43-45

An airplane flew ① **high** above the deep blue seas far from any land. Flying the small plane was a student pilot who was sitting alongside an experienced flight instructor. As the student looked out the window, she was filled with ② **wonder** and appreciation for the beauty of the world. Her instructor, meanwhile, waited patiently for the right time to start a surprise flight ③ **emergency** training exercise. When the plane hit a bit of turbulence, the instructor pushed a hidden button. Suddenly, all the monitors inside the plane flashed several times then went out completely! Now the student was in control of an airplane that was flying well, but she had no indication of where she was or where she should go. She did have a map, but no other instruments. She was at a loss and then the plane shook again. When the student began to panic, the instructor said, "Stay ④ **calm** and steady. You can do it". Calm as ever, the instructor told her student, "Difficult times always happen during flight. The most important thing is to ⑤ **focus on** your flight in those situations". Those words encouraged the student to ⑥ **focus on** flying the aircraft first. "Thank you, I think I can make it", she said, "As I've been ⑦ **training** , I should search for visual markers". Then, the student carefully flew low enough to see if she could find any ships making their way across the surface of the ocean. Now the instructor and the student could see some ships. Although the ships were far apart, they were all sailing in a line. With the line of ships in view, the student could see the way to home and safety. The student looked at her in ⑧ **relief** , who smiled proudly back at her student.

기호	어색한 표현		올바른 표현
(　　)	＿＿＿＿＿	⇨	＿＿＿＿＿

2024 고1 6월 모의고사

❶ voca   ❷ text   ❸ [/]   ❹ _____   ❺ quiz 1   ❻ quiz 2   ❼ quiz 3   ❽ quiz 4   ⑨ quiz 5

☑ **다음 글을 읽고 물음에 답하시오.** (18)

Dear Reader, We always ^{감사하다}_____ your support. As you know, our service is now ^{이용 가능하다} _____ through an app. There has never been a better time to ^{전환하다} _____ to an online membership of TourTide Magazine. (가) 신의 현재 인쇄본 구독료에서 50% 할인된 가격으로 1년 치를 온라인으로 구독할 수 있습니다. Get new issues and daily web pieces at TourTide.com, read or listen to TourTide Magazine via the app, and get our members-only newsletter. You'll also gain access to our editors' selections of the best articles. Join today! Yours, TourTide Team

1. 1)힌트를 참고하여 각 빈칸에 알맞은 단어를 쓰시오.

2. 2)위 글에 주어진 (가)의 한글과 같은 의미를 가지도록, 각각의 주어진 단어들을 알맞게 배열하시오.

(가) discount / off   your / of / print / can / current / A   a / you / year / online / a   full / access / 50% / reading. / subscription,

☑ **다음 글을 읽고 물음에 답하시오.** (19)

(가) 우체통에서 걸어올 때 내 심장은 빠르게 뛰고 있었다. In my hands, I held the letter from the university I had applied to. I thought my grades were good enough to cross the line and my application letter was well-written, but was it enough? I hadn't slept a wink for days. As I carefully ^{찢다} _____ into the paper of the envelope, the letter slowly ^{나타나다} _____ with the opening phrase, "It is our great pleasure..". I shouted with joy, "I am in"! As I held the letter, I began to ^{상상하다} _____ about my college life in a faraway city.

3. 3)힌트를 참고하여 각 빈칸에 알맞은 단어를 쓰시오.

4. 4)위 글에 주어진 (가)의 한글과 같은 의미를 가지도록, 각각의 주어진 단어들을 알맞게 배열하시오.

(가) walked / was / the / As / my / heart / rapidly. / beating / mailbox, / from / I

☑ 다음 글을 읽고 물음에 답하시오. (20)

(가) 방이 지저분한 것은 결국 부정적인 감정과 파괴적 인 사고로 이어질 수 있다. Psychologists say that having a disorderly room can ⁿⁿⁿⁿⁿ^{나타내다} _____ a ^{혼란스러운} _____ mental state. (나) 정리 전문가 중 한 명은 방청소를 시작하는 순간 당신은 인생을 변화시키고 새로운 관점을 얻기 시작한다고 말한다. When you clean your surroundings, positive and good ^{분위기} _____ follows. You can do more things efficiently and neatly. So, clean up your closets, organize your drawers, and arrange your things first, then peace of mind will follow.

5. 5)힌트를 참고하여 각 빈칸에 알맞은 단어를 쓰시오.

6. 6)위 글에 주어진 (가) ~ (나)의 한글과 같은 의미를 가지도록, 각각의 주어진 단어들을 알맞게 배열하시오.

(가) can / thinking. / add / and / to / feelings / destructive / room / a messy / negative / up / Having

(나) experts / One / also / and / gaining / changing / you / start / the / says / your / you / life / perspective. / room, / moment / that / of / tidying / the / your / new / cleaning / professional / start

☑ 다음 글을 읽고 물음에 답하시오. (21)

(가) 농지의 토양은 단일 작물 재배를 위한 완벽한 환경이어야 한다. This is achieved by adding nutrients in the form of fertilizer and water by way of irrigation. During the last fifty years, engineers and crop scientists have helped farmers become much more efficient at supplying exactly the right amount of both. World usage of fertilizer has tripled since 1969, and the global capacity for irrigation has almost doubled; we are feeding and watering our fields more than ever, and our crops are loving it. ⓐ Fortunately, these luxurious conditions have also excited the attention of certain agricultural desirables. Because of farm fields are loaded with nutrients and water relative to the natural land that surrounds them, it is desired as luxury real estate by every random weed in the area.

7. 7)밑줄 친 ⓐ에서, 어법 혹은 문맥상 어색한 부분을 찾아 올바르게 고쳐 쓰시오.

ⓐ	잘못된 표현	바른 표현
	( ) ⇨ ( )	
	( ) ⇨ ( )	
	( ) ⇨ ( )	
	( ) ⇨ ( )	

8. 8)위 글에 주어진 (가)의 한글과 같은 의미를 가지도록, 각각의 주어진 단어들을 알맞게 배열하시오.

(가) the / a / be / field / environment / monoculture / is / farm / The / to / of / for / soil / forced / growth. / perfect

☑ 다음 글을 읽고 물음에 답하시오. (22)

ⓐ When it comes to help out, you don't have to do much. All you have to do are come around and show that you care. If you notice someone who is lonely, you could go and sit with them. If you work with someone who eats lunch all by them, and you go and sit down with them, they will begin to be more social after a while, and they will owe it all to you. A person's happiness comes from ^{문맥 상 들어갈 단어} _____. (가) 세상에는 모든 이가 자신을 잊었거나 무시한다고 느끼는 사람들이 너무 많다. Even if you say hi to someone passing by, they will begin to feel better about themselves, like someone cares.

9. 9)힌트를 참고하여 각 빈칸에 알맞은 단어를 쓰시오.

10. 10)밑줄 친 ⓐ에서, 어법 혹은 문맥상 어색한 부분을 찾아 올바르게 고쳐 쓰시오.

ⓐ   잘못된 표현   바른 표현

(   ) ⇨ (   )

(   ) ⇨ (   )

(   ) ⇨ (   )

11. 11)위 글에 주어진 (가)의 한글과 같은 의미를 가지도록, 각각의 주어진 단어들을 알맞게 배열하시오.

(가) the   world / or   ignored / too / like / There / many / has / them. / people / who / feel / out   in / forgotten / everyone / them / are

☑ 다음 글을 읽고 물음에 답하시오. (23.)

We often try to make cuts in our challenges and take the easy route. When taking the quick exit, we fail to ^{얻다} _____ the strength to compete. We often take the easy route to improve our skills. Many of us never really work to achieve mastery in the key areas of life. These skills are key tools that can be useful to our career, health, and ^{번영} _____. Highly successful athletes don't win because of better equipment; they win by facing ^{어려움} _____ to gain strength and skill. They win through preparation. It's the mental preparation, winning mindset, strategy, and skill that set them apart. (가) 힘은 저항이 가장 적은 길을 택하는 것이 아니라 맞서 싸우는 데서 나온다. Hardship is not just a lesson for the next time in front of us. Hardship will be the greatest teacher we will ever have in life.

12. 12)힌트를 참고하여 각 빈칸에 알맞은 단어를 쓰시오.

13. 13)위 글에 주어진 (가)의 한글과 같은 의미를 가지도록, 각각의 주어진 단어들을 알맞게 배열하시오.

(가) Strength / least / taking / struggle, / of / from / resistance. / from / not / the path / comes

☑ 다음 글을 읽고 물음에 답하시오. (24)

Your behaviors are usually a ^{반사} _____ of your identity. (가) 당신이 하는 행동은 당신이 스스로를 어떤 사람이라고 믿고 있는지를 나타낸다. — either consciously or nonconsciously. Research has shown that once a person believes in a particular aspect of their identity, they are more likely to act according to that belief. For example, people who identified as "being a voter" were more likely to vote than those who simply claimed "voting" was an action they wanted to perform. ⓐ Similarly, the person who accepts exercise as the part of their identity doesn't have to convince them to train. Doing the right thing is easy. After all, when your behavior and your identity perfectly match, you are no longer to pursue behavior change. You are simply acting like the type of person you already believe <yourself/you to be.

14. 14)힌트를 참고하여 각 빈칸에 알맞은 단어를 쓰시오.

15. 15)밑줄 친 ⓐ에서, 어법 혹은 문맥상 어색한 부분을 찾아 올바르게 고쳐 쓰시오.

   ⓐ   잘못된 표현   바른 표현
   (   ) ⇨ (   )
   (   ) ⇨ (   )

16. 16)위 글에 주어진 (가)의 한글과 같은 의미를 가지도록, 각각의 주어진 단어들을 알맞게 배열하시오.

(가) What / an indication / the type / you / are. / of / do is / that / you / person / believe / you / of

☑ **다음 글을 읽고 물음에 답하시오.** (25)

The above graph shows the electronic waste collection and recycling rate by region in 2016 and 2019. In both years, Europe showed the highest electronic waste collection and recycling rates. The electronic waste collection and recycling rate of Asia in 2019 was lower than in 2016. The Americas ^{기록하다} _____ second in 2016 and third in 2019, with 17 percent and 9 percent respectively. In both years, the electronic waste collection and recycling rates in Oceania ^{머무르다} _____ under 10 percent. Africa had the lowest electronic waste collection and recycling rates in both 2016 and 2019, showing the smallest gap between 2016 and 2019.

17. 17)힌트를 참고하여 각 빈칸에 알맞은 단어를 쓰시오.

☑ **다음 글을 읽고 물음에 답하시오.** (26)

Fritz Zwicky, a memorable astrophysicist who coined the term 'supernova', was born in Varna, Bulgaria to a Swiss father and a Czech mother. At the age of six, he was sent to his grandparents who ^{돌보다, 2단어} _____ him for most of his childhood in Switzerland. There, he received an advanced education in mathematics and physics. In 1925, he emigrated to the United States and continued his physics research at California Institute of Technology (Caltech). He developed numerous theories that have had a ^{지대한} _____ influence on the understanding of our universe in the early 21st century. After being ^{임용하다} _____ as a professor of astronomy at Caltech in 1942, he developed some of the earliest jet engines and holds more than 50 ^{특허} _____, many in jet propulsion.

18. 18)힌트를 참고하여 각 빈칸에 알맞은 단어를 쓰시오.

☑ **다음 글을 읽고 물음에 답하시오.** (29)

(가) 수렵 채집 생활 방식은 인류에게 "자연스러운" 것으로 묘사될 수 있으며, 그것을 추천할 만한 많은 것이 있는 것으로 보인다. Examination of human remains from early hunter-gatherer societies has suggested that our ancestors enjoyed ^{풍부한} _____ food, obtainable without excessive effort, and suffered very few diseases. ⓐ If this is true, it is not clear that so many humans settled in temporary villages and developed agriculture, growing crops and domesticating animals: cultivating fields was hard work, and it was in farming villages that epidemic diseases first took root. Whatever its immediate effect on the lives of humans, the development of settlements and agriculture ^{의심할 여지 없이} _____ led to a high increase in population density. This period, known as the New Stone Age, was a major ^{전환점} _____ in human development, opening the way to the growth of the first towns and cities, and eventually leading to settled "civilizations".

19. 19)힌트를 참고하여 각 <u>빈칸에 알맞은</u> 단어를 쓰시오.

20. 20)밑줄 친 ⓐ에서, 어법 혹은 문맥상 어색한 부분을 찾아 올바르게 고쳐 쓰시오.

ⓐ	잘못된 표현		바른 표현
(	)	⇨ (	)
(	)	⇨ (	)

21. 21)위 글에 주어진 (가)의 한글과 같은 의미를 가지도록, 각각의 주어진 단어들을 알맞게 배열하시오.

(가) The hunter-gatherer lifestyle, / it. / can / had much / which / be described / to have / "natural" / as / beings, / appears / to human / to recommend

☑ 다음 글을 읽고 물음에 답하시오. (30)

Many human and nonhuman animals save commodities or money for future consumption. (가) 이러한 행동은 즉각적인 보상보다 지연된 보상을 선호하는 것을 드러내는 듯하다.: the agent gives up some immediate pleasure in exchange for a future one. ⓐ <u>Thus the undiscounted value of the future reward should be greater than the discounted value of the present one. However, in some cases the agent does not wait for the envisioning occasion but uses their savings premature.</u> For example, early in the year an employee might set aside money to buy Christmas presents but then spend it on a summer vacation instead. Such cases could be examples of weakness of ^{의지} ____. ^즉 _____, the agents may judge or resolve to spend their savings in a certain way for the greatest benefit but then act differently when ^{유혹} _____ for immediate pleasure appears.

22. 22)힌트를 참고하여 각 <u>빈칸에 알맞은</u> 단어를 쓰시오.

23. 23)밑줄 친 ⓐ에서, 어법 혹은 문맥상 어색한 부분을 찾아 올바르게 고쳐 쓰시오.

ⓐ	잘못된 표현		바른 표현
(	)	⇨ (	)
(	)	⇨ (	)
(	)	⇨ (	)
(	)	⇨ (	)

24. 24)위 글에 주어진 (가)의 한글과 같은 의미를 가지도록, 각각의 주어진 단어들을 알맞게 배열하시오.

(가) preference / delayed / one / an / behavior / a / of / reward / over / seems / to / reveal / This / a / immediate

☑ **다음 글을 읽고 물음에 답하시오.** (31.)

ⓐ The costs of interruptions are well-documenting. Martin Luther King Jr. lamenting them when he was described "that lovely poem that didn't get writing because someone knocked on the door". Perhaps the most famous literary example happened in 1797 when Samuel Taylor Coleridge started writing his poem Kubla Khan from a dream he had but then ⓑ was visited by an expected guest. For Coleridge, by incidence , the untimely visitor came at a particularly bad time. He forgot his perspiration and left the work unfinishing. While there are many documented cases of sudden disruptions that have had significant ^{결과} _____ for professionals in critical roles such as doctors, nurses, control room operators, stock traders, and pilots, they also impact most of us in our everyday lives, slowing down work ^{생산성} _____ and generally increasing stress levels.

25. 25)힌트를 참고하여 각 빈칸에 알맞은 단어를 쓰시오.

26. 26)밑줄 친 ⓐ~ⓑ에서, 어법 혹은 문맥상 어색한 부분을 찾아 올바르게 고쳐 쓰시오.

ⓐ   잘못된 표현   바른 표현

(   ) ⇨ (   )

(   ) ⇨ (   )

(   ) ⇨ (   )

(   ) ⇨ (   )

ⓑ   잘못된 표현   바른 표현

(   ) ⇨ (   )

(   ) ⇨ (   )

(   ) ⇨ (   )

(   ) ⇨ (   )

☑ **다음 글을 읽고 물음에 답하시오.** (32.)

There's a lot of scientific evidence ^{입증하다} _____ that focused attention leads to the reshaping of the brain. In animals rewarded for noticing sound (to hunt or to avoid being hunted for example), we find much larger auditory centers in the brain. In animals rewarded for sharp eyesight, the visual areas are larger. Brain scans of violinists provide more evidence, showing dramatic growth and expansion in regions of the cortex that represent the left hand, which has to finger the strings ^{정확히} _____, often at very high speed. Other studies have shown that the hippocampus, which is vital for spatial memory, is enlarged in taxi drivers. (가) 요점은 우리가 어디에 주의를 기울이고 무엇을 연습하느냐에 따라 뇌의 물리적 구조가 달라진다는 것이다.

27. 27)힌트를 참고하여 각 <u>빈칸에 알맞은</u> 단어를 쓰시오.

28. 28)위 글에 주어진 (가)의 한글과 같은 의미를 가지도록, 각각의 주어진 단어들을 알맞게 배열하시오.

(가) is / the   brain / that / and   what / we / according / The   point / we / attention / our / to   where / doing. / practice / of / the physical architecture / changes / direct

☑ 다음 글을 읽고 물음에 답하시오. (33)

How did the human mind ^{진화하다} _____? (가) <u>한 가지 가능성은 다른 인간 부족과의 경쟁과 갈등이 우리 두 뇌가 그렇게 진화하도록 했다는 것이다.</u> A human tribe that could out-think its enemies, even slightly, possessed a vital advantage. The ability of your tribe to imagine and predict where and when a hostile enemy tribe might strike, and plan ^{그에 따라} _____, gives your tribe a significant military advantage. The human mind became a weapon in the ^{투쟁} _____ for survival, a weapon far more ^{결정적인} _____ than any before it. And this mental advantage was applied, over and over, within each succeeding generation. (나) <u>상대보다 더 우수한 생각을 할 수 있는 부족은 전투에서 승리할 확률이 높았고, 이러한 정신 적 우위를 담당하는 유전자를 자손에게 물려주었다.</u> You and I are the ^{후손} _____ of the winners.

29. 29)힌트를 참고하여 각 <u>빈칸에 알맞은</u> 단어를 쓰시오.

30. 30)위 글에 주어진 (가) ~ (나)의 한글과 같은 의미를 가지도록, 각각의 주어진 단어들을 알맞게 배열하시 오.

(가) the / human / conflicts / caused / possibility / did. / evolve / brains / they / way / that / our / with / is / competition / tribes / and / One / to / other

(나) could / advantage / more / its / the   genes / offspring. / succeed / was / out-think / likely / on / in / for / responsible / then / mental / to / that / opponents / its / battle / would / The tribe / and / to / this / pass

☑ **다음 글을 읽고 물음에 답하시오.** (34.)

To find the hidden ^{잠재력} _____ in teams, instead of brainstorming, we're better off shifting to a process called brainwriting. The ^{초기의} _____ steps are solo. You start by asking everyone to generate ideas separately. Next, you pool them and share them anonymously among the group. To ^{유지하다} _____ independent judgment, each member evaluates them on their own. Only (가) <u>그러고 나서야 팀이 함께 모여 가장 유망한 옵션을 선택하고 다듬는다.</u> By developing and assessing ideas individually before choosing and elaborating them, teams can surface and advance possibilities that might not get attention ^{그렇지 않았더라면} _____. This brainwriting process makes sure that all ideas are brought to the table and all voices are brought into the conversation. It is especially effective in groups that struggle to achieve ^{집단지성} _____.

31. ³¹⁾힌트를 참고하여 각 빈칸에 알맞은 단어를 쓰시오.

32. ³²⁾위 글에 주어진 (가)의 한글과 같은 의미를 가지도록, 각각의 주어진 단어들을 알맞게 배열하시오.

(가) and refine / the team / promising / then / come / to select / does / options. / together / the most

☑ **다음 글을 읽고 물음에 답하시오.** (35.)

Simply giving employees a sense of ^{들어갈 단어} _____ — a feeling that they are in control, that they have genuine decision-making authority — can radically increase how much energy and focus they bring to their jobs. One 2010 study at a manufacturing plant in Ohio, for instance, carefully examined assembly-line workers who were empowered to make small decisions about their schedules and work environment. They designed their own uniforms and had ^{권한} _____ over shifts while all the manufacturing processes and pay scales stayed the same. Within two months, ^{생산성} _____ at the plant increased by 20 percent, with workers taking shorter breaks and making fewer mistakes. (가) <u>자신들이 통제권을 쥐고 있다는 느낌을 직원들에게 부여한 것이 그들이 업무에 끌어들이는 자기 통제력을 향상시켰다.</u>

33. ³³⁾힌트를 참고하여 각 빈칸에 알맞은 단어를 쓰시오.

34. ³⁴⁾위 글에 주어진 (가)의 한글과 같은 의미를 가지도록, 각각의 주어진 단어들을 알맞게 배열하시오.

(가) of / improved / self-discipline / how / employees / a / their / sense / they / much / brought / control / Giving / jobs. / to

☑ **다음 글을 읽고 물음에 답하시오.** (36.)

ⓐ As businesses shift some core business activities to digital, such as sales, marketing, or archiving, that is assumed that the impact on the environment will be less positive. However, digital business activities can still be threatened by the environment. In some cases, the harm of digital businesses can be even less hazardous. A few decades ago, offices used to have much more paper waste since all documents were digital based. When workplaces shifted from paper to digital documents, invoices, and emails, it was a ^{유망한} _____ step to save trees. However, the cost of the Internet and electricity for the environment is ^{간과하다} _____. A recent Wired report declared that most data centers' energy source is ^{화석연료} _____. When we store bigger data on clouds, increased carbon emissions make our green clouds gray. The carbon footprint of an email is smaller than mail sent via a post office, but still, it causes four grams of CO_2, and it can be as much as 50 grams if the ^{첨부} _____ is big.

35. 35)힌트를 참고하여 각 빈칸에 알맞은 단어를 쓰시오.

36. 36)밑줄 친 ⓐ에서, 어법 혹은 문맥상 어색한 부분을 찾아 올바르게 고쳐 쓰시오.

ⓐ	잘못된 표현		바른 표현
(	)	⇨ (	)
(	)	⇨ (	)
(	)	⇨ (	)
(	)	⇨ (	)
(	)	⇨ (	)

☑ **다음 글을 읽고 물음에 답하시오.** (37.)

ⓐ Problems often arise if an familiar species is suddenly introduced to an ecosystem. Britain's red and grey squirrels provide a clear example. When the grey arriving from America in the 1870s, both squirrel species competed for the different food and habitat, which put the native red squirrel populations under pressure. The grey had the edge because it can adept its diet; it is able, for instance, to eat green acorns, while the red can only digest mature acorns. (가) 숲의 같은 지역 내에서 회색 다람쥐는 붉은 다람쥐가 한 입 먹기도 전에 식량 공급을 파괴할 수 있다. Greys can also live more densely and in varied habitats, so have survived more easily when woodland has been destroyed. As a result, the red squirrel has come close to ^{멸종} _____ in England.

37. 37)힌트를 참고하여 각 빈칸에 알맞은 단어를 쓰시오.

38. 38)밑줄 친 ⓐ에서, 어법 혹은 문맥상 어색한 부분을 찾아 올바르게 고쳐 쓰시오.

ⓐ 　　잘못된 표현　　　　　　　바른 표현

(　　　　　　　　) ⇨ (　　　　　　　　　)

(　　　　　　　　) ⇨ (　　　　　　　　　)

(　　　　　　　　) ⇨ (　　　　　　　　　)

(　　　　　　　　) ⇨ (　　　　　　　　　)

39. 39)위 글에 주어진 (가)의 한글과 같은 의미를 가지도록, 각각의 주어진 단어들을 알맞게 배열하시오.

(가) before / destroy / squirrels / the food supply / can / a bite. / the same / area / red / even have / grey / squirrels / of forest, / Within

☑ **다음 글을 읽고 물음에 답하시오.** (38.)

Growing crops forced people to stay in one place. Hunter-gatherers typically moved around ^{자주} _____, and they had to be able to carry all their ^{소유물} _____ with them every time they moved. In particular, mothers had to carry their young children. As a result, hunter-gatherer mothers could have only one baby every four years or so, ^{간격을 두다} _____ their births so that they never had to carry more than one child at a time. Farmers, on the other hand, could live in the same place year after year and did not have to worry about transporting young children long distances. (가) 한곳에 정착하게 된 사회는 출산 간격을 4년에서 약 2년으로 단축할 수 있었다 ⓐ This meant that each woman could have more children than her hunter-gatherer counterpart, which n turn resulted from rapid population growth among farming communities. A decreased population was actually an advantage to agricultural societies, because farming required small amounts of human labor.

40. 40)힌트를 참고하여 각 빈칸에 알맞은 단어를 쓰시오.

41. 41)밑줄 친 ⓐ에서, 어법 혹은 문맥상 어색한 부분을 찾아 올바르게 고쳐 쓰시오.

ⓐ 　　잘못된 표현　　　　　　　바른 표현

(　　　　　　　　) ⇨ (　　　　　　　　　)

(　　　　　　　　) ⇨ (　　　　　　　　　)

(　　　　　　　　) ⇨ (　　　　　　　　　)

42. 42)위 글에 주어진 (가)의 한글과 같은 의미를 가지도록, 각각의 주어진 단어들을 알맞게 배열하시오.

(가) place / one / were / years / able / their birth / Societies / from / four / down in / to shorten / intervals / to about two. / that / settled

☑ **다음 글을 읽고 물음에 답하시오.** (39.)

Spending time as children allows animals to learn about their environment. Without childhood, animals must rely more fully on hardware, and therefore be less flexible. Among migratory bird species, those that are born knowing how, when, and where to migrate — those that are migrating entirely with instructions they were born with — sometimes have very inefficient migration routes. ⓐ <u>These birds, born knowing how to migrate, don't adept easily.</u> So when lakes dry up, forest becomes farmland, or climate change pushes breeding grounds farther north, those birds that are born knowing how to migrate keep flying by the old rules and maps. By comparison, birds with the shortest childhoods, and those that migrate with their parents, tend to have the most efficient migration routes. (가) <u>유년기는 문화적 정보의 전달을 촉진하며, 문화는 유전자보다 더 빠르게 진화할 수 있다</u> Childhood gives ^{본문 단어 찾아서 변형} _____ in a changing world.

43. 43)힌트를 참고하여 각 <u>빈칸에 알맞은</u> 단어를 쓰시오.

44. 44)밑줄 친 ⓐ에서, 어법 혹은 문맥상 어색한 부분을 찾아 올바르게 고쳐 쓰시오.

ⓐ	잘못된 표현		바른 표현
(	) ⇨ (	)
(	) ⇨ (	)

45. 45)위 글에 주어진 (가)의 한글과 같은 의미를 가지도록, 각각의 주어진 단어들을 알맞게 배열하시오.

(가) information, / can / culture / on   of / and / genes. / cultural / evolve / the   passing / faster   than / facilitates / Childhood

☑ **다음 글을 읽고 물음에 답하시오.** (40.)

Over the last several decades, scholars have developed standards for how best to create, organize, present, and ^{보존하다} _____ digital information for future generations. (가) <u>그러나 대부분의 경우 장애가 있는 사람들의 요구는 여전히 무시되어 왔다</u> As a result, many of the otherwise most valuable digital resources are useless for people who are deaf or hard of hearing, as well as for people who are blind, have low vision, or have difficulty distinguishing particular colors. While professionals working in educational technology and commercial web design have made significant progress in meeting the needs of such users, (나) <u>디지털 프로젝트를 만드는 일부 학자들은 이러한 요구를 고려하지 못하는 경우가 너무 많다.</u> This situation would be much improved if more projects ^{수용하다} _____ the idea that we should always keep the largest possible audience in mind as we make design decisions, ensuring that our final product serves the needs of those with disabilities as well as those without.

46. 46)힌트를 참고하여 각 빈칸에 알맞은 단어를 쓰시오.

47. 47)위 글에 주어진 (가) ~ (나)의 한글과 같은 의미를 가지도록, 각각의 주어진 단어들을 알맞게 배열하시오.

(가) remained / the / with / of   people / neglected / needs / are / has / What / part, / however, / for   the   most / disabilities.

(나) creating / to take / digital / these / all too often / scholars / projects / some / needs into / account. / fail

☑ **다음 글을 읽고 물음에 답하시오.** (41~42.)

All humans, ^{어느 정도} _____, seek activities that cause a degree of pain in order to experience pleasure, whether this is found in spicy food, strong massages, or stepping into a too-cold or too-hot bath. The key is that it is a '^{안전한 위협} _____'. The brain ^{감지하다} _____ the stimulus to be painful but ultimately nonthreatening. ⓐ Interestingly, this could be contrary to the way humor works: a 'safe threat' that causes pleasure by playfully conforming to norms. We feel uncomfortable, but safe. In this context, which survival is clearly not in danger, the desire for pain is actually the desire for a reward, not ^{고통} _____ or punishment. This reward-like effect comes from the feeling of mastery over the pain. (가) 칠리를 먹는 습관을 자세히 들여다볼수록 이는 더욱 분명하게 드러난다. When the active ingredient of chillies — capsaicin — touches the tongue, it stimulates exactly the same ^{수용체} _____ that is activated when any of these tissues are burned. (나) 우리 몸이 위험 신호를 보내고 있지만 실제로는 완전히 안전하다는 것을 알면 쾌감이 생긴다. All children start off hating chilli, but many learn to ^{도출하다} _____ pleasure from it through repeated exposure and knowing that they will never experience any real harm. Interestingly, seeking pain for the pain itself appears to be uniquely human. The only way scientists have trained animals to have a ^{선호} _____ for chilli or to self-harm is to have the pain always directly associated with a pleasurable ^{보상} _____.

48. 48)힌트를 참고하여 각 빈칸에 알맞은 단어를 쓰시오.

49. 49)밑줄 친 ⓐ에서, 어법 혹은 문맥상 어색한 부분을 찾아 올바르게 고쳐 쓰시오.

ⓐ	잘못된 표현		바른 표현
(	)	⇨ (	)
(	)	⇨ (	)
(	)	⇨ (	)

50. 50)위 글에 주어진 (가) ~ (나)의 한글과 같은 의미를 가지도록, 각각의 주어진 단어들을 알맞게 배열하시오.

(가) The / more / remarkable it / closer / at your / the / seems. / habit, / you / chilli-eating / look

(나) body is / that we / firing / that / produces / signals, / are / actually completely / but / pleasure. / off danger / our / safe, / Knowing

☑ **다음 글을 읽고 물음에 답하시오.** (43~45.)

An airplane flew high above the deep blue seas far from any land. Flying the small plane was a student pilot who was sitting alongside an experienced flight instructor. As the student looked out the window, she was filled with wonder and ^{감탄} _____ for the beauty of the world. Her instructor, meanwhile, waited patiently for the right time to start a surprise flight emergency training exercise. When the plane hit a bit of turbulence, the instructor pushed a hidden button. Suddenly, all the monitors inside the plane flashed several times then went out completely! Now (가) <u>교육생은 잘 날고 있는 비행기를 조종하고 있었지만, 그녀는 자신이 어디에 있는지, 어디로 가야 하는지 알 방도가 없었다.</u> She did have a map, but no other instruments. She was at a loss and then the plane shook again. ⓐ <u>When the student began to panic, the instructor said, "Stay calmly and steady. You can do it". Calm as ever, the instructor told her student, "Difficult times always are happened during flight. The most important thing is to focus on your flight in those situations".</u> Those words ^{격려하다} _____the student to focus on flying the aircraft first. "Thank you, I think I can make it", she said, "As I've been trained, I should search for visual markers". Then, (나) <u>교육생은 바다 표면을 가로지르는 배가 보이는지 확인할 수 있을 정도로 충분히 낮게 조심히 비행하였다.</u> Now the instructor and the student could see some ships. Although the ships were far apart, they were all sailing in a line. With the line of ships in view, the student could see the way to home and safety. The student looked at her in relief, who smiled ^{자랑스럽게} _____ back at her student.

51. 51)힌트를 참고하여 각 <u>빈칸에 알맞은</u> 단어를 쓰시오.

52. 52)밑줄 친 ⓐ에서, 어법 혹은 문맥상 어색한 부분을 찾아 올바르게 고쳐 쓰시오.

ⓐ   잘못된 표현   바른 표현

(   ) ⇨ (   )

(   ) ⇨ (   )

53. 53)위 글에 주어진 (가) ~ (나)의 한글과 같은 의미를 가지도록, 각각의 주어진 단어들을 알맞게 배열하시오.

(가) was / an / go. / well, / she / the   student / should / she / control / was / indication / or   where / had / in / airplane / she / of where / no / flying / of / but / was / that

(나) making / carefully / the surface / to see if / of / flew / find / she / way across / any / their / ships / the ocean. / the student / enough / could / low

보듬영어

정답

WORK BOOK

———

2024년 고1 6월 모의고사 내신대비용 WorkBook & 변형문제

Prac 1 **Answers**

1) has
2) subscription
3) access
4) get
5) rapidly
6) cross
7) with
8) to
9) messy
10) negative
11) destructive
12) disorganized
13) says
14) gaining
15) efficiently
16) neatly
17) arrange
18) is achieved
19) During
20) become
21) exactly
22) watering
23) Unfortunately
24) Because
25) relative
26) are desired
27) helping
28) show
29) them
30) social
31) it
32) who
33) has
34) themselves
35) to make
36) taking
37) improve
38) prosperity
39) because of
40) mental
41) set
42) taking
43) have
44) identity
45) that
46) either
47) or
48) more
49) identified
50) to perform
51) themselves
52) Doing
53) match
54) yourself
55) both
56) rate
57) respectively
58) remained
59) showing
60) was born
61) most
62) advanced
63) continued
64) being
65) astronomy
66) holds
67) be described
68) has
69) suffered
70) permanent
71) domesticating
72) Whatever
73) leading

74) Many
75) one
76) uses
77) prematurely
78) it
79) differently
80) appears
81) them
82) literary
83) was visited
84) coincidence
85) left
86) many
87) slowing
88) increasing
89) that
90) rewarded
91) rewarded
92) provide
93) represent
94) which
95) Other
96) spatial
97) that
98) where
99) what
100) evolve
101) did
102) possessed
103) predict
104) plan
105) gives
106) it
107) was applied
108) succeeding
109) its
110) was
111) its
112) descendants
113) process
114) initial
115) separately
116) anonymously
117) independent
118) refine
119) them
120) that
121) are brought
122) struggle
123) giving
124) that
125) increase
126) were empowered
127) had
128) increased
129) taking
130) employees
131) that
132) less
133) threaten
134) more
135) have
136) When
137) is neglected
138) that
139) increased
140) is
141) arise
142) which
143) because
144) adapt
145) mature
146) have
147) densely
148) been destroyed
149) extinction
150) to stay

151) could
152) spacing
153) transporting
154) were
155) counterpart
156) increased
157) because
158) to learn
159) more
160) inefficient
161) don't
162) keep
163) have
164) evolve
165) What
166) neglected
167) useless
168) distinguishing
169) have
170) creating
171) take
172) that
173) serves
174) extent
175) that
176) perceives
177) similar
178) violating
179) uncomfortable
180) where
181) effect
182) remarkable
183) is activated
184) produces
185) repeated
186) appears
187) directly
188) experienced
189) wonder
190) patiently
191) completely
192) that
193) indication
194) other
195) during
196) to focus
197) it
198) to see
199) sailing
200) who

1) has
2) subscription
3) access
4) get
5) rapidly
6) cross
7) with
8) to
9) messy
10) negative
11) destructive
12) disorganized
13) says
14) gaining
15) efficiently
16) neatly
17) arrange
18) is achieved
19) During
20) become
21) exactly
22) watering
23) Unfortunately
24) Because
25) relative
26) are desired
27) helping
28) show
29) them
30) social
31) it
32) who
33) has
34) themselves
35) to make
36) taking
37) improve
38) prosperity
39) because of
40) mental
41) set
42) taking
43) have
44) identity
45) that
46) either
47) or
48) more
49) identified
50) to perform
51) themselves
52) Doing
53) match
54) yourself
55) both
56) rate
57) respectively
58) remained
59) showing
60) was born
61) most
62) advanced
63) continued
64) being
65) astronomy
66) holds
67) be described
68) has
69) suffered
70) permanent
71) domesticating
72) Whatever
73) leading

74) Many
75) one
76) uses
77) prematurely
78) it
79) differently
80) appears
81) them
82) literary
83) was visited
84) coincidence
85) left
86) many
87) slowing
88) increasing
89) that
90) rewarded
91) rewarded
92) provide
93) represent
94) which
95) Other
96) spatial
97) that
98) where
99) what
100) evolve
101) did
102) possessed
103) predict
104) plan
105) gives
106) it
107) was applied
108) succeeding
109) its
110) was
111) its
112) descendants
113) process
114) initial
115) separately
116) anonymously
117) independent
118) refine
119) them
120) that
121) are brought
122) struggle
123) giving
124) that
125) increase
126) were empowered
127) had
128) increased
129) taking
130) employees
131) that
132) less
133) threaten
134) more
135) have
136) When
137) is neglected
138) that
139) increased
140) is
141) arise
142) which
143) because
144) adapt
145) mature
146) have
147) densely
148) been destroyed
149) extinction
150) to stay

151) could
152) spacing
153) transporting
154) were
155) counterpart
156) increased
157) because
158) to learn
159) more
160) inefficient
161) don't
162) keep
163) have
164) evolve
165) What
166) neglected
167) useless
168) distinguishing
169) have
170) creating
171) take
172) that
173) serves
174) extent
175) that
176) perceives
177) similar
178) violating
179) uncomfortable
180) where
181) effect
182) remarkable
183) is activated
184) produces
185) repeated
186) appears
187) directly
188) experienced
189) wonder
190) patiently
191) completely
192) that
193) indication
194) other
195) during
196) to focus
197) it
198) to see
199) sailing
200) who

Answers

1) appreciate
2) available
3) membership
4) subscription
5) membersonly
6) beating
7) applied
8) cross
9) application
10) tore
11) emerged
12) held
13) fantasy
14) faraway
15) messy
16) negative
17) destructive
18) disorderly
19) disorganized
20) tidying
21) perspective
22) positive
23) efficiently
24) arrange
25) field
26) forced
27) monoculture
28) fertilizer
29) irrigation
30) supplying
31) tripled
32) irrigation
33) watering
34) crops
35) luxurious
36) agricultural
37) undesirables
38) relative
39) desired
40) random
41) helping
42) care
43) lonely
44) themselves
45) social
46) owe
47) attention
48) forgotten
49) ignored
50) passing
51) cares
52) cuts
53) challenges
54) acquire
55) compete
56) improve
57) mastery
58) prosperity
59) hardship
60) preparation
61) apart
62) struggle
63) least
64) resistance
65) Hardship
66) reflection
67) identity
68) indication
69) aspect
70) belief
71) identified
72) claimed
73) perform

74) identity
75) convince
76) match
77) pursuing
78) astrophysicist
79) coined
80) term
81) after
82) emigrated
83) theories
84) profound
85) universe
86) appointed
87) astronomy
88) patents
89) propulsion
90) hunter-gatherer
91) had
92) Examination
93) remains
94) has
95) obtainable
96) excessive
97) few
98) permanent
99) domesticating
100) cultivating
101) epidemic
102) settlements
103) agriculture
104) population
105) density
106) civilizations
107) commodities
108) consumption
109) preference
110) delayed
111) immediate
112) pleasure
113) future
114) discounted
115) greater
116) undiscounted
117) present
118) envisioned
119) prematurely
120) aside
121) weakness
122) resolve
123) benefit
124) temptation
125) interruptions
126) lamented
127) written
128) knocked
129) literary
130) visited
131) coincidence
132) inspiration
133) unfinished
134) documented
135) professionals
136) productivity
137) demonstrating
138) attention
139) reshaping
140) rewarded
141) auditory
142) visual
143) cortex
144) precisely
145) hippocampus
146) spatial
147) enlarged
148) direct
149) evolve
150) competition

151) conflicts
152) evolve
153) out-think
154) possessed
155) predict
156) hostile
157) strike
158) military
159) weapon
160) decisive
161) mental
162) succeeding
163) opponents
164) succeed
165) offspring
166) brainstorming
167) shifting
168) brainwriting
169) separately
170) anonymously
171) independent
172) evaluates
173) does
174) promising
175) assessing
176) elaborating
177) surface
178) advance
179) brought
180) effective
181) collective
182) agency
183) control
184) genuine
185) authority
186) increase
187) manufacturing
188) examined
189) empowered
190) uniforms
191) authority
192) stayed
193) productivity
194) taking
195) mistakes
196) control
197) self-discipline
198) shift
199) digital
200) negative
201) threaten
202) hazardous
203) based
204) promising
205) neglected
206) fossil
207) emissions
208) gray
209) sent
210) attachment
211) arise
212) exotic
213) arrived
214) competed
215) habitat
216) pressure
217) adapt
218) mature
219) densely
220) varied
221) have
222) destroyed
223) extinction
224) Growing
225) stay
226) Hunter-gatherers
227) possessions

228) time
229) years
230) spacing
231) transporting
232) settled
233) shorten
234) intervals
235) counterpart
236) rapid
237) farming
238) advantage
239) agricultural
240) labor
241) children
242) learn
243) hardware
244) flexible
245) migratory
246) instructions
247) inefficient
248) born
249) adapt
250) farther
251) comparison
252) facilitates
253) passing
254) culture
255) evolve
256) genes
257) flexibility
258) digital
259) future
260) neglected
261) disabilities
262) valuable
263) useless
264) distinguishing
265) professionals
266) progress
267) meeting
268) creating
269) fail
270) account
271) improved
272) embraced
273) largest
274) needs
275) disabilities
276) without
277) pain
278) pleasure
279) spicy
280) massages
281) threat
282) stimulus
283) nonthreatening
284) humor
285) violating
286) norms
287) where
288) reward
289) punishment
290) mastery
291) remarkable
292) stimulates
293) activated
294) burned
295) danger
296) derive
297) repeated
298) seeking
299) human
300) preference
301) directly
302) associated
303) pleasurable
304) flew

305) student
306) experienced
307) appreciation
308) surprise
309) emergency
310) turbulence
311) indication
312) loss
313) panic
314) steady
315) Calm
316) encouraged
317) markers
318) low
319) safety
320) relief

1) appreciate
2) available
3) membership
4) subscription
5) membersonly
6) beating
7) applied
8) cross
9) application
10) tore
11) emerged
12) held
13) fantasy
14) faraway
15) messy
16) negative
17) destructive
18) disorderly
19) disorganized
20) tidying
21) perspective
22) positive
23) efficiently
24) arrange
25) field
26) forced
27) monoculture
28) fertilizer
29) irrigation
30) supplying
31) tripled
32) irrigation
33) watering
34) crops
35) luxurious
36) agricultural
37) undesirables
38) relative
39) desired
40) random
41) helping
42) care
43) lonely
44) themselves
45) social
46) owe
47) attention
48) forgotten
49) ignored
50) passing
51) cares
52) cuts
53) challenges
54) acquire
55) compete

56) improve
57) mastery
58) prosperity
59) hardship
60) preparation
61) apart
62) struggle
63) least
64) resistance
65) Hardship
66) reflection
67) identity
68) indication
69) aspect
70) belief
71) identified
72) claimed
73) perform
74) identity
75) convince
76) match
77) pursuing
78) astrophysicist
79) coined
80) term
81) after
82) emigrated
83) theories
84) profound
85) universe
86) appointed
87) astronomy
88) patents
89) propulsion
90) hunter-gatherer
91) had
92) Examination
93) remains
94) has
95) obtainable
96) excessive
97) few
98) permanent
99) domesticating
100) cultivating
101) epidemic
102) settlements
103) agriculture
104) population
105) density
106) civilizations
107) commodities
108) consumption
109) preference
110) delayed
111) immediate
112) pleasure
113) future
114) discounted
115) greater
116) undiscounted
117) present
118) envisioned
119) prematurely
120) aside
121) weakness
122) resolve
123) benefit
124) temptation
125) interruptions
126) lamented
127) written
128) knocked
129) literary
130) visited
131) coincidence
132) inspiration

133) unfinished
134) documented
135) professionals
136) productivity
137) demonstrating
138) attention
139) reshaping
140) rewarded
141) auditory
142) visual
143) cortex
144) precisely
145) hippocampus
146) spatial
147) enlarged
148) direct
149) evolve
150) competition
151) conflicts
152) evolve
153) out-think
154) possessed
155) predict
156) hostile
157) strike
158) military
159) weapon
160) decisive
161) mental
162) succeeding
163) opponents
164) succeed
165) offspring
166) brainstorming
167) shifting
168) brainwriting
169) separately
170) anonymously
171) independent
172) evaluates
173) does
174) promising
175) assessing
176) elaborating
177) surface
178) advance
179) brought
180) effective
181) collective
182) agency
183) control
184) genuine
185) authority
186) increase
187) manufacturing
188) examined
189) empowered
190) uniforms
191) authority
192) stayed
193) productivity
194) taking
195) mistakes
196) control
197) self-discipline
198) shift
199) digital
200) negative
201) threaten
202) hazardous
203) based
204) promising
205) neglected
206) fossil
207) emissions
208) gray
209) sent

210) attachment
211) arise
212) exotic
213) arrived
214) competed
215) habitat
216) pressure
217) adapt
218) mature
219) densely
220) varied
221) have
222) destroyed
223) extinction
224) Growing
225) stay
226) Hunter-gatherers
227) possessions
228) time
229) years
230) spacing
231) transporting
232) settled
233) shorten
234) intervals
235) counterpart
236) rapid
237) farming
238) advantage
239) agricultural
240) labor
241) children
242) learn
243) hardware
244) flexible
245) migratory
246) instructions
247) inefficient
248) born
249) adapt
250) farther
251) comparison
252) facilitates
253) passing
254) culture
255) evolve
256) genes
257) flexibility
258) digital
259) future
260) neglected
261) disabilities
262) valuable
263) useless
264) distinguishing
265) professionals
266) progress
267) meeting
268) creating
269) fail
270) account
271) improved
272) embraced
273) largest
274) needs
275) disabilities
276) without
277) pain
278) pleasure
279) spicy
280) massages
281) threat
282) stimulus
283) nonthreatening
284) humor
285) violating
286) norms

287) where
288) reward
289) punishment
290) mastery
291) remarkable
292) stimulates
293) activated
294) burned
295) danger
296) derive
297) repeated
298) seeking
299) human
300) preference
301) directly
302) associated
303) pleasurable
304) flew
305) student
306) experienced
307) appreciation
308) surprise
309) emergency
310) turbulence
311) indication
312) loss
313) panic
314) steady
315) Calm
316) encouraged
317) markers
318) low
319) safety
320) relief

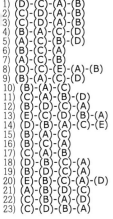

Quiz 1 **Answers**

1) (D)-(C)-(A)-(B)
2) (C)-(D)-(A)-(B)
3) (C)-(D)-(A)-(B)
4) (B)-(A)-(C)-(D)
5) (A)-(C)-(B)-(D)
6) (B)-(C)-(A)
7) (A)-(C)-(B)
8) (D)-(C)-(E)-(A)-(B)
9) (B)-(A)-(C)-(D)
10) (B)-(A)-(C)
11) (C)-(A)-(B)-(D)
12) (B)-(D)-(C)-(A)
13) (E)-(C)-(D)-(B)-(A)
14) (D)-(B)-(A)-(C)-(E)
15) (B)-(A)-(C)
16) (B)-(C)-(A)
17) (C)-(A)-(B)
18) (D)-(B)-(C)-(A)
19) (B)-(D)-(C)-(A)
20) (E)-(B)-(C)-(A)-(D)
21) (A)-(B)-(D)-(C)
22) (C)-(B)-(A)-(D)
23) (C)-(D)-(B)-(A)

Quiz 2 **Answers**

1)
[정답] ④ ⓓ, ⓔ
[해설]
ⓓ prescription ⇨ subscription
ⓔ assess ⇨ access

2)
[정답] ① ⓑ, ⓓ
[해설]
ⓑ applied ⇨ applied to
ⓓ does ⇨ was

3)
[정답] ⑤ ⓐ, ⓓ, ⓔ, ⓖ
[해설]
ⓐ positive ⇨ negative
ⓓ organized ⇨ disorganized
ⓔ say ⇨ says
ⓖ neat ⇨ neatly

4)
[정답] ② ⓐ, ⓒ, ⓔ
[해설]
ⓐ flawed ⇨ perfect
ⓒ fertilization ⇨ fertilizer
ⓔ becoming ⇨ become

5)
[정답] ⑤ ⓐ, ⓒ, ⓖ, ⓗ
[해설]
ⓐ help ⇨ helping
ⓒ less ⇨ more
ⓖ passes ⇨ passing
ⓗ care ⇨ cares

6)
[정답] ② ⓒ, ①
[해설]
ⓒ shortcut ⇨ mastery
① most ⇨ least

7)
[정답] ④ ①, ⓚ
[해설]
① mismatch ⇨ match
ⓚ promise ⇨ change

8)
[정답] ② ⓑ, ⓒ, ⓔ
[해설]
ⓑ coins ⇨ coined
ⓒ born ⇨ was born
ⓔ had ⇨ have

9)
[정답] ⑤ ⓑ, ⓕ, ⓗ, ①
[해설]
ⓑ have ⇨ have had
ⓕ disease ⇨ diseases
ⓗ were ⇨ was
① what ⇨ that

10)
[정답] ② ⓑ, ⓙ
[해설]
ⓑ to release ⇨ to reveal
ⓙ delayed ⇨ immediate

11)
[정답] ④ ⓗ, ⓘ
[해설]
ⓗ documents ⇨ documented
ⓘ produce ⇨ productivity

12)
[정답] ⑤ ⓓ, ⓖ, ⓘ, ⓙ
[해설]
ⓓ are rewarded ⇨ rewarded
ⓖ auditory ⇨ spatial
ⓘ that ⇨ what
ⓙ to do ⇨ doing

13)
[정답] ④ ⓔ, ⓖ, ⓚ
[해설]
ⓔ romantic ⇨ hostile
ⓖ less ⇨ more
ⓚ ascendants ⇨ descendants

14)
[정답] ③ ⓒ, ⓓ, ⓖ
[해설]
ⓒ collaboratively ⇨ separately
ⓓ unanimously ⇨ anonymously
ⓖ interdependently ⇨ individually

15)
[정답] ② ⓐ, ⓓ, ⓘ
[해설]
ⓐ given ⇨ giving
ⓓ decrease ⇨ increase
ⓘ taken ⇨ taking

16)
[정답] ③ ⓐ, ⓔ, ⓖ, ⓚ
[해설]
ⓐ which ⇨ that
ⓔ less ⇨ more
ⓖ less ⇨ more
ⓚ dwindled ⇨ increased

17)
[정답] ⑤ ⓑ, ⓒ, ⓖ, ⓙ
[해설]
ⓑ arrive ⇨ arrived from
ⓒ different ⇨ same
ⓖ less ⇨ more
ⓙ prosperity ⇨ extinction

18)
[정답] ④ ⓑ, ⓔ, ⓙ, ⓜ
[해설]
ⓑ assessions ⇨ possessions
ⓔ space ⇨ spacing
ⓙ less ⇨ more
ⓜ small ⇨ large

19)
[정답] ② ⓔ, ⓗ
[해설]
ⓔ efficient ⇨ inefficient
ⓗ shortest ⇨ longest

20)
[정답] ④ ⓐ, ⓕ, ⓗ, ⓘ
[해설]
ⓐ That ⇨ What
ⓕ procedures ⇨ progress
ⓗ smallest ⇨ largest
ⓘ with ⇨ without

21)
[정답] ⑤ ⓙ, ⓜ
[해설]
ⓙ dangerous ⇨ safe
ⓜ inference ⇨ preference

22)
[정답] ④ ⓒ, ⓕ, ⓖ
[해설]
ⓒ emergence ⇨ emergency
ⓕ neglect ⇨ focus on
ⓖ training ⇨ trained

Quiz 3 **Answers**

1)
[정답] ①
[해설]
1개
⑦ assess ⇨ access

2)
[정답] ④
[해설]
4개
② applied ⇨ applied to
③ appliance ⇨ application
⑤ been slept ⇨ slept
⑦ making ⇨ make

3)
[정답] ③
[해설]
3개
① positive ⇨ negative
⑤ say ⇨ says
⑦ neat ⇨ neatly

4)
[정답] ④
[해설]
5개
① flawed ⇨ perfect
④ While ⇨ During
⑥ less ⇨ more
⑦ less ⇨ more
⑨ desirables ⇨ undesirables

5)
[정답] ③
[해설]
5개
② eat ⇨ eats
③ less ⇨ more
⑤ separation ⇨ attention
⑦ passes ⇨ passing
⑧ care ⇨ cares

6)
[정답] ③
[해설]
4개
④ useless ⇨ useful
⑥ successive ⇨ successful
⑦ luck ⇨ hardship
⑧ winning ⇨ struggle

7)
[정답] ③
[해설]
5개
② be ⇨ are
③ general ⇨ particular
⑤ was ⇨ were
⑥ less ⇨ more
⑨ training ⇨ to train

8)
[정답] ②
[해설]
3개
③ born ⇨ was born
⑤ had ⇨ have
⑥ appointing ⇨ being appointed

9)
[정답] ②
[해설]
6개
① artificial ⇨ natural
② have ⇨ have had
③ remains ⇨ remains from
⑧ were ⇨ was
⑨ hardly ⇨ hard
⑩ what ⇨ that

10)
[정답] ③
[해설]
4개
① assumption ⇨ consumption
② to release ⇨ to reveal
⑤ past ⇨ future
⑦ discounted ⇨ undiscounted

11)
[정답] ②
[해설]
3개
① appreciated ⇨ lamented
⑦ finished ⇨ unfinished
⑧ documents ⇨ documented

12)
[정답] ④
[해설]
6개
① demonstrated ⇨ demonstrating
② rewarding ⇨ rewarded
⑥ that ⇨ which
⑦ auditory ⇨ spatial
⑧ indirect ⇨ direct
⑩ to do ⇨ doing

13)
[정답] ④
[해설]
4개
① collaboration ⇨ competition
② evolving ⇨ to evolve
④ highly ⇨ slightly
⑥ to give ⇨ gives

14)
[정답] ②
[해설]
4개
④ unanimously ⇨ anonymously
⑦ interdependently ⇨ individually
⑧ brainstorming ⇨ brainwriting
⑨ affective ⇨ effective

15)
[정답] ①
[해설]
2개
③ which ⇨ that
⑨ taken ⇨ taking

16)
[정답] ③
[해설]
6개
① which ⇨ that
⑤ less ⇨ more
⑥ were used ⇨ used
⑦ less ⇨ more
⑪ dwindled ⇨ increased
⑬ detachment ⇨ attachment

17)
[정답] ③
[해설]
5개
① are ⇨ is
⑤ adopt ⇨ adapt
⑦ less ⇨ more
⑨ less ⇨ more
⑩ prosperity ⇨ extinction

18)
[정답] ③
[해설]
6개
③ general ⇨ particular
⑤ space ⇨ spacing
⑥ less ⇨ more

⑦ different ⇨ same
⑧ settling ⇨ transporting
⑫ dwindled ⇨ increased

19)
[정답] ②
[해설]
4개
① Spend ⇨ Spending
⑥ adopt ⇨ adapt
⑧ shortest ⇨ longest
⑪ inefficiency ⇨ flexibility

20)
[정답] ③
[해설]
4개
④ worthless ⇨ valuable
⑥ procedures ⇨ progress
⑦ neglected ⇨ embraced
⑨ with ⇨ without

21)
[정답] ②
[해설]
5개
⑤ risky ⇨ safe
⑦ reward ⇨ punishment
⑧ less ⇨ more
⑩ dangerous ⇨ safe
⑬ inference ⇨ preference

22)
[정답] ④
[해설]
6개
① highly ⇨ high
② wander ⇨ wonder
③ emergence ⇨ emergency
④ calmly ⇨ calm
⑤ neglect ⇨ focus on
⑥ neglect ⇨ focus on

Quiz 4 **Answers**

1)
[정답]
① aggravate ⇨ appreciate
② unavailable ⇨ available
④ prescription ⇨ subscription
⑥ listen ⇨ listen to

2)
[정답]
① slowly ⇨ rapidly
② applied ⇨ applied to
④ does ⇨ was
⑥ was emerged ⇨ emerged

3)
[정답]
① positive ⇨ negative
② constructive ⇨ destructive

③ disorder ⇨ disorderly
④ organized ⇨ disorganized
⑤ say ⇨ says
⑥ less ⇨ more
⑦ neat ⇨ neatly

4)
[정답]
① flawed ⇨ perfect
② multiculture ⇨ monoculture
④ While ⇨ During
⑥ less ⇨ more
⑦ less ⇨ more
⑧ barren ⇨ luxurious
⑨ desirables ⇨ undesirables
⑩ artificial ⇨ natural
⑪ undesired ⇨ desired

5)
[정답]
④ doubt ⇨ owe
⑤ separation ⇨ attention

6)
[정답]
① detours ⇨ cuts
② inquire ⇨ acquire
③ shortcut ⇨ mastery
④ useless ⇨ useful
⑤ High ⇨ Highly
⑥ successive ⇨ successful
⑦ luck ⇨ hardship
⑧ winning ⇨ struggle

7)
[정답]
④ less ⇨ more
⑥ less ⇨ more
⑦ Conversely ⇨ Similarly
⑧ isn't ⇨ doesn't
⑨ training ⇨ to train
⑩ mismatch ⇨ match
⑪ promise ⇨ change

8)
[정답]
① memorial ⇨ memorable

9)
[정답]
① artificial ⇨ natural
② have ⇨ have had
③ remains ⇨ remains from
⑤ limited ⇨ abundant
⑥ disease ⇨ diseases
⑦ temporary ⇨ permanent
⑨ hardly ⇨ hard
⑩ what ⇨ that

10)
[정답]
① assumption ⇨ consumption
② to release ⇨ to reveal
③ immediate ⇨ delayed
⑤ past ⇨ future

⑥ inflated ⇨ discounted
⑦ discounted ⇨ undiscounted
⑧ determination ⇨ weakness
⑨ consistently ⇨ differently
⑩ delayed ⇨ immediate

11)
[정답]
③ literal ⇨ literary
⑤ untime ⇨ untimely
⑥ perspiration ⇨ inspiration
⑦ finished ⇨ unfinished

12)
[정답]
④ are rewarded ⇨ rewarded
⑤ less ⇨ more
⑦ auditory ⇨ spatial
⑩ to do ⇨ doing

13)
[정답]
① collaboration ⇨ competition
③ were ⇨ did
④ highly ⇨ slightly
⑦ less ⇨ more

14)
[정답]
① on ⇨ off
② together ⇨ solo
③ collaboratively ⇨ separately
⑥ requirements ⇨ options
⑦ interdependently ⇨ individually
⑧ brainstorming ⇨ brainwriting
⑨ affective ⇨ effective
⑩ independent ⇨ collective

15)
[정답]
⑥ during ⇨ while
⑧ dwindled ⇨ increased
⑪ Given ⇨ Giving

16)
[정답]
① which ⇨ that
② more ⇨ less
③ positive ⇨ negative
④ benefit ⇨ harm
⑤ less ⇨ more
⑥ were used ⇨ used
⑧ promised ⇨ promising
⑨ overestimated ⇨ neglected
⑩ green ⇨ fossil
⑪ dwindled ⇨ increased
⑫ transmissions ⇨ emissions
⑬ detachment ⇨ attachment

17)
18)
[정답]
③ general ⇨ particular
④ year ⇨ years
⑧ settling ⇨ transporting

⑨ lengthen ⇨ shorten
⑪ steady ⇨ rapid
⑫ dwindled ⇨ increased

19)
[정답]
① Spend ⇨ Spending
② less ⇨ more
③ software ⇨ hardware
④ more ⇨ less
⑤ efficient ⇨ inefficient
⑥ adopt ⇨ adapt
⑦ what ⇨ how
⑧ shortest ⇨ longest
⑩ slower ⇨ faster
⑪ inefficiency ⇨ flexibility

20)
[정답]
④ worthless ⇨ valuable
⑤ distinguishes ⇨ distinguishing
⑥ procedures ⇨ progress
⑦ neglected ⇨ embraced
⑧ smallest ⇨ largest

21)
[정답]
① seeks ⇨ seek
② if ⇨ whether
⑤ risky ⇨ safe
⑥ regret ⇨ reward
⑦ reward ⇨ punishment
⑨ different ⇨ same
⑩ dangerous ⇨ safe
⑪ hatred ⇨ pleasure
⑫ deprive ⇨ derive
⑬ inference ⇨ preference

22)
[정답]
⑦ training ⇨ trained

Quiz 5 **Answers**

1) 감사하다 - appreciate // 이용 가능하다 - available // 전환하다 - switch
2)
　(가) At a 50% discount off your current print subscription, you can access a full year of online reading.
3) 찢다 - tore // 나타나다 - emerged // 상상하다 - make a fantasy
4)
　(가) As I walked from the mailbox, my heart was beating rapidly.
5) 나타내다 - indicate // 혼란스러운 - disorganized // 분위기 - atmosphere
6)
　(가) Having a messy room can add up++to negative feelings and destructive thinking.
　(나) One of the professional tidying experts says that the moment you start cleaning your room, you also start changing your life and gaining new perspective.
7)
　ⓐ

Fortunately ⇨ Unfortunately

desirables ⇨ undesirables

Because of ⇨ Because

it is ⇨ they are

8)

(가) The soil of a farm field is forced to be the perfect environment for monoculture growth.

9) 문맥 상 들어갈 단어 - attention

10)

ⓐ

help ⇨ helping

are ⇨ is

them ⇨ themselves

11)

(가) There are too many people out in the world who feel like everyone has forgotten them or ignored them.

12) 얻다 - acquire // 번영 - prosperity // 어려움 - hardship

13)

(가) Strength comes from struggle, not from taking the path of least resistance.

14) 반사 - reflection

15)

ⓐ

them ⇨ themselves

to pursue ⇨ pursuing

16)

(가) What you do is an indication of the type of person you believe that you are.

17) 기록하다 - ranked // 머무르다 - remained

18) 돌보다, 2단어 - looked after // 지대한 - profound // 임용하다 - appointed // 특허 - patents

19) 풍부한 - abundant // 의심할 여지 없이 - undoubtedly // 전환점 - turning point

20)

ⓐ

that ⇨ why

temporary ⇨ permanent

21)

(가) The hunter-gatherer lifestyle, which can be described as "natural" to human beings, appears to have had much to recommend it.

22) 의지 - will // 즉 - That is // 유혹 - temptation

23)

ⓐ

undiscounted ⇨ discounted

discounted ⇨ undiscounted

envisioning ⇨ envisioned

premature ⇨ prematurely

24)

(가) This behavior seems to reveal a preference of a delayed reward over an immediate one

25) 결과 - consequences // 생산성 - productivity

26)

ⓐ

well-documenting ⇨ well-documented

lamenting ⇨ lamented

was described ⇨ described

writing ⇨ written

ⓑ

expected ⇨ unexpected

incidence ⇨ coincidence

perspiration ⇨ inspiration

unfinishing ⇨ unfinished

27) 입증하다 - demonstrating // 정확히 - precisely

28)

(가) The point is that the physical architecture of the brain changes according to where we direct our attention and what we practice doing.

29) 진화하다 - evolve // 그에 따라 - accordingly // 투쟁 - struggle // 결정적인 - decisive // 후손 - descendants

30)

(가) One possibility is that competition and conflicts with other human tribes caused our brains to evolve the way they did.

(나) The tribe that could out-think its opponents was more likely to succeed in battle and would then pass on the genes responsible for this mental advantage to its offspring.

31) 잠재력 - potential // 초기의 - initial // 유지하다 - preserve // 그렇지 않더라면 - otherwise // 집단지성 - collective intelligence

32)

(가) then does the team come together to select and refine the most promising options.

33) 들어갈 단어 - agency // 권한 - authority // 생산성 - productivity

34)

(가) Giving employees a sense of control improved how much self-discipline they brought to their jobs.

35) 유망한 - promising // 간과하다 - neglected // 화석연료 - fossil fuels // 첨부 - attachment

36)

ⓐ

that ⇨ it

positive ⇨ negative

be threatened by ⇨ threaten

less ⇨ more

digital ⇨ paper

37) 멸종 - extinction

38)

ⓐ

familiar ⇨ exotic

arriving ⇨ arrived

different ⇨ same

adept ⇨ adapt

39)

(가) Within the same area of forest, grey squirrels can destroy the food supply before red squirrels even have a bite.

40) 자주 - frequently // 소유물 - possessions // 간격을 두다 - spacing

41)

ⓐ

from ⇨ in

A decreased ⇨ An increased

small ⇨ large

42)

(가) Societies that settled down in one place were able to shorten their birth intervals from four years to about two.

43) 본문 단어 찾아서 변형 - flexibility

44)

ⓐ

adept ⇨ adapt

shortest ⇨ longest

45)

(가) Childhood facilitates the passing on of cultural information, and culture can evolve faster than genes.

46) 보존하다 - preserve // 수용하다 - embraced

47)

(가) What has remained neglected for the most part, however, are the needs of people with disabilities.

(나) some scholars creating digital projects all too often fail to take these needs into account.

48) 어느 정도 - to an extent // 안전한 위협 - safe threat // 감지하다 - perceives // 고통 - suffering // 수용체 - receptor // 도출하다 - derive // 선호 - preference // 보상 - reward

49)

ⓐ

contrary ⇨ similar

conforming to ⇨ violating

which ⇨ where

50)

(가) The closer you look at your chilli-eating habit, the more remarkable it seems.

(나) Knowing that our body is firing off danger signals, but that we are actually completely safe, produces pleasure

51) 감탄 - appreciation // 격려하다 - encouraged // 자랑스럽게 - proudly

52)
ⓐ
calmly ⇨ calm
are happened ⇨ happen

53)
(가) the student was in control of an airplane that was flying well, but she had no indication of where she was or where she should go.
(나) the student carefully flew low enough to see if she could find any ships making their way across the surface of the ocean.